MODERN SOUTHEAST ASIA SERIES
Stephen F. Maxner, *General Editor*

the battle at
ngok tavak

Allied Valor and Defeat in Vietnam

Bruce Davies

Texas Tech University Press

First published 2008 by Allen & Unwin Book Publishers,
83 Alexander Street, Crows Nest NSW 2065 Australia

Original Copyright © 2008 Bruce Davies

Published in the United States by Texas Tech University Press,
Box 41037, Lubbock, TX 79409-1037 USA
By arrangement with Allen & Unwin Publishers,
83 Alexander Street, Crows Nest NSW 2065 Australia

North American Edition, Copyright © 2009 by Texas Tech University Press

The acid-free paper used in this book meets the minimum requirements of ANSI/NISO
Z39.48-1992 (R1997). ∞

Library of Congress Cataloguing-in-Publication Data will be available.

Printed in the United States of America

First North American Edition

09 10 11 12 13 14 15 16 17 / 9 8 7 6 5 4 3 2 1

Texas Tech University Press
Box 41037
Lubbock, Texas 79409-1037 USA
800.832.4042
ttup@ttu.edu
www.ttup.edu

*For all of the warriors who fought at Ngok Tavak
and whose souls wandered in the wilderness for so long*

*And for Anne, my wife, 1946–2007;
without her my spirit would have broken long ago*

CONTENTS

The War Zone

South
Vietnam
&
Cambodia

NORTH
VIETNAM

Tchepone
Khe Sanh
Quang Tri
Hue

Da Nang

I CORPS
Kham Duc

LAOS

Ngok Tavak
Quang
Ngai
Duc
Pho

Kontum

Pleiku

Qui Nhon

SOUTH
VIETNAM

II CORPS

CAMBODIA
Ban Me Thuest

Kratie
Nha Trang

Pnom Penh
Snoul
Cam Ranh

Prey Veng
"The Fishhook"
III CORPS

Hau Nghia

Sihanoukville
(Kompong Som)
"Parrot's
Beak"
Long
An
Vung Tau

Can Tho

IV
CORPS

I Corps Tactical Zone

War in the Northern Provinces, Department of the Army, 1975.

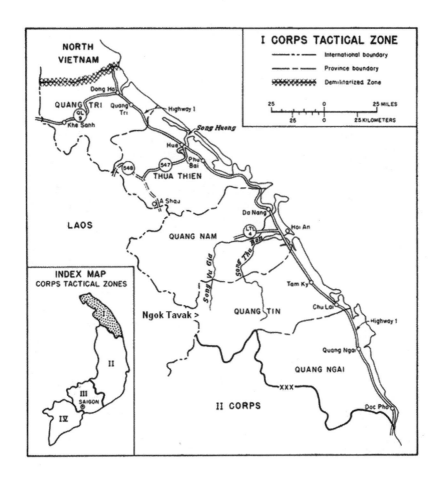

Little Ngok Tavak–Position Layout Diagram

Opposite: Note that the magnetic north–south orientation is from the top right to bottom left corners. The overall dimensions of the bottom part of the diagram are 50 metres by 70 metres. The inner fort area, which was surrounded by a 2-metre-high earthen berm, was 33 metres by 50 metres. Two platoons of Nungs were located at the western end of what was the old 'parade ground', marked LZ, one platoon on the northwestern quadrant and the other facing southwest. The 11th Company command post was at the northwestern end of the fort's floor with the third Nung platoon distributed around the eastern wall of the fort. The Marine howitzers were located during the first few days in the 'old vehicle park' and then moved on 8 and 9 May up into the fort's floor area. The Civilian Irregular Defense Group (CIDG) from Kham Duc was put in the vehicle park area, which is the little bump immediately beneath the words 'CIDG PLAT'. The gradient from the vehicle park to the fort's floor was around 50 metres in height over 150 metres in distance. The diagram this map is based on was drawn immediately after the battle in 1968.

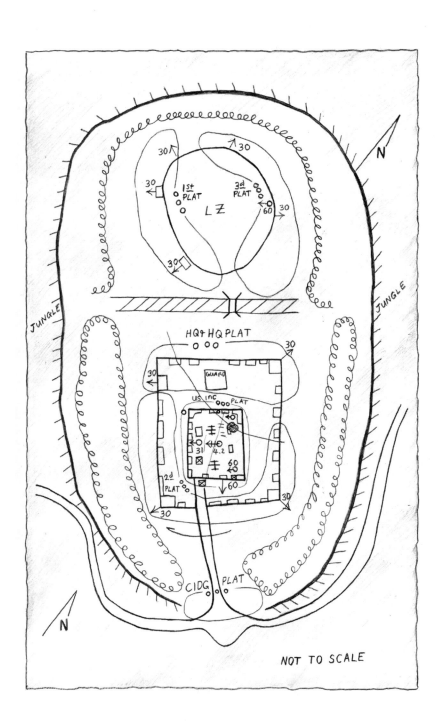

Ngok Tavak Forward Operating Base 1:50,000

The forward operating base was on Little Ngok Tavak hill just to the top right of the sign QL 14, Grid Reference 964 009. Kham Duc camp was 7 kilometres in a straight line over the main Ngok Tavak feature. Contour intervals are in metres.

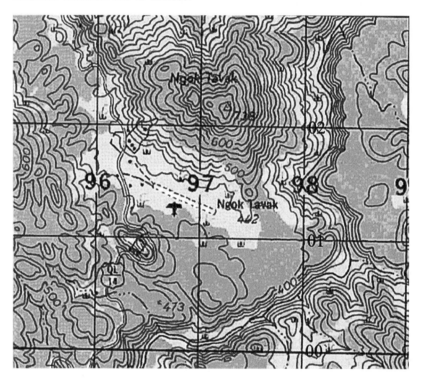

FOREWORD
Jack Shulimson

I have never met Bruce Davies except through the internet. In fact, I still know very little about his personal life except that he had been in Vietnam as an Australian adviser to the South Vietnamese and that he also served with the US Army Special Forces-controlled 'Mike Force'. He contacted me through a friend stating that he had read my history, *US Marines in Vietnam, The Defining Year 1968*, which contained a brief account of the overrunning of the Special Forces outpost at Ngok Tavak in May of that year. In our brief electronic correspondence, Bruce told me that he was writing a book on the subject and wanted to know if I could help him with source material. I answered a few questions and soon realised that he knew much more about this particular incident than I did. He had ploughed through most of the available sources including US, Vietnamese and Australian, besides conducting his own correspondence and interviews with survivors and relatives of the fallen. Bruce then asked me to read and comment upon his manuscript. I found it a most impressive work—well written and exceptionally well researched. The author was obviously someone who was familiar with the terrain and had an extensive knowledge of the weaponry and military tactics.

What was it that made this small hill outpost called Ngok Tavak more exceptional than many of the other outposts lost during the Vietnam War? To answer that question, it is necessary to provide a bit of context. The extensive fighting during May 1968 has been improperly dubbed 'Mini-Tet' in comparison to the enemy Tet Offensive in January and February. In actuality there was nothing 'mini' about this May combat. Moreover, the heaviest losses in one month for US and South Vietnamese forces occurred in May.

The basic difference between the two 'Tet Offensives' was the element of surprise. While the allies expected an offensive in January, they did not expect the intensity and extent of the enemy attacks. There was little surprise to the attacks in May. The US and Vietnamese forces were aware and ready for this second onslaught. For the most part, the allies turned back most of the North Vietnamese and Viet Cong assaults and inflicted heavy losses upon the enemy troops. There were exceptions, however, to this general situation and the struggle for Ngok Tavak was one of the exceptions.

While it was usual for the communist forces to target a relatively isolated and exposed outpost such as Ngok Tavak, there were several factors that made this incident unique. I remember that one of the reasons that piqued my interest when I wrote my 1968 history was the odd fact that a Marine artillery platoon with two 105 mm howitzers was there in support of an Army Special Forces unit. The nearest Marine command was nearly 100 kilometres away. Even more unusual was that two of the Marines, fighting as infantrymen, were awarded the Navy Cross, the second highest medal for heroism, and the entire platoon received the Meritorious Unit Commendation award for its actions on the hill.

There were several other factors that made Ngok Tavak a special case. Basically, the outpost overlooked the main Special Forces camp at Kham Duc some 7 kilometres to the north. The mission of the Special Forces was to monitor North Vietnamese infiltration across the Laos border approximately 16 kilometres away. The make-up of the defenders also posed problems. The force at Ngok Tavak consisted of approximately 113 personnel of a South Vietnamese Civilian Irregular Defense Group (CIDG) Mobile Strike Force Company, eight US Army Special Forces advisers, and three members of an Australian Army training team.

This mixed make-up of troops was not a happy marriage. Neither the Americans nor the Australians trusted the loyalty or fighting capability of the Vietnamese irregulars. On the other hand, while the command relations at Ngok Tavak were unimpaired, there were obvious shortfalls up above. There had been irritations between Marines and the Army Special Forces over the existence and control of these border outposts, as well as differences between the top Marine commander in Vietnam, Lieutenant General Robert E. Cushman, and the overall US commander, Army General William C. Westmoreland.

In any event, anything that could go wrong did go wrong. Missed communications, poor tactical decisions, treachery, lack of proper supplies all played a role. At Ngok Tavak, according to Marine records, out of the 43 Marines and one Navy Corpsman who made up the Marine platoon, thirteen were dead and twenty were wounded and only eleven escaped unscathed. Bruce Davies describes how the defenders of Ngok Tavak left the bodies of eleven of the Marine dead and one US Army Special Forces sergeant behind when they evacuated the outpost. In the end, the American command also decided to evacuate Kham Duc.

One of Bruce's accomplishments in this history is his ability to thread his way through the maze of command relations, conflicting stories, national and service rivalries and resentments, faulty memories, and missing documents to bring forth a coherent account. As significant as this may be, his major contribution is his depiction of the aftermath and the final return of both the survivors and, 30-something years later, what remained of the fallen. From interviews and correspondence, he portrays with deep empathy the grief and loss suffered by the parents, wives, sweethearts and siblings of the American troops who died on that forlorn hill. Some refused to believe the men were dead and instead claimed some were still alive and held prisoner somewhere in North Vietnam. The cruellest aspect was the lack of any physical remains. The author describes the efforts of a small, dedicated group of Vietnam veterans who did not give up hope of finding the physical evidence of the dead men that they knew were left on that hilltop. Because of their untiring efforts and pressure upon both Vietnamese and US authorities over the years, enough remains were collected to provide definite DNA identification of five of the American dead. There was also circumstantial evidence to believe that the remaining seven were among the bits and pieces that could not be identified. Bruce fittingly ends his narrative in October 2005 with the interment at Arlington Cemetery of a coffin containing the unidentified remains and the presentation of twelve folded flags to the next of kin of those who died at Ngok Tavak.

Dr Jack Shulimson, now retired, is the former Senior Vietnam Historian and Head of the Histories Section, US Marine Corps History and Museums Division. Dr Shulimson did his undergraduate work at the University of Buffalo, now the State University of New York at Buffalo. He earned his Masters Degree in History at the University of Michigan, Ann Arbor, and his doctorate in American Studies at the University of Maryland, College Park.

PREFACE

A Chinese mercenary–US Special Forces infantry company, commanded by an Australian, was sent on a mission near the Laos border in South Vietnam in 1968. Some weeks later, a US Marine two-gun artillery detachment was landed on the remote base to provide fire support. Their mission was to find an enemy force, but the Allied troops were routed and forced to retreat. They left behind the bodies of eleven American marines and a Special Forces sergeant; an American medic was missing. What was the story behind this eclectic mix of troops seemingly dropped in the middle of an enemy-infested wilderness? It was a puzzling tactical decision that aroused my curiosity. The more one asked, the greater the puzzle. Not only did the story become a challenge, but the puzzle also appeared to expand into an enigma. In addition, the battle at Ngok Tavak occurred just before a battle debacle at nearby Kham Duc, which smothered the story of what happened on this lonely hilltop on 10 May 1968.

There are many small articles about Ngok Tavak on the internet and printed in military magazines, but they do no more than invite greater constructive scrutiny. As a result, my research led me through many of the old unit reports and many other official and personal papers that explained what took place at this isolated outpost. Naturally, not everything is written down and some things that are recorded attract criticism from those who were there. Thus began my search to find those who were in the battle and to record their memories. John White was the first contact and this story would not be as comprehensive as it is without his assistance. He led me to Tim Brown, whose assistance was paramount. Tim also opened the door to some of the American survivors of the battle, as well as some families and members of Vietnam Veterans of America. Bob Mascharka helped me get connected with Marine pilots and crew who flew into the besieged camp, a few of whom walked out after two of their helicopters were destroyed. Bob Adams, Don Cameron (DCM, MM), Jon Davis, Dave Fuentes (now deceased), Jim Garlitz, William Loman, Eugene Makowski, 'Jack' Matheney, Dean Parrett, Charles Reeder, Greg Rose, Henry Schunck (Navy Cross), Ray Scuglik, Paul Swenarski and Scott 'Doc' Thomas are some of those who survived the battle and allowed me to reignite their memories so that first-hand experiences could be included in this book. Kenneth Benway added some detailed pre-battle background, and his photographs of Ngok Tavak, which he permitted me to use, are unique.

Janice Kostello was a mine of family information, as were Dennis King, Sherry Perry and Patricia Zajack. It was a challenge for me to peer back into their grief and to record their emotions for public consumption. That they allowed this took great courage. Harry Albert's excellent video record of the Team Bravo return to Vietnam in 1995 was also an outstanding reference. Many others assisted with the story and one feels embarrassed by not being able to mention everyone here, but their names appear throughout the text and in the bibliography. To those people, please accept my sincere thank you for your efforts.

This was not an easy story to dissect and it contains some provocative and controversial comments and conclusions. Where there are two sides to the story, they have been presented in what I hope is a fair balance that will allow readers to decide what happened. But, in the end, I must accept responsibility for the book and any errors that it might contain, which I hope are few.

Without the guidance of Angela Handley, Senior Editor at Allen & Unwin, and Anne, my wife, who died during the writing of this book, the manuscript would have been just another jumble of words. And it would never have made the shelf without the support of Ian Bowring, my publisher.

A note on usage: I have used the westernised spelling of place names such as Vietnam and Danang, rather than Viet Nam and Da Nang.

Bruce Davies
Point Lonsdale, Victoria

PROLOGUE

Ngok Tavak was a battle of treachery, courage, defeat and compassion. It probably barely registered on the main board in the Military Assistance Command Vietnam Combat Operations Center in Saigon. But, as with all fire-fights, for those intent on killing the other side face-to-face, it was *the* battle of the war and the result carried with it emotional burdens that may never be erased. Ngok Tavak was an annoying pinprick in the side of a North Vietnamese Army force, which planned to destroy a larger prey at Kham Duc. The battle pitched a disparate grouping of allies against a battle-hardened enemy that had recently experienced the mighty firepower available to the Americans. Ironically, this battle was fought on a piece of land that was a dilapidated area of defence built by the French many years previously.

Ngok Tavak was built to a favoured design of berms, parapets and parados in France's war against the Viet Minh. This military outpost aided a tactical plan that was to:

> Find the enemy and destroy his units one by one. Unfortunately most of our [France's] difficulties came in trying to find his units. On the other hand, whenever our units found themselves isolated, the enemy attacked without warning, in superior numbers, and with much vigour. [The enemy force] . . . condensing into a storm whose violence is quickly over . . . leaving behind it only a blue sky . . . and some ruins.[1]

In 1968, this 'fort' was now no more than the remains of earthen walls and an interior court that the jungle had no desire to consume. The thunderclouds of the 1968 war now rolled around Ngok Tavak, and their vanguard was the 40th Battalion, 1st Regiment of the 2nd North Vietnamese Army Division. Awaiting them was a mixture of US Army Special Forces troops—with three Australians—a United States Marine Corps artillery detachment and an infantry contingent that consisted of Nung mercenaries and a suspect Vietnamese group from Kham Duc.

the battle at
ngok tavak

PART 1 THE WARRIORS

'But I don't want to go among mad people,' Alice remarked.
'Oh, you can't help that,' said the Cat:
'We're all mad here. I'm mad, you're mad.'
'How do you know I'm mad?' said Alice.
'You must be,' said the Cat, 'or you wouldn't have come here.'
Lewis Carroll, *Alice's Adventures in Wonderland*, 1865

1 PATHWAYS TO A BATTLE

Observe your enemy, for they first find out your faults.
Antisthenes, 445–365 BC

The 2nd North Vietnamese Army Division

The 2nd North Vietnamese Army (NVA) Division—or the now frequently used term People's Army of Vietnam (PAVN)—is recorded as forming in Quang Nam Province in October 1965 when one of its regiments, the 21st, came down from the North. The other divisional elements included Regiment 1, which was a People's Liberation Army Forces (PLAF) unit, and Battalion 70. The PLAF were more generally known as Viet Cong. The 1st Regiment was formed from Quang Da's provincial military forces, which consisted of the 19th Battalion and then added to by the amalgamation of a series of units designated with the letters RQ; there were possibly five provincial battalions—RQ20B, RQ21, RQ23, RQ24 and RQ25—that were absorbed to form the regiment. Quang Da was the northern half of what South Vietnam called Quang Nam Province. It included the districts from the town of Hoi An to Danang City. Battalion 70 was classified as a 'regroupee' formation. Regroupees were Viet Minh soldiers who went north following the 1954 Armistice and re-infiltrated south to fight the new enemy in the 1960s. Regiment 31 (aka 3rd) joined the division from North Vietnam in 1966. There was also an independent 31st NVA Regiment listed as operating in the Danang region during 1968. Most of the Marine reports showed that the 3rd Regiment was a 2nd Division unit; however, the Marine command chronologies do not always show the 3rd and one of the 31st regiments as different formations. This inconsistency was explained by Marine Corps

3

intelligence as a stratagem by the North Vietnamese to confuse. Latter-day (North) Vietnamese monographs about the division identify the regiment under divisional command as the 31st, although its original designator was 64A of the 320th Division. Douglas Pike wrote in 1986:

> PAVN ... employed over the years an almost endless variety of troop unit names, special designations ... code designations. Many ... only used for a few months. Some are highly descriptive although not informative ... [and] some are so vague as to be meaningless ... for instance, *Cluster Two*.[1]

Obviously, in this case the deception worked.

An establishment chart of the 2nd NVA Division is shown here:

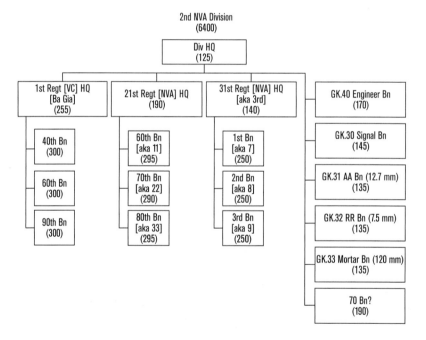

The chart shows the principal units of the division with estimated numbers of personnel taken from various US intelligence reports of the day, which were their best guesses. Each of the regiments also had supporting arms companies such as: reconnaissance, engineers, anti-aircraft and mortar as well as signal and medical troops. The 70th Battalion is listed separately with a question mark. The battalion was recorded as an original unit of the division, but apparently it was not absorbed by any of the division's regiments. Perhaps being a Viet Minh regroupee unit gave the 70th Battalion a special privilege. At some stage, the battalion may have moved to NVA Group 44. There was also a 24th Battalion, a rear service element, which reported to divisional headquarters. When senior retired NVA officers were interviewed in 1995, one of them said the battalions of the 1st (Ba Gia) Regiment had approximately 400 men each in 1968.[2] But it is difficult to provide accurate manning figures given that an NVA/VC (Main Force) battalion's generally reported *maximum* field strength was around 450–500; however, most fought under strength. As an example, NVA Senior General Chu Huy Man, Military Region 5 commander, wrote in 2004, 'one battalion [of the 2nd NVA Division] with about 200 fighting men...[in 1968]... underestimated the enemy's troops'.[3] An average planning figure of 1200 personnel per regiment would not be far off the mark and it would be unlikely that a battalion strength exceeded 300 men. There were other Main Force and Local Force VC units located within the division's area of operations and some of these were: the already mentioned 70th Battalion as well as the 72nd and 74th VC infantry battalions, the 409th Sapper Battalion and seven independent VC infantry companies. An NVA Artillery Regiment, 368B, supported the division in early 1968, but it was not a divisional unit. The division had a number of aliases, such as: Thon An 520, Ham Tu 2, 620th Division, Nong Truong 2 and Ta–310. Military Assistance Command Vietnam (MACV) and III Marine Amphibious Force (MAF) listed the unit as Nong Truong 2 in 1968.[4] Nong Truong meant a unit had responsibility for a regional zone, in this case the zone centred on the lowlands of southern I Corps that was probably referred to as Work Site 2, which included the bottom half of Quang Nam Province and the Province of Quang Tin. The 2nd NVA Division had also operated in Quang Ngai Province, but this region was not its major area of operations in 1968. The division's mission was to support guerrilla action and to provide protection for PLAF political action cells operating against the government of South Vietnam. One of its essential objectives was to oppose and defeat the South's pacification program of clearing, holding and building better infrastructure in the lowlands where there were lucrative rice fields and higher population centres, especially in the extensive valleys of Thuong Duc, An Hoa, Hiep Duc and Que Son that were to the west and southwest of Hoi An. The division could also threaten the security of Danang should it control this southerly avenue to the city. These valleys also provided an escape route back into Laos with the Special Forces camp and training facility at Kham Duc being a minor hindrance near the border, but that could be easily bypassed and it was, often.

During the April to September period of 1967, the 2nd NVA Division clashed repeatedly with units of the United States Marine Corps that included heavy battles against the 1st, 5th and 7th Marines in the Que Son Valley. These engagements hurt both sides. Also in 1967, the US Army's Task Force Oregon—later redesignated the 23rd or American Division—deployed units into this area of operations to increase the number of Allied forces operating in the northern Quang Tin and southern Quang Nam provincial regions. On 5 December 1967, Le Huu Tru, the commander of the 2nd NVA Division and the political commissar, Nguyen Minh Duc, as well as the commanders of the 21st and 31st regiments and some of the staff officers, were killed by American helicopter gunships. Giap Van Cuong and Nguyen Ngoc Son were appointed divisional commander and deputy political commissar respectively. In late January 1968, the 2nd NVA Division's Headquarters moved from their mountain redoubt into an area known as the Go Noi Island, immediately west of Hoi An, probably to prepare for an attack upon Duy Xuyen District, also west of Hoi An, and Danang as well. North Vietnamese Group 44, an NVA headquarters group, which commanded all of the independent units, and was thought to be of equal importance as the 2nd NVA Division, was also reported to be in the area. Senior Colonel Vo Thu, the former Chief of Staff of Military Region 5 and, briefly, commander of the 3rd NVA Division, commanded Group 44.

Throughout January, and the February 1968 Tet Offensive, the 2nd NVA Division fought a series of battles against Americal, USMC and Korean units around the southern outskirts of Danang and to the west of Hoi An. By 9 February, the NVA assaults had been defeated and they are reported to have 'suffered severe casualties' in January and 'heavy casualties' in February. Lieutenant General Cushman, USMC,

Commanding General, III Marine Amphibious Force, said that the 2nd NVA Division seemed to be withdrawing and he ordered his units to continue to attack. All of the battle reports indicated that the NVA were moving back into the embrace of the jungle-clad mountains. The commander of the 1st Marine Division said that the NVA and the Viet Cong units 'got their signals mixed' during the assault on Danang and this caused a confused and inept attack that resulted in their defeat. General Chu Huy Man confirmed this in 2004.[5]

It is difficult to analyse the numbers of enemy casualties reported and not question how the 2nd NVA Division remained intact and with any form of combat efficacy. The American Division recorded significant successes against the 2nd NVA Division in January 1968 with claims, when the fighting ended in mid-January, of over 1000 enemy dead, which prompted Major General Samuel W. Koster, the Commanding General of the American Division, to boast, somewhat prematurely, that 'the 2nd NVA suffered losses that impaired its future effectiveness'.[6] In a message of complete contradiction Major General Donn J. Robertson, Commanding General, 1st Marine Division, told his superior headquarters on 5 February: 'The fighting during the preceding week had drawn down the strength of the ARVN and the two Marine battalions and the enemy division [2nd NVA] still had uncommitted units that it could throw into the fray.'[7] Even more startling are the claims that more than 4500 enemy, including the division's senior commanders (confirmed), were reported killed in the period November 1967 to 29 February 1968 by the American Division during *Operation Wheeler–Wallowa* that was conducted in the 2nd NVA Division's area of deployment. What is not shown in these statistics is the number of wounded, which, at a conservative estimate, would be at least three wounded in need of evacuation to every one soldier killed, and the challenges of getting them to a hospital without helicopters or vehicles is not discussed. The US ratio of killed in action to wounded was 1:5.6.[8] These figures also do not show the casualties inflicted on the NVA by other Allied forces that fought in contiguous areas of operations.[9] Bearing in mind the mix of enemy units in the region, for any military collective to recover from this battlefield hammering is remarkable. But what is more noteworthy is that surviving elements of the 2nd NVA Division redeployed over 80 kilometres, across country, under constant threat, to a safe haven from where they could take their revenge on the defenders of Kham Duc and Ngok Tavak.

Soldiers of the sea

I Corps was synonymous with the United States Marine Corps. The Corps' humble introduction to the five provinces of the northern segment of South Vietnam started when a Marine helicopter squadron, HMM-163, set up a base at Danang in September 1962. The first ground troops, which included an infantry detachment, under the command of Major Alfred M. Gray, a future Commandant of the Corps, went out to Khe Sanh in June 1964, where they established a radio-monitoring site on Tiger Tooth Mountain to the north of the village. Marine Detachment, Advisory Group 1, was the first Marine ground unit into South Vietnam. The Marine disembarkation at Red Beach on the northern edge of Danang City in March 1965, however, is seen as the beginning of the American *ground war*.

The Marine Corps force in I Corps grew from that March landing into III Marine Amphibious Force, which had nearly 120,000 personnel under its control by January 1968. That force also included two US Army divisions and is best described as being a field army in size. The Marine field force consisted of two reinforced divisions, the 1st and the 3rd, and their areas of operation divided the Corps Tactical Zone so that the 3rd Division protected the Demilitarised Zone in Quang Tri Province. The 1st Division had the responsibility for the area from Hue south to near Hoi An in Quang Nam Province. There had been considerable shuffling of the major formations in I Corps immediately prior to the attacks of Tet 1968 so that the Army's 1st Cavalry Division (Airmobile) filled the remaining expanses in Thua Thien in the north, and the Americal covered Quang Tin–Quang Ngai in the south. South Vietnam's two infantry divisions in I Corps were also matched to these operational zones with the 1st ARVN Division alongside the 3rd Marine Division and the 2nd ARVN Division worked in concert with the Americal Division. The 1st Marine Division was supported by the ARVN 51st Regiment in Quang Nam and the 2nd Republic of Korea Brigade that the American commanders could ask nicely to assist, but of whom they could demand nothing.

With four-fifths of its area immediately abutting either North Vietnam or Laos, I Corps contained the most dangerous battlefields in Vietnam for the Americans, which prompted Lieutenant General Victor H. Krulak, Commanding General, Fleet Marine Force Pacific, to comment that 'the bulk of the war is in the I Corps Tactical Zone'.[10] The danger was compounded by the artillery capability of the NVA and the infiltration routes inside Laos. The Ho Chi Minh Trail brought new men and supplies through topography that helped the northerners outmanoeuvre allied military formations who had an area just on 18,000 square kilometres and a population of nearly three million people to protect. In the western section, the Annamite Mountains were rugged with some peaks reaching heights of 2000 metres. These rolled down to the coastal plains where the food and most of the Vietnamese people were; Montagnards lived in the hills.

Tet and fresh blood

The battle that started during the night of 30–31 January 1968 in I Corps and rolled down through South Vietnam was called the Tet Offensive. Its ferocity startled the allies, but the fact that there was an attack did not surprise. The toll on both sides was high with 14,344 enemy claimed to have been killed by III MAF and ARVN units during February 1968, the main period of Tet. Three thousand eight hundred and forty-three weapons were captured. The American forces in III MAF lost 796 men killed in action, another 83 died of wounds, and 3221 were wounded.[11] Those figures do not include the Korean brigade or the South Vietnamese casualties.

It was now time for both sides to consolidate and lick their wounds. The North Vietnamese regional commander, General Chu Huy Man, decided to withdraw his Main Force units, which he wrote about later: 'Vo Chi Cong [NVA Military Region 5 Commissar] and I reviewed the situation and decided to use small units ... while we sent the bulk of our forces out into the rural countryside to ... secure and maintain our strategic posture.'[12] The pressing question for allied intelligence was, where were they going? It was a question that was never adequately answered and as a result would cause the Americans considerable tactical unease. Prior to General Man's decision, two prisoners captured in the Go Noi

Island area described the typical hardships the Viet Cong units had suffered. Luu Van Niem, a platoon leader, said the battalion was always short of food. The morale of the battalion was low because the experienced soldiers were afraid of being killed by the Marine firepower. Thinh Van Ba, who was a stretcher-bearer in the same unit, confessed: 'The company is short of food; they are tired and afraid of the bombings.'[13] Also, although their unit was a Local Force battalion it had received North Vietnamese as replacements for its losses. This was common following Tet 1968 when Viet Cong losses were high, even though VC units may have had a high percentage of northerners in their ranks they were still known as VC and not NVA formations.

The American government was also worried. President Johnson bought into the operational picture by asking General Earle G. Wheeler, Chairman of the Joint Chiefs of Staff, to find out if General William Westmoreland, Commander, US Military Assistance Command Vietnam, wanted more help. There was a slightly terse exchange between Westmoreland and Wheeler when all that MACV requested was another C-130 squadron. Westmoreland was told, 'The United States Government is not prepared to accept defeat in South Vietnam. In summary, if you need more troops, ask for them.'[14] On 12 February, the president approved an Army brigade and the 27th Marines to move to Vietnam. The Marine regiment included the 2nd Battalion 13th Marines, an artillery battalion that would, in the near future, deploy a platoon of two 105 mm howitzers to Ngok Tavak. The rapid deployment of the regiment and its associated administrative difficulties are detailed in Dr Jack Shulimson's *The Defining Year*; some of the manpower challenges are described here.

> At a meeting at the White House later on the 12th . . . the Joint Chiefs of Staff . . . [directed] . . . the movement of a reinforced regiment from the 5th Marine Division to Vietnam, with one battalion moving by sea and the other two by air. Air transport would begin by 14 February, and the entire regiment was to be in Vietnam by 26 February. The Commandant [USMC] promptly directed Lieutenant General Victor H. Krulak to prepare Regimental Landing Team (RLT) 27 for deployment to Vietnam by the afternoon of 14 February. Battalion Landing Team (BLT) 1/27, normally stationed in Hawaii,

was already at sea, having embarked on board amphibious shipping for a four-month training deployment on 10 and 12 February. On 13 February, General Krulak simply cancelled the training exercise and directed the battalion to steam directly to Da Nang. Not only was the BLT seriously under strength . . . nearly 400 embarked Marines and sailors did not meet the criteria for assignment to Vietnam. Nearly 100 infantrymen waived a disqualifying factor and volunteered to deploy with the regiment.[15]

One of those was Private First Class William H. Loman, Jr., whose family had a long history of military service with American forces that dated back to pre-United States days. Loman enlisted in February 1965 and following recruit training he served his first year in Vietnam with H Battery, 3rd Battalion, 11th Marines, which was based at Chu Lai. Loman recalled joining Delta Battery, 2nd Battalion, 13th Marines, in 1967.

Hawaii held very bad days for me. There was never any thought of the unit going into Vietnam, it was never discussed and the general idea was that we were in existence only to fill holes left by units [who had gone] to Vietnam. No combat was ever thought of or trained for. We did the standard field training there in Hawaii, but these folks were in pre Vietnam mindset as far as I was concerned. I don't know how many in the howitzer platoon, other than myself, had served in Vietnam; it wasn't discussed. Finally in February 1968, we deployed out of Hawaii on what was to become a Pacific curse [sic], Okinawa, Philippines, Australia etc. We loaded out of Hawaii and were out about three days when orders changed to go to Vietnam. I had to sign a waiver to go back in, I had a brother over at Danang. I was actually happy to be going back in even though I was disappointed about not getting to see the world. I was hit up [asked a lot of questions] by quite a few Marines about what it was like. I told them, keep your head and butt down and do what you are told and you'll make it. I also told them not to take the traditional idea that artillery is behind the line with grunts [infantry] on the perimeter. There were no actual lines in Vietnam.[16]

Captain Conrad Kinsey, who had served a year in Vietnam during 1965–66, was assigned as battery commander of D Battery, 2nd Battalion, in October 1967. He remembered his unit's deployment to Vietnam in February 1968.

In about the first week of February 1968 we departed from Pearl Harbor on our 'Grand Tour' of the Orient. On the 4th or 5th day out of Pearl we received orders cancelling our 'Tour' and directing us to Danang. Anyone with less than one year back from Vietnam was to be detached unless specifically volunteering to waive their time back. Most of the junior enlisted men waived the time back requirement. But we were hit hard in the staff NCO and officer ranks where none waived their time back, electing instead to keep their marriage. Nearly all of D Battery's staff and officers were lost. While we were in transit to Danang [a]... very innovative training program [was developed] to prepare the battery for action. In many ways we brainwashed the men to believe that they were the best cannoneers in the Corps. On 28th of February we arrived at Danang. A more ragtag outfit has never been observed landing to go to war. Because we departed Hawaii for a training cruise people had brought some of the most incongruous items. One sergeant had brought two Japanese motor scooters to be repaired in Japan. One officer debarked carrying a golf bag over one shoulder and a banjo over the other. Another sergeant was carrying a guitar and someone had an eight-foot surfboard.[17]

Bob Adams, who had been Conrad Kinsey's Executive Officer in the mortar battery prior to Kinsey's assignment to D Battery, found he had been transferred to the position of S-4 (Logistics Officer) in the 1/27 Battalion Landing Team (BLT) when he returned from a live firing exercise to Kaneohe, Hawaii.

I thought of myself as artilleryman, not a grunt. I didn't like the idea... but I made the best of it. I was to write an embarkation plan [for the 'Grand Tour'] we were told that we would be meeting many dignitaries... all officers were to take their summer dress uniforms... NCOs were to take a coat. It all sounded like fun and games. After a week or so we were informed that we would be going to a live fire exercise at Danang. [The mother of all live fire exercises!] It was something of a logistical nightmare when we arrived at Danang to off-load. We had all of our underage Marines who were not allowed to go ashore. We also had a number of Marines who had just returned from Vietnam; they were not allowed ashore either. The first night ashore was a bit freaky; the BLT infantry side was a little over half strength. The artillerymen... suddenly found themselves in the line units of the BLT and without weapons.[18]

Lance Corporal Tim Brown's memories of Battery D's training and preparation prior to their unexpected deployment to Vietnam were more robust.

Because of [my] assignment to a Fleet Marine Force Pacific unit rather than immediate deployment to Vietnam, which was the exception... I and my fellow Marines... benefited from cross-training in several areas, more physical conditioning, live firing, field exercises and tropical climate acclimation as an intact unit... for almost a full year. Delta Battery, a six-gun 105 mm howitzer unit along with Whiskey Battery, a 4.2-inch [107 mm] mortar unit, had been detached from the 2nd Battalion, 13th Marines, 5th Marine Division in California to Kaneohe Bay, Oahu, Hawaii. There, along with elements of the 27th Marine Regiment, we formed an amphibious reaction force for the Pacific area. Many of the NCOs had at least one Vietnam tour under their belt, as did many of our officers, some with Korean War combat experience as well. Following my return to Hawaii from Christmas leave in December 1967, the level of training... [and] the degree of discipline administered by our officers began to noticeably increase... so there was a prevailing feeling among us all that something out of the ordinary was about to come our way. Sometime in late January 1968, we were officially informed that we would depart by ship for a cruise to the Philippines, Okinawa, Japan and back to Kaneohe Bay. For us, it was an exciting adventure to exotic places, fun foreign women and so forth although there were some old salts that insisted that our real destination was

'Nam'. While that notion lingered in the back of my mind, I chose to believe the official description of the mission. We had all been told to pack our civilian clothes as well as dress uniforms along with our combat gear.

The force, then organised as a battalion landing team, sailed aboard three ships: USS *Vancouver*, USS *Bexar* and USS *Washburn*. The *Vancouver* departed on 10 February, the others followed on 12 February 1968. Tim Brown remembered leaving Pearl Harbor.

As we departed . . . most of us stood on deck along the railing, each I'm sure with many mixed emotions as we passed through that narrow historic channel leading us into the deep blue waters of the Pacific. I must admit that many old WW2 movies flashed through my mind . . . being young and naïve, I had glorious thoughts that I, like my Dad before me, and my brother, was off to land on the beach of some far away hostile island . . . as a mean and dangerous Marine to defeat the enemy of my country at the time. Soon after, seasickness hit many of us, some seriously, plus a long voyage on military ships is no cruise. Stacked four high in unbearable heat, poor ventilation, awful food and the rocking and rolling of the ship made the ride over seem worse that the eventual destination.

General Krulak's order to change the destination was issued on 13 February, as Lance Corporal Tim Brown recalled.

On about the 3rd or 4th day . . . just after evening chow, the ship's captain came over the PA system . . . Now hear this . . . Now hear this . . . just like in the aforementioned war movies, and he advised all hands that the ship had just received orders changing our destination to Danang. You, at first, could hear a pin drop, it was so quiet and then all hell broke loose with . . . they can't do this, my wife and family are stranded in Hawaii, or hell, I just got back from Nam three months ago, and there were a fair number of, see I told you so as well. Needless to say the tone and mood of everyone changed at this point and the next day we began to prepare for war. While I don't recall the exact date we pulled in to Danang, it was after dark when we dropped anchor and we could not offload until after sunrise the next morning. We could not sleep, so most of us stayed on deck and watched the show off in the distant hills. A distant raging storm combined with a stateside fireworks show was the best way I could describe [the action]. The mood was quiet and sombre . . . this was the real deal . . . I realized the moment of truth had finally arrived. I experienced feelings of fear, excitement and loneliness. The next day, we headed off to Hill 34 [southwest of Danang], which was to be our fire support base over the next several months.[19]

The potpourri army

The Australian Army Training Team Vietnam (AATTV)—Australian advisers—was the first Australian unit committed to the war when it arrived in Saigon in the middle of 1962. Although the Australian government had directed that AATTV, or the Team as it was colloquially known, was not to be involved in combat, the commander of AATTV was soon seeking to get his men involved in more active tasks. In October 1962, he took advantage of an offer made by the US Special Forces to attach Australians to their village defence program. Sergeant Ray Simpson was sent to a village near Lao Bao, which was on Route 9 very near the border with Laos, and then to the village of Khe Sanh with detachment A-131 of the 1st Special Forces Group (SFG). The groundwork for more Australians to be assigned to Special Forces had been established. Ray Simpson would later be awarded the Victoria Cross (US Medal of Honor equivalent) for conspicuous gallantry for actions with a Mike Force unit under the command of the 5th Special Forces Group. He would be one of three Victoria Cross recipients who were decorated with the highest award for gallantry while attached to US Special Forces. There were only four VCs bestowed during the war; all were granted to members of AATTV.

The Buon Enao experiment was considered to be the beginning of the formation of a Montagnard force that would evolve into the Civilian Irregular Defense Group (CIDG). Buon Enao was a small Montagnard village along Route 21, just to the east of Ban Me Thuot in Darlac Province. The idea was to train and arm the villagers who would pledge allegiance to the South Vietnamese government to stop their defection to the North Vietnamese controlled forces. This program, started by the CIA and handed on to the Special Forces under *Operation Switchback* in 1963, brought a change in administrative matters, but not attitude. Dislike between the Montagnard and Vietnamese prevailed. During the period 1963–65, Buon Enao grew into a 1000-man group that was known as the *Truong Son Force*, which was led by Australian Captain Barry Petersen.

Also, from December 1962 to February 1963, the US Army Special Forces trained and armed 18,000 strike-force warriors. CIDG camps were built in all four tactical zones of South Vietnam with a strong emphasis post-1963 on border surveillance. From the camps the CIDG would 'conduct guerrilla warfare—long-range patrol activities to deny the border areas to the Viet Cong by detection, interdiction, harassment, and elimination of the infiltration routes parallel to or through the border control zone'.[20] In reality, the program was beset with problems that stopped the camps watching over the border routes effectively. To begin with, the camps were too far apart; they had 'a density of one company per 28 miles [45 kilometres]'. There were command disagreements between the CIDG, the Vietnamese Special Forces and their US Special Forces and Australian advisers, who were often required to command, not advise. Nevertheless, although the camps could not prevent the movement of enemy forces, they were kept open to provide locations to gather information that was fed back into the intelligence stream. The camps, however, were prone to attack by night and this weakness was exploited by the enemy whenever a camp became too much of an annoyance. The CIDG was also susceptible to infiltration by the Viet Cong. In 1964, the forerunner of Mobile Strike Force companies (Mike Force) was set up with the specific aim of being a reserve or reinforcement troops for camps under attack. Mike Force units deployed both Montagnard and Nung as their principal fighters, with both groups entering into mercenary contracts with the US Special Forces. The Mike Force role was expanded later to include raids, ambushes, combat patrols and small-scale conventional combat operations.

In September 1965, Captain Geoff Skardon commanded Detachment A-107 when it reopened the camp at Tra Bong in Quang Ngai Province. Other Australians now held positions in the 'C' Team in

Danang and with the Nung Force as well, which was also in the Danang area. At the end of December 1965, twenty out of a total of 88 Australian advisers in South Vietnam were deployed in Special Forces positions. This association strengthened over the next two years to the point where an Australian captain commanded the Mike Force in Danang, which consisted of four companies (11, 12, 14 and 16), and Australians also commanded companies and platoons within that force. The Mike Force companies were frequently deployed in I Corps to assist camps such as Tien Phuoc, Sa Huynh, Thuong Duc and Lang Vei (near Khe Sanh). In January 1968, the Australians with Special Forces had spread to the head-quarters at Nha Trang and into the Mike Force located at Pleiku, but the total number remained unchanged at twenty. In 1965, the concept of operations for the CIDG changed to a more offensive task. They were to seek and fight the enemy, to clear and secure an area, which was a more conventional warfare function and one, many knew, for which the CIDG was neither trained nor equipped. Australian Captain Peter Ray, who commanded 14th Mike Force Company and the Danang Mike Force in 1967, remembered:

> The I Corps Mike Force companies were being sent off on what were at times quite unrealistic tasks given their level of training and their numbers. Furthermore Lt Col Schungel (senior SF officer, I Corps) committed the Mike Force elements to operations, which were unsound, with an inadequate level of support, even down to insufficient radios for the basic nets. He was undoubtedly a most courageous man who believed in leading from the very front, but I believe that he was tactically naïve. In the past, the Mike Force had been thrown into situations with very little information on the situation—in other words they went in blind. On this particular night [a camp was under attack] we had a good understanding of the situation and briefed Mal [Captain Malcolm McCallum] accordingly. It was fairly obvious to me that if Mal's company moved directly from the LZ to the 'A camp' it would pass through an obvious killing ground, and I gave him a direct order that under no circumstances was he to move along that route. This was fortuitous because as it transpired the enemy had prepared an ambush in that area for the reaction company, but that wasn't the end of it. As was

his way, Lt Col Daniel Schungel had gone out to the camp to take over the situation. He ordered Mal to move through the area in question and Mal refused to on the basis that I had given him a direct order not to do so, which probably saved himself and his men, but did not endear him or me to the colonel.[21]

In 2006, Malcolm McCallum confirmed that he had refused to go down an obvious ambush alley, as he delightfully explained: 'I did not want to be the title of a lesson learnt at the Australian Jungle Warfare Training Centre on what not to do in the relief of a garrison under attack.' He had a vision of the Centre's students sniggering at his stupidity as the instructors outlined what that fool McCallum had done by blundering into an obvious trap.[22]

One of the CIDG camps built at Lang Vei, just west of Khe Sanh on Highway 9 near the Laos border, was attacked on 7 February 1968, during the Tet Offensive. North Vietnamese hit the camp with a heavy mortar bombardment that was followed by an attack by amphibious tanks (PT-76) and supporting infantry who used satchel charges, tear gas and flame-throwers to breach the camp's defences. Lieutenant Colonel Daniel F. Schungel, Commander, Company C, US Special Forces, was in the camp at the time and fought through the battle until a relief force of MACV-SOG commanded by Major George Quamo rescued them. The Lang Vei battle casualties were very heavy. Ten of the Special Forces soldiers were either missing or thought to be dead and thirteen were wounded. Three of the missing had been captured and were released in 1973. More than 300 of the CIDG troops were either killed or went missing. The battle also caused some recrimination against the Marines by the Army's Green Berets. The Marines located at the Khe Sanh Combat Base (KSCB), approximately 10 kilometres to the east of Lang Vei, had practised reinforcing the Special Forces camp, but in attempting to emulate a tactical avoidance of possible ambushes they found a 19-hour cross-country effort unworkable. Even though the KSCB was being shelled at the same time as the Lang Vei assault, and was also under threat of a ground attack, they provided artillery support to the Green Berets that included 'Firecracker'—a new shell not previously used in Vietnam—but they did not send reinforcements. General Westmoreland was aware of this. He was in the command post at Danang at the time, but he did not 'interfere' with the ground commander's decision. The lack of reinforcements dismayed Colonel Jonathan Ladd, Commander, 5th Special Forces Vietnam, and he allegedly called General Creighton Abrams Deputy Commander MACV for assistance. Abrams supposedly told him to work it out with the Marine air commander to get the troops out of Lang Vei, Ladd said in a 1984 interview with Ted Gittinger in Washington, D.C.[23] In the *Valley of Decision* by John Prados and Ray Stubbe, however, General Westmoreland is credited with directing Lieutenant General Cushman to provide the helicopters for the rescue.[24] Colonel Ladd remained critical of the Marine Corps' actions, or lack thereof, in the relief of Lang Vei. He never forgave the Marine Corps, especially Colonel David Lowndes, the commander at Khe Sanh, for refusing entry to the combat base by the Montagnard survivors of the Lang Vei battle.

When Lang Vei was overrun, the camp at Kham Duc, which was located at the western edge of Quang Tin Province, 75 kilometres west of Tam Ky, was the last border-surveillance camp remaining in I Corps. Little Ngok Tavak, just 7 kilometres to its southwest, was a derelict and empty old French 'fort' that the Special Forces used as a forward operating base. It really wasn't a fort, but more a cleared area on a little hill that had earthen berms, or walls, that provided some protection for the occupants. Route 14 bordered its eastern slope. There was space to land helicopters at the western end and there was a 700-metre pierced steel planking (PSP) airstrip 500 metres to its northeast that could be used by light tactical aircraft. The 738-metre-high feature named Ngok Tavak overshadowed the strip, and it would be incorrectly referred to in later reports as the Special Forces forward operating base for Kham Duc.

One Vietnam veteran, who had served with US Special Forces in 1968, said that he thought Lieutenant Colonel Schungel, who had been trapped inside the Lang Vei camp when it was overrun, was known to carry a grudge against the Marine Corps thereafter. He allegedly displayed his displeasure in a Machiavellian manner by requesting that two Marine howitzers be placed at Ngok Tavak to support a Special Forces reconnaissance force that was located there. This, so it was said, was to ensure the Marines would not leave him in the lurch again if his camps were attacked. Dr Jack Shulimson, a highly respected Marine Corps historian, said in 2006:

> the two outposts were important to monitor the movements of the NVA, especially the 2d NVA Division. In Cushman's mind also must have been the criticism he received from Westmoreland and Abrams for not reinforcing in January [1968] the Special Forces Camp at Lang Vei in the north near Khe Sanh. They probably assumed that they would be able to reinforce the camps [Kham Duc/Ngok Tavak] if they came under attack and that the two pieces would be sufficient to provide enough protection.[25]

Well prior to this, in 1967, Lieutenant General Lewis W. Walt, Commanding General, III MAF, in a signal message dated 6 May 1967, directed the following responsibilities for the relief and reinforcement of CIDG camps in southern I Corps.

> Pending published changes to references (A) and (B) [letters of instruction to subordinate generals] responsibility for relief/ reinforcement of CIDG camps is assigned as follows: 1st Mar Div [Marine Division] (1) Tien Phuoc. (2) Kham Duc. (3) Thuong Duc. Task Force Oregon [later Americal Division]. (1) Tra Bong. (2) Ha Tanh. (3) Minh Long. (4) Ba To.

Copies of this message were sent to: the Deputy Senior Advisor, I Corps, who was the III MAF officer responsible for the operational control of Company C, 5th SFG; 5th SFG (Airborne) Nha Trang; and Company C, 5th SFG (Airborne) Danang.[26] On 6 September 1967, Major General Donn J. Robertson, Commanding General, 1st Marine Division, promulgated his detailed, 38-page, operational plan 303–67, which provided for the assistance to the three camps allotted to his division. Later in the year, due to the relocation of American units, the Commanding General, III MAF, directed an amendment to the geographical area of responsibility between the 1st Marine Division and the Americal Division by signal message dated 3 October 1967. The 1st Marine Division's plan 303-67 was modified and reissued on 7 November 1967 as Operation Plan 303-68. The Marine division was now responsible for the Thuong Duc camp only. The new demarcation between the two divisions was 12 kilometres to the north of Kham Duc, along the east–west (latitude) gridline 20. This made the Army's American Division accountable for the relief and/or reinforcement of Kham Duc and the change was reflected in the American Division's *Golden Valley* plan.[27] If Lieutenant Colonel Schungel's plot was to goad a Marine reaction to an enemy attack on Ngok Tavak–Kham Duc by putting Marine howitzers there, then his scheme was misguided. Furthermore, it is considered that such a secret plan did not exist because Schungel's request was for some artillery in support; he had no influence over where those guns would come from.

Mike Force

Captain John White and Warrant Officers Don Cameron and Frank Lucas, Australian advisers, were assigned to the Danang Mike Force on 19 February 1968. John White graduated from the Royal Military College, Duntroon, in 1963 and was posted as a platoon commander to the 2nd Battalion of the Royal Australian Regiment. He subsequently served as an instructor at the Officer Cadet School, Portsea. Captain White had not served in a combat operational area prior to his assignment to AATTV in 1968. However, the renowned Major Felix Fazekas, who was the senior instructor on the Tropical Warfare (TW) Advisers' Course at Australia's Jungle Training Centre, wrote this glowing assessment of John White's performance on the 11/67 TW course: 'Captain White was the outstanding officer of the course, who set an excellent example in all phases of training. Recommended for service in the field with AATTV.'[28] His grade was 'B'— above average, 'A', was rarely issued—and the report was signed off by the then Lieutenant Colonel (later major general) Ron Grey. John White's two brothers were also in the Defence Force: Peter in the Army and Michael, the Navy. Don Cameron was on his second tour of Vietnam. He had served previously with the Nung Force in Danang during his service with AATTV in 1965–66. Don had also served in Korea, where he had been awarded the Military Medal for bravery. Frank Lucas was also on his second tour with AATTV, having served with the unit in 1965–66; he, too, had done time with the Nungs. The three Australians were allocated to the 11th Company, White as the company commander and the two warrant officers as platoon commanders. The chart of a Mike Force company below is the official organisation, but like most military establishments, the 'rice-paddy', or operational, strength was less than these numbers. John White's 11th Company consisted of the command group, which, beside him, had the two Australian warrant officers, three enlisted US Special Forces soldiers, three Vietnamese Special Forces personnel and three interpreters. There were 122 Nungs in the company, which made the sub-unit 134 in total.

A Mobile Strike Force (Mike Force) Company

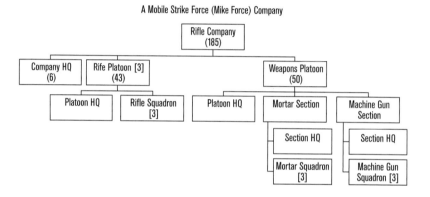

The Mike Force in Danang was under the command of Major Adam Husar, US Special Forces, when Captain John White arrived, a time he remembered nearly 40 years later.

My arrival at Da Nang Mike Force was a low-key event. I did not have any idea what was going on, neither in SVN, I Corps, Da Nang area nor Mike Force. There was neither orientation briefing nor induction. I was introduced to the USSF [Special Forces] people I was to work with in my company and that was about it. We were on an operational footing from then on, in that we could be sent as a reaction force or on an operation as we were. There was a barracks for my company and Nungs seemed to come and go. Sometimes there would be up to 100 people there and sometimes 20. I had no idea what was going on. In the first week of my being there, I took the company onto the sand hills nearby to look at how we would do a company attack and it was a mixture of US tactics,

French, Vietnamese and whatever. Basically, there was no standard approach. We stayed in this situation (I demanded a briefing from my commander but that was so vague that I was none the wiser) for a couple of weeks and then we were told we were going on an operation in the Kham Duc area. Then things started to happen. Firstly, soldiers started to turn up and the barracks started to fill. What I did not know was the local tong/triad controlled things in a loose way and they had a hand in filling vacancies and taking commissions. I had no idea how good the incumbents were and the USSF guys told me we just had to take what we got. My thoughts were quite different. I think the USSF got caught in a bit of a self-made trap where they wanted to demonstrate clearly that they were the commanders. In doing this they did not generally consult with their Nungs. My approach was to involve the Nungs, as they would have to fight with and depend on one another. I asked around and found out there was a respected Nung, whom I nicknamed 'Tiger' (he liked the name), and I appointed him my Nung commander. A lot of the people who called themselves Nungs were actually Chinese cowboys from Da Nang and I had no idea who was who. I explained to Tiger that, as far as I was concerned he was my Nung commander, he was in charge of selecting who went with us and he would be responsible for them. I doubled his pay and we had a good arrangement. Tiger then walked through the ranks, gave the nod to most, told about 20 to go away and we now had a company of about 130 men. Then back to the sand hills to look at our company tactics. I worked out a dual command approach: I would discuss what we were going to do with the three platoon commanders—Warrant Officers Don Cameron and Frank Lucas and Sergeant Swicegood—and give them, along with the specialist USSF, their orders. I would then brief Tiger and he would pass the information down through the Nung chain-of-command that I asked him to set up. There was never any doubt that the Australians–Americans were in charge but this approach saved time and confusion. Tiger was a natural leader, a good soldier and a very tough man. The Nungs did what he said and he never abused his power. We spent a couple of weeks training, firing weapons and being kitted out. The training comprised minor tactics and the Nungs knew more about this than we did. My approach was to find out what they did and tell the Australians/US that was how we were going to do it also. It was simpler, safer and easier to adapt to their known approach rather than confuse them with major changes. There was no need to teach them about weapons. Each Nung had his favourite weapon and our job was more to provide ammunition for it. Mostly they carried M16s, M79s and a few favoured their carbines. These soldiers had been at war for years and they knew what they wanted.[29]

Where in the CTZ is the 2nd NVA?

The movements of the 2nd NVA Division confounded the allied intelligence agencies—it was a real will-o'-the-wisp unit. American intelligence reports for the first two months of 1968 had tagged the NVA unit fairly accurately, but these reports were written after the event and as Captain (later colonel) James F. Humphries remembered:

> Tracking the elusive NVA division from its hidden base areas into the Que Son or Hiep Duc valley areas was no simple task. Except for information provided by some defectors and the occasional radio intercept, though, it was we infantry, or cavalry soldiers who most often found the enemy—usually where we did not expect him to be. I personally feel that we knew too little about the NVA and VC units whom we fought, and my opinion is not an isolated one.[30]

In January and February, the clashes between the 2nd NVA and the US forces, both Army and Marines, assisted with the identification and tracking of the division's units, but the whereabouts and plans of the North Vietnamese following those battles were less clear. The 1st Marine Division's Command Chronology for March 1968 identified Main Force (enemy) units in its area of operations as:

> The Headquarters of the 2nd NVA Division was last located in the vicinity of [grid reference] ZC 1628 [approximately 25 kilometres northeast of Kham Duc] on 22 March. The 1st VC Regiment was reported at ZC 1845 on 19 March [approximately 40 kilometres west of Hoi An]. The 3rd Regiment was ... in the vicinity of AT

9419 [approximately 25 kilometres northwest of the Special Forces camp at Tien Phuoc]. The 21st regiment was in the vicinity of AT 8328 [approximately 30 kilometres to the southeast of the Special Forces camp at Thuong Duc and the same distance northeast of Kham Duc].[31]

These locations contradicted the information released with the 27th Marines operation order signed off on 22 March that included an intelligence summary provided with the 1st Marine Division's Operation Order 301-68, which put the 2nd NVA Division's headquarters at Que Son—30 kilometres southwest of Hoi An—with two regiments, the 3rd (aka 31st of the 2nd Division) and the 21st, near Go Noi Island, which was just to the west of Hoi An, and the 1st Regiment was 20 kilometres to the west of Tam Ky. In April, however, the NVA division did not rate a mention in the 1st Marine Division's command report. The 5th Special Forces Group submitted a more ominous account for the period January–April 1968 in which they said:

> The presence of the 31st NVA Regiment near Thuong Duc (A–109), the 2nd NVA Division command post and the 3rd Regiment, 2nd NVA Division near Kham Duc (A-105), and the 1st (and possibly the 21st) NVA regiments near Tien Phuoc (A-102) posed serious threats to the three camps as the quarter ended. [Note that the report refers to the 31st and the 3rd regiments and in this case it is assumed that the 31st is the independent regiment previously mentioned.]

Their observations continued with another warning.

> The VC are using the CIDG recruiting programs as means for infiltrating agents into the CIDG. Investigation following a recent attack on a CSF [Camp Strike Force] outpost revealed that several VC had infiltrated the ranks of the CIDG . . . a total of 27 actual or suspected VC . . . were subsequently apprehended.[32]

III Marine Amphibious Force, Periodic Intelligence Report number 18-68 dated 5 May 1968, supported the locations of the NVA units listed by the 5th Special Forces in their quarterly report. Intelligence agencies across the board all warned that one of the enemy's primary courses of action was considered to be an attack on isolated units and outposts with up to one reinforced regiment. Two changes were implemented to American plans in April and May 1968 that refined the provision of assistance to Special Forces camps in southern I Corps. Change 3 to the 1st Marine Division's Operation Order 301-68, dated 10 April 1968, gave the 7th Marines the mission to be prepared to provide a relief force for the CIDG camp at Thuong Duc. The same order directed 27th Marines to be prepared also to provide a relief force for Thuong Duc, but that company-sized force, if deployed, would be under the operational control of the 7th Marines who had the primary obligation. The Americal Division's *Golden Valley* plan (Relief/Reinforcement of CIDG Camps) was amended on 4 May 1968 so that the 1st Battalion, 46th Infantry Battalion's Task Force from the Americal Division had the duty to relieve/reinforce the Kham Duc Special Forces/CIDG camp. That directive included this analysis on the enemy's capabilities:

> The enemy has the freedom of movement, available time, and resources to prepare detailed attack plans to assault isolated US SF/CIDG camps.
>
> The enemy possesses the capability to marshal forces in secure areas of his choosing in an attempt to overwhelm a particular camp before a relief force may react effectively. The enemy can be expected to establish ambushes along major avenues of approach likely to be used by ground forces. [33]

The document concluded:

> US SF/CIDG camps will be attacked during the hours of darkness, reduced visibility and inclement weather. Reinforcement or relief force...for Kham Duc [and Ngok Tavak]...would require a minimum of 2½ hours for 1 company and nine hours for four companies and an artillery battery [to arrive at the location].[34]

To further complicate the intelligence picture, Major Thomas McGan, who commanded Detachment B of the 1st Military Intelligence Battalion, wrote several reports on the Kham Duc area in March and April 1968. This is a summary of the main points.

Air force intelligence reported ... a new road under construction at YC 779 028 [approximately 30 kilometres to the southwest of Kham Duc and inside Laos] [Three weeks later] ... an overflight revealed that the road construction had moved approximately twelve kilometres to the southeast. Two spot reports on 28 February revealed that the highway had actually extended east [to within] ... 1000 metres from Highway 14 [the main route inside Vietnam that went to Ngok Tavak and Kham Duc]. The road is a three-lane, graded dirt, fair weather road. Aircraft dropping 750-pound [340-kilogram] bombs have successfully inflicted heavy damage to major sections of the highway [inside Vietnam] ... these road cuts have not been repaired. Anti-aircraft fire has been very extensive in this area ... [with] .30 cal and .50 cal ... being used ... there have not been any reports of 37mm fire. However ... in Laos ... destroyed parts of the road have been repaired. South of the new road and down Highway 14 ... work has been detected on a trail extending northeast [a track than ran parallel to Highway 14, but separated from it by a major ridgeline].

Major McGan's reports provided trends of possible enemy action and he also corrected errors in grid references that were used in his first summary of 14 March. The road was first sighted closer to the border with Vietnam than the first report indicated. Major McGan's analyses continued:

Extensive construction on a new highway from Laos to Vietnam indicates that the enemy is seeking a new route for supplies and troop movement. The road extends ... east into Vietnam and to Highway 14, 10 km south of Kham Duc [this distance was an error, the road was around 25 kilometres south]. There has been no movement north on Highway 14 toward the special forces camp, but instead new construction extends north west [sic northeast] to the Dak Mi River and would probably be used to supply the enemy forces in the Tam Ky, Hoi An and Da Nang areas. It appears at this time that most of the enemy's fire power is defensive as heavy weapons have not been detected. A friendly patrolling unit has been moved to Ngok Tavak, 7 km south of Kham Duc . . . and repairs are being made to the airstrip at that location. They have reported two small probing attacks but none have been serious enough to cause damage. [When interviewed in 2006, Captain John White, the Australian patrol commander, denied his position had been probed.] It appears that the enemy is continuing their plan of extending the road in an easterly direction.[35]

An intelligence estimate update promulgated by HQ 5th SFGA on 28 April 1968 provided the following information: 'collateral intelligence reports indicate that the 2nd NVA Div HQ . . . has moved [from a position close to the Laos border] to vicinity of YB 9689 as of 21 April 1968 [approximately 12 kilometres due south of Ngok Tavak]'. Documents were also found that indicated an NVA soldier who had been released from a regimental hospital may have come from 'Factory 10', which was an alias for the 3rd NVA Regiment, 2nd NVA Division. Further information that came from III MAF intelligence said that the HQ, 2nd NVA Division, had a strength of 125 and the 2nd Battalion, 3rd Regiment, had 200 personnel. The 5th SFGA paper continued:

> [Recent and present significant activities:] An old French road that runs from . . . where it leads off Hwy 14 in a north-easterly direction, and ends at the western bank of the Dak Mi river, has been widened and reconditioned. There has been heavy foot traffic detected on a trail leading east off Hwy 14 [approximately 20 kilometres south of Ngok Tavak]. Trail activity south of Ngok Tavak on Hwy 14, to the new road has been light. [Enemy capabilities:] Attack isolated units and outposts with up to one reinforced regiment. Camp Kham Duc is the vulnerable camp to an enemy armored attack in Quang Tin Province. Although there have been no reports of armor in this area.[36]

The location of the 2nd NVA Division in 1968 is also shown in a Vietnamese record on the division's activities. *Second Division, Volume 1,* published in 1989, acknowledged the fighting that took place during the Tet of 1968, which is corroborated in some aspects by Senior General Chu Huy Man's comments in *Time of Upheaval*. It is easy to discount some of the extravagant claims of victory over American units and the numbers of casualties that the NVA caused, as some of the US accounts must also be questioned. But, included in the 2nd Division's records are valuable accounts of where they were and what it was they intended to achieve in battle. Some excerpts are repeated below, with, first of all, a constructive piece of self-criticism about its Tet skirmishes.

> During these operations [Tet], the division's cadre and soldiers were further tempered in battle and tested in combat on new, unfamiliar battlefields and on difficult terrain, moving constantly and fighting without adequate preparations and supplies etc. However, the quality and efficiency of the division was not high. The division was unable to carry out its mission of annihilating large enemy units and could not dominate the battlefield, and its effectiveness in supporting local revolutionary movements was limited.[37]

Following the deaths of the divisional commander and senior staff officers in December 1967, the new NVA commanders realised that the division had been over-extended immediately prior to Tet when it had been required to attack Que Son instead of resting and preparing for the main assault. Nevertheless, the acknowledged flawed attack plan on Danang that used only one battalion went ahead, but 'the single battalion from 2nd Division was only able to get one platoon into the city'. General Chu Huy Man decided soon after that 'the bulk of our forces [would be withdrawn] and sent out into the rural countryside to destroy enemy forces and maintain our strategic posture'.[38] This decision was recorded in *Second Division, Volume 1*:

> In response to urgent battlefield requirements, in early March 1968 the Military Region Headquarters ordered the division to turn around and march back to the west to destroy Kham Duc district capital and district military headquarters, to clear Route 14, and open a road for our supply trucks from the main strategic transportation corridor [the Ho Chi Minh Trail] down to the coastal lowlands.

The North Vietnamese Army's analysis on how to attack Kham Duc concluded that Ngok Tavak should be neutralised as well. Furthermore, the NVA examined the problem of how to prevent the Americans from interfering with their preparatory phase. They decided:

> Given the enemy's deployment of forces at that time, the only force that could support Kham Duc was the US Americal Division. The division decided to establish a new combat area [which] would tie down the mobile elements of the Americal Division. During this campaign, therefore, the [2nd NVA] division would have to fight in two different widely separated locations. The Division (minus) would be responsible for destroying the Kham Duc complex. The 31st Regiment, reinforced, would establish a combat area [further to the east in an arc to the north of Tien Phuoc] and . . . lure in troops of the Americal Division . . . and tie them down in that area. This combat area would begin its operations 7 to 10 days before the main operation [at Kham Duc].[39]

The NVA had rightly forecast that the only additional troops available to help Kham Duc had to come from the Americal Division and they would engage that division to disrupt its plans and to destroy any force that came to the rescue of the camp. The battle dice had been thrown; now the warriors prepared for combat.

2 INTO THE CAULDRON

The battleground

Kham Duc was now the only border camp in the northern five provinces of South Vietnam. The primary mission of the strike force (indigenous troops) at Kham Duc was to control the population and resources, interdict infiltration, and to conduct reconnaissance, surveillance and combat operations. The camp also had the task of training all Civilian Irregular Defense Group troops in I Corps. The main village, 800 metres northwest of the camp, held 272 people, of which only 15 per cent were civilian merchants and families; the remainder were dependants of the camp strike force.[1] President Ngo Dinh Diem, who was murdered in Saigon on 2 November 1963, had used the Kham Duc area as a 'hunting lodge', and a solid airfield was constructed in the valley to allow the president access by air, although the surrounding mountains made approaches and departures difficult. He reportedly once moved an entire regiment of the 2nd ARVN Division (South Vietnamese) to the area to protect him while he hunted tiger and other big game.

The American Special Forces first came to the district in August 1963, as 1st Lieutenant (later colonel) Wayne Long, USA SF (Ret.) recalled.

My team, commanded by Captain Joe Schwar, was detached upon arrival and placed under operational control of the CIA. Our job was to take command of two CIA-recruited Border Surveillance Battalions (Indigenous troops of course) and commence shallow penetration recce and strike missions into Laos. The team was split, with half under Schwar deploying to Khe Sanh, and myself commanding the other half . . . to Kham Duc. There was a Vietnamese Special Forces team with each battalion. Our higher HQ was the CIA station at Danang under Tucker Guggerman. Australian Captain Guy Boileau was a liaison officer to the station. Our first operation was in November, and from then until our redeployment in February 1964 we averaged three operations a month. We had an active area; 'Charles' didn't like us screwing around in his rear areas while he was in the process of constructing the 'Trail' road system.

Long remembered using the Ngok Tavak fort located 7 kilometres to the southwest of Kham Duc, but he did not recall an airstrip in the area.

Ngok Tavak served two purposes for us. Initially it was a base for a half battery of ARVN 105 howitzers, the other half as at Kham Duc [and therefore, capable of supporting each other] and they provided pretty effective forward based indirect covering fire for us. Then as ops moved closer to the border, Ngok Tavak became a Forward Operating Base (FOB). The ARVN redeployed the half battery back to Kham Duc since their main mission was to provide defensive indirect fire for that place.

Colonel Long described the Ngok Tavak camp's layout:

It was a bermed compound about 75 to 100 metres off the road to the west on a small ridge that ran roughly at right angles to Highway 14. There was a double-apron barbed wire barrier outside the berms and about 8 or 10 lightly revetted artillery positions in a 360-degree arc inside the walls. The revetments always seemed to be half-full of water and I wondered how the ARVN could man the three guns that were deployed there. The supporting infantry had a few automatic weapon positions with light overhead cover and sandbags. The living shelters were two or three poorly sandbagged buildings with corrugated tin roofs and a chicken coop and a pigsty inside the walls, all pretty squalid.[2]

Wayne Long also said that after they came back to Kham Duc, there were signs that the VC also used the Ngok Tavak camp as a stopover from time to time. They tried to ambush them there, but were not successful. Other Special Forces men who served in the area after 1964 also recalled using the site infrequently, more as a one-day stopover, rest-up and resupply base prior to further patrolling. By 1968, the berms and pits were overgrown owing to lack of full-time use. The old parade ground and the fort's inner space, however, were flat, open and denuded of flora, except for a light copse of trees that provided a boundary between the two parts of the position. Kenneth Benway, a Special Forces medic, who went to Ngok Tavak with John White's 11th Company in March 1968, described the airstrip that was about 500 metres to the north of the fort area.

> I believe the airstrip matting was easily more than ten years old. I was told by a member of the USSF at Kham Duc that the airstrip at Ngok Tavak was of French origin. That has stuck in my mind very clearly since then. Once on the ground, and we walked its length, I was surprised at how stout and still-serviceable the matting— Pierced Steel Planking—(PSP) type metal matting, composed of approximately 10 feet by three feet [3 metres by 1 metre] sections linked together, corrugated with approximately three inch holes through which the elephant grass was growing. The matting sections were beginning to show a dark patina of corrosion, but I believe they were still sturdy enough to have been serviceable for air operations. [A 5th SFGA report dated 18 March 1968 said that the strip was recently overhauled.] The foundation ... appeared to be well packed, with a layer of fine gravel. It seemed to me that the airstrip was built by very competent engineers; further reinforcing my understanding that it was of French construction.[3]

Detachment B of the 1st Military Intelligence Battalion provided this information on the terrain around Kham Duc–Ngok Tavak in March 1968:

> Kham Duc is located in Quang Tin Province 90 km west of Tam Ky near the Laotian border. The terrain in the vicinity is very rough with mountain peaks reaching the elevation of 4000 and 5000 feet [1220 and 1525 metres]. Heavy canopy and underbrush cover the

mountains and valleys, making traffic difficult by foot. Highway 14 extending parallel along the Dak Se River...is a single lane road in ill repair that is now being used only for foot traffic. It extends... south past Kham Duc [and Ngok Tavak]. Most of the bridges along the road...are in poor condition and are unusable to vehicular traffic. Weather conditions are poor during the [south] monsoon [April to October] and limit air traffic considerably.[4]

Go get 'em

Company C, 5th Special Forces, located at Danang, came up with a plan to supplement the information-gathering agencies that were operating around Kham Duc in early 1968 by putting a Mike Force company on the ground to the south of the camp in March. Captain John White's 11th Company was selected. White remembered that the concept of the operation was not described very well.

> Prior to leaving for our task I was given a briefing by the Mike Force operations officer. The CO of Mike Force (LTCOL Schungel) sat in on the briefing but added little. I am not exaggerating when I say the briefing went something like this: 'the enemy is moving north along the axis of Route 14. We want you to take your company to Kham Duc and reconnoitre south, make contact with the enemy, see if you can take some prisoners and gather some intelligence.' The rest of the briefing was about transport, radios etc. There was not one mention that the enemy was 2 NVA Div—which they knew and I did not find out until about a week before we were over-run [5th SFG reports disagree with this assertion], where the enemy was up to with regard to its advance, how long the operation was meant to last, etc. I shudder now to think how ill-prepared we were but I naively thought that these people knew what they were doing, that my activities were part of a big plan and that more information would flow forth in due course. So, off we went to Kham Duc, about an hour's flight by C-130. I do not know what date this was. Capt Chris Silva was the USSF commander at Kham Duc and made us feel welcome. He knew little more than I did about the tactical and strategic situation but he was helpful with briefings on

the local topography. We stayed at Kham Duc about 48 hours and then set off south along Route 14, which we were told was safe to advance along.[5]

It is at this point that the official reports and individual memories begin to differ, as Kudelk, a cartoonist, so aptly portrayed in *The Australian* newspaper: 'War is long periods of boredom punctuated by moments of sheer terror followed by years and years of arguing about what actually happened.'[6] Captain White said, many years later:

> The old French fort that I subsequently named Ngok Tavak after an adjacent small mountain, lay on Route 14 and when we came upon it on the second day, I thought it was ideal for us to lie up while we began patrolling to the south to see what was happening.[7]

Ngok Tavak, however, was a well-known FOB. Not only did Wayne Long remember its use in 1963, Specialist Fourth Class Mark R. Chase, a member of A1/324 Special Forces team was killed in action at Ngok Tavak—an outpost of Kham Duc—on 4 March 1965. Although John White does not recall being told to use Ngok Tavak, all of the reports indicate that he was directed to go there and to establish a base from which he could operate further to the south. The Military Intelligence Detachment B's report dated 7 April 1968 said, for example, that 'a friendly patrolling unit [11th Company] has been moved to Ngok Tavak, 7 km south of Kham Duc'. The Mobile Strike Force, Danang, monthly report for March 1968, which was signed by Warrant Officer Haberley, an Australian, also recorded that '11 Coy moved to Ngok Tavak to establish [an] FOB'. John White continued his explanation:

> The fort was easily defendable but at the same time overgrown. I figured that we could establish a good patrol base there with a minimum of disturbance and effort and, when we were compromised, we could move to another base somewhere else in the very thick jungle that covered the whole area. I was very clear with the troops that they were not to cut down timber and make [it] obvious that we [were] there.[8]

Specialist Fourth Class Kenneth Benway (later lieutenant colonel), who was 11th Company's medic during the deployment until approximately 20 April 1968, has a different recollection of the move to and set up at Ngok Tavak.

Captain John White, commander of 11th Company, informed me in roughly late March 1968 (I'm not sure of the date) that we were going to Ngok Tavak. We flew to Kham Duc probably by C-130, as we did it in one lift, and we remained at Kham Duc for several days preparing for a ground movement to Ngok Tavak to establish an operational base. It seems to me that we had a helicopter available for a reconnaissance of the route to Ngok Tavak. We made a company-sized ground tactical move to Ngok Tavak in one day. I recall leaving Kham Duc wire before dawn and arriving on Ngok Tavak late afternoon. I cannot recall how long was originally allocated for the move during planning. It may well be that we played it by ear and the tactical situation permitted a one-day move. There were no other [friendly] forces occupying Ngok Tavak when we arrived.[9]

There are significant differences of opinion on what happened when 11th Company arrived at Ngok Tavak and it may seem to be unnecessarily captious to highlight the disparity, but this information is at the core of understanding what was to happen here. Was this a base that was occupied on the move, with no knowledge of its previous history, and only to be used temporarily while patrolling further south, or was it a defined location set in place by a tactical plan devised by Company C, 5th Special Forces, White's commanding headquarters? Benway had no doubt that this was going to be a base camp.

When we got there, the three tiers breaking out into the open plain at the top of the position were heavily overgrown. The top of Ngok Tavak was a relatively flat, and open area, roughly shaped like an hourglass, with a line of trees bisecting the position. On one lobe was the command bunker—later referred to as the fort—and the other lobe was the helicopter-landing zone. We established interlocking sectors of fire for the automatic weapons. We selectively cleared vegetation to improve fields of fire for small arms. We then dug at least two bunkers, improving each with sandbags, but I cannot recall at what point the bags were flown in. We emplaced a 60 mm mortar and a command bunker was developed, as well as a supply bunker closer to the helipad. [John White's command bunker was in the northwestern corner of the inner fort area and should not be confused with other so-called bunkers scattered around the fort's interior.] We continued to improve the position and to run local security patrols and nightly ambushes as part of the defensive plan.[10]

Photographs taken of the position prior to 20 April show a very bare hilltop with soldiers of an apparently unconcerned reconnaissance force not wearing shirts or carrying basic equipment and weapons. Some are seen in a game of 'baseball', which made them appear to be oblivious to the potential danger around them. Prior to the surge in interest in what the enemy may have been up to around Kham Duc, the camp had a reputation—maybe unjust—as being a bit of an in-country R&R centre. This might have had an influence upon how the hazards faced by this operation were viewed. Perhaps they had been lulled into a false sense of security by their operational briefing and little contact with the enemy after their arrival in March. Benway said, 'During my time at Ngok Tavak through approximately 20 April, I did not hear a shot fired in anger.'[11] Warrant Officer Haberley, who was then the adjutant of Mike Force in Danang, wrote in his report to AATTV for April 1968: '11 Coy [company]: This coy had two contacts during the month... both contacts were light and involved local VC units (Ngoc Tavak South).'[12] Several of the official monthly reports on activities in the area also give an account of an enemy probe against the Ngok Tavak position in late March. The Mobile Strike Force (AATTV) monthly report for March 1968 said that 'the position was probed by a squad-sized element on 28 March 68'. This was followed by these comments from the 5th Special Forces in a paper dated 31 May: 'probe of Ngok Tavak by unknown size enemy force using automatic and semi-automatic weapons and mortars, 29 March 2230 hours to 30 March 0010 hours. Result: friendly negative, enemy unknown.' The 1st Military Intelligence Battalion's Detachment B made a similar comment. John White, however, denied that such an attack happened when he was interviewed in 2006.

He believed that 'any firing that took place was his Nungs shooting at peacocks that had come down to feast on the scraps of their meals that had been thrown over the wire and that the birds had set off trip flares. This spooked the Nungs into thinking an enemy force was nearby and they opened fire.' John White did not recall any report being lodged by him on the incident; the alleged probe was a mystery to him.[13] Nevertheless, any firing of this magnitude that prompted a formal report to be raised, even if it was to cover an embarrassing false contact, should have raised a concern that the position was compromised and it was time to go elsewhere. But they did not and as White explained:

> So, a-patrolling we went. The only people I was confident in for patrolling were the three platoon commanders. The other Special Forces soldiers were excellent, but were weapons, medical and communications specialists. I took out the first patrol, which lasted about three days . . . [we] headed south. I could see that there had been some activity around the place, but not much worth bothering about—local Montagnard VC according to my Nungs; certainly not major troop movements. And so we passed our time. The fort was too good a position to give up so we continued to patrol from there for a couple of weeks before we started to make contact.[14]

Kenneth Benway recalled that the patrols down Route 14 went out perhaps every five days or so.

> Patrols typically ran 24–48 hours. I accompanied Warrant Officer Cameron on one of these patrols . . . where we examined a steel bridge over a stream, and surveilled it for a day or so. No enemy activity was noted. I also accompanied Staff Sergeant Clay Aiken, Special Forces, on several combat patrols. On one of these . . . our point [leading] man 'Tiger' suddenly opened fire (single shot), taking down a very nice deer, which was much welcomed by the Nungs back at camp, as we had been subsisting on dehydrated indigenous rations for several weeks. Aiken and I were not overly thrilled with the action, however. We returned to camp, as our patrol had clearly been compromised, if any NVA were indeed in the area. Tiger was a hero at dinner, though![15]

Resupply to Ngok Tavak was a challenge. The road was not trafficable; helicopters were used several times a week, but they were considered to be uneconomical for bulk delivery so a twin-engine Caribou was used to airdrop rations and ammunition during April, which Ken Benway recalled:

> G11 camouflaged cargo parachutes were employed and we used one at the fort to provide overhead shade protection from the blazing sun. We lost one load and my recollection is that the pallet had ammunition and it landed about 100 meters long to the east. I recall spending several days searching for the pallet and its huge chute, but could never locate it. It would have blended perfectly with the heavy vegetation and likely hung in some tall trees for years. Other pallets included rations, sandbags and it seemed to me a couple of live pigs were included in the drop that the Nungs were looking forward to with great enthusiasm.[16]

The helicopter flights alone would have been sufficient to alert any NVA and/or VC force in the area that their enemy was conducting an operation somewhere along Route 14 to the south of Kham Duc. Ngok Tavak, with its airstrip and previously used French fort, was a logical area to check for any activity.

Patrolling from Ngok Tavak continued, but on 18 April the two Australian warrant officers were deserted by their troops when an enemy force hit them not far from where a surveillance patrol had clashed with an NVA platoon on 8 March. The AATTV Headquarters description of the contact is recorded in the unit's monthly report:

> On 18 Apr 68, at 1530 hrs, WO Lucas and WO Cameron were with a mobile strike force patrol near Ngok Tavak, eight kilometres SOUTH of KHAN DUC [sic]. The patrol was ambushed by an NVA force and the two advisers and the leading section were cut off and were missing. However, the two advisers and some survivors managed to return to the Special Forces A Team camp at KHAN DUC [sic] on the afternoon of 19 Apr 1968. A detailed report of this incident is awaited.[17]

That report did not agree with the April report from Danang that said contact was light and against Local Force VC. No further report on the incident was filed by AATTV. Don Cameron, one of the 'missing', provided the following account of the ambush in 2006:

> When we got into position on Ngok Tavak Frank [Lucas] and I took the platoon out to give them a bit of experience and we struck the enemy and our valiant troops decided they didn't want to be there and all took off. Frank and I managed to move down to a river, cross it and set up a position on the far side. They had captured our radio operator with the radio and all the codes, which caused a bit of consternation back at base. During the night they must have been torturing this chap, he screamed and yelled all the night. The next day, choppers flew all around the area. And Willie Swicegood [US Special Forces soldier with 11th Company] went out on the chopper, strapped himself in and was at the open door and he flew back and forwards along the river until I flashed an air panel and he gave us the thumb up that he had seen us. I had already indicated to Willie that we would go to a spot to which I had pointed and it took us all day to get there. There was a bit of a hut there and not long after a helicopter came in and landed, whereupon our troops all came out of the bushes and tried to take over the helicopter. We restored order and got the first group back to the position and then returned for another group. When we returned to the base [Ngok Tavak, not Kham Duc] Captain White told us he was just about to advise HQ that we were missing in action.[18]

The 5th Special Forces After Action Report dated 31 May 1968 said this about the action:

> 181530 [date/time] April: OPN P-63 ambushed from a distance of 20 metres at YB 935929 [nearly 10 map kilometres to the south-southwest of Ngok Tavak] by an unknown size NVA force with semi-automatic and automatic weapons. Results: friendly 1 MSF MIA, 1 MSF WIA, 1 PRC-25 radio lost: enemy unknown.[19]

A further contact with the enemy was recorded on 23 April at map reference YB 986 965—approximately 5 map kilometres to the southeast of Ngok Tavak—on a feature that rose to over 915 metres (3000 feet). Five VC were involved—they fled north—and one Mobile Strike Force soldier was wounded.

A pattern of military activity had now been established around Ngok Tavak, one that alerted both sides. As John White said: 'We continued to patrol from there. We knew something was going on because at night we could hear these explosions to the south and I reported this to Danang. I received nothing back from Danang.'[20] The explosions were most likely from the US bombing of the 'new' road coming in from Laos to join Route 14 some 17 map kilometres south of Ngok Tavak, which had been under air force surveillance and action for weeks. White also mentioned this in his 'Venison and Valour' article, written in 1972 for *Australian Infantry*: 'The only indication . . . was the sound of bombing on the so called Ho Chi Minh Trail about 20 kilometres to our west.' The 1st Military Intelligence Battalion had reported in March and April 1968 that 'repairs on the road damaged by airstrikes have been slow and bombing has continued every day'. There was a lot of speculation by the 5th Special Forces Group and the Military Intelligence Battalion on what the enemy's intentions were. There was scope for the enemy to reinforce their units in the area with divisional units coming from North Vietnam and from the Central Highlands—II Corps Tactical Zone—within South Vietnam. This appeared to be unlikely, however, as the construction and the signs of troop movement indicated a flow towards the lowlands of Tam Ky and Hoi An on the parallel, to Route 14, 'old French' trail. There was little or no movement north of any significance detected along Route 14 towards Ngok Tavak and Kham Duc. Captured documents and statements by POWs identified transportation and logistics units as the main organisations in this western district. For example, the 559th Transport Group that had a primary responsibility to keep the supply routes open, particularly in Laos, was a well-known user of these trails. The North Vietnamese firepower in the area was classified as defensive anti-aircraft 12.7 mm and .30 calibre machine guns that were being used to protect the camps and work sites. The 5th SFGA's ominous warning that the North Vietnamese could attack isolated units and outposts with up to one reinforced regiment and the enemy's past success against isolated outposts located on main infiltration routes, brought one simple conclusion. This was to: 'Increase reconnaissance and combat operations along Highway 14, south and west of Ngok Tavak, to provide information on enemy strength and identification, and interdiction of the enemy's LOCs [lines of communication] and base/operational areas.'[21] John White's boss, Lieutenant Colonel Schungel, didn't know what the NVA intentions were or who they were; he wanted Captain White to find out and tell him.

Headquarters III MAF and the Americal Division had little interest in the Special Forces camps, although there was a reinforcement plan in place to come to their rescue when under serious attack. The camps were too far distant from their centre of interest and elements of the 2nd NVA Division were causing the Americans some combat heartburn down in their old haunts around the Que Son Valley where the Marines established another 2nd NVA hunting unit. On 27 April 1968, III MAF set up *Operation Quick Track*, which was commanded by Lieutenant Colonel John F. Kelly from its G-2 (Intelligence) staff. Its task was:

> To crack the 2D NVA Division, which had retreated southwest to the Laotian border. With his command post on Hill 55 south of Danang, Lieutenant Colonel Kelly's task force consisted of a small headquarters, the provisional company of the 1st Reconnaissance Company, a detachment of Sub-Unit 1, 1st Radio Battalion (signal Intelligence capability) and 14th Company Mobile Strike Force Company. The 1st Marine Division and the 1st Marine Aircraft Wing would provide support when necessary. Task Force Kelly began its first inserts on 30 April and would continue the operation into May.[22]

The 14th Company was a sister unit to John White's 11th Company. Task Force Kelly did not operate in the area of Route 14 out near the border with Laos, and this additional effort to track the 2nd NVA confirmed that the intelligence picture of this major enemy formation's location was blurred.

The danger signs at Ngok Tavak should have been evident by now. A small indigenous force with no heavy weapon support; a unit that might get some ground attack aircraft if the weather permitted was locked on a piece of real estate with everything but a flashing neon sign that said, 11th Company located here. Not that the North Vietnamese needed a sign; they already knew—and had known for some weeks—that the Ngok Tavak position was occupied. John White knew he should not stay there and he advised Danang that he was going to move base, but he was told to stay at the fort for 'a short while longer'. This decision-making process also indicated that Captain White did not have tactical flexibility; he was nailed to Ngok Tavak whether he liked it or not. White's force was there to conduct reconnaissance, and there is a misconception contained in some latter-day articles that his force could head for the hills and easily switch to going after the enemy in some form of tactical hit-and-run offensive role. They could not. The Nung company was not established as a mobile guerrilla force; its task was to conduct reconnaissance and there was no battlefield support plan in place for it to operate as a guerrilla force. An attempt to use them as such at this stage would have been fraught with extreme danger.[23] Eleventh Company's only option, if they lost their reconnaissance mobility and came under too much pressure, was to 'withdraw back to Kham Duc'.[24] Plans were also in train that appeared to rescind any idea of a withdrawal.

3 BATTLE PLANS

The 1st VC Regiment's Headquarters, April 1968

The attacks by the 2nd NVA Division against the American's 196th Brigade in the Hiep Duc–Que Son valleys during January had been unnecessary. Although they had hurt the Americans, the battles had stretched the division's resupply capabilities and, even worse, did not permit their warriors a time of rest prior to the coming major offensive during Tet. That they had suffered a setback during their attack upon Danang was predictable—the plan was weak—but General Chu Huy Man had permitted it to go ahead. With Vo Chi Cuong, he had then decided to withdraw the 2nd Division to the mountains, where the Americans were afraid to venture. There the division could rest, resupply and integrate their replacement manpower prior to implementing Man's plan to 'secure and maintain our strategic posture'. General Man ordered the 2nd NVA Division to break contact with the allied forces down on the coastal plains in March 1968 and to move to rest and refit and also to reconnoitre, a task in which they were known to be meticulous. The retired NVA commanders said in 1995 that they had been in the Ngok Tavak area for 'a long time'; they were there almost certainly for most of April. Comrade 'T'— the political officer, whose name is obliterated in the general's report—had returned from Hanoi and flew into an insane rage when he heard the Division had 'retreated'. He criticised the NVA military for being incompetent. General Man had gritted his teeth, and kept his silence, but in a private conversation with the Deputy Military Commander, who had burst into tears over T's outburst, he permitted himself a brief moment of laughter at 'the peasant's' anger. Comrade T, he confided, always flew to Hanoi when the big battles were about to begin. General Man had issued a directive to Giap Van Cuong, Commander 2nd NVA; it was an ambitious plan. He had split the division into two fighting arms. One regiment was to tie down the Americans in the valleys; the remainder of the division was to disappear back to their camps near Laos where they would link up with the 70th Transport Regiment, a unit that was under the 559th Transport Group's control. In complete confidence, the general told the senior officers that they were going to destroy Kham Duc and they would do it with such ferocity that the imperialists would be overawed and would retreat.

The Ba Gia Regiment (1st VC Regiment) was given the task of the initial attack, which would include sweeping aside the small outpost at Ngok Tavak. For the time being, however, they were to rest in the valleys to the east of Route 14, along the edges of the Dak Mi River, opposite the new road that came from Laos. There was some bombing, which did not cause them any harm—every veteran knew how to protect himself from the bombs—and the occasional spotting aircraft that flew this way was good for their entertainment. As Captain Phan, from unit GK.31 Anti-Aircraft said:

> They were like insects, noisy pests that we could crush with a single swipe, but we played with them so we did not tell them what weapons we had. The transport regiment sometimes used their heavy vehicle to make false trails that lured them into a valley where we frightened them with 12.7 mm that were dug so deep they never see them. We had 23 mm guns there too, but they kept silent. Our gunners followed the insects with their fingers and complained that they could have destroyed the planes with one blow, but the anti-aircraft unit commanders, Dang Ding Truong and Le Huu Tuu, would not permit them to fire.

Major Dang Ngoc Mai's 40th Battalion, 1st VC Regiment, was to destroy the Ngok Tavak camp, following which the battalion was to move quickly and to be available as a reserve for the regiment during its assault on Kham Duc. His attack would commence in the early hours and the regimental support weapons would mortar Kham Duc at the same time to confuse and frighten the defenders.

Reconnaissance units had been sent out when they had come here from their battles in the Que Son. It was now April and the 13th Reconnaissance Company had a good picture of what was going on at Ngok Tavak and one of the reconnaissance scouts from the company was called to provide his information on what he had seen. He reported:

> The Tui Nung [Nung thugs] were like water buffaloes when they patrolled, they 'snorted and grunted' and stomped around in a herd, but did nothing. They were easy to watch, and to hide from their big patrols was very easy. Perhaps, he said, they could scare the schoolgirls and the women in the alleys of Danang, and boast that they were great warriors, but they did not worry him. Tui Nung— he spat with anger—one shot and they run 1000 kilometres with the nguy [puppets].

Captain Nguyen Xuan, Commander of the 60th Battalion, also reported his information to the headquarters.

> The reconnaissance patrols had watched the enemy. The Local Force Montagnard unit reported every day; they had seen the first patrol sent out by the 'long-nose' at Ngok Tavak and had followed others from a safe distance to observe and learn their tactics. If it was safe, they attacked [probably a euphemism for fired upon] the puppet troops to watch what happened. Once, the traitor puppets ran away and deserted their American masters [this would have been the two Australian warrant officers]. They could now get close to the camp to watch and make drawings of the Ngok Tavak position.

Then Captain Xuan waited while the staff drew an outline of the latest details on the mud-map. The regimental reconnaissance officer pointed to an area where two of the 'Americans' (Australians) had their tent; it was easily found as the tent had water containers around it to catch the rain. (Warrant Officer Don Cameron moved the containers later, thinking that the enemy had spotted their location—his action proved to be fortuitous, as the containers would be targeted by rocket-propelled grenades in the coming attack.) All of the officers stood, as a mark of respect, when Lieutenant Colonel Nguyen Van Tri, Commander of the

1st VC Regiment, joined their group. He was satisfied that their preparations would meet Giap Van Cuong's expectations. It was time, he said, to make sure that the soldiers were settled and that the new men from the north were accepted as comrades. He was concerned that some of the new equipment might not be understood and he told Nguyen Ngoc Dong, Commander, GK.40 Engineer Battalion, to make sure that the training on the flame-throwers, satchel bombs and tear gas was done thoroughly and in time for an attack deadline of early May 1968. A message from the divisional commander was read out to the gathered officers:

> We must remain hidden from the puppet regime until our battlefield preparation is finished. Military Region Headquarters has despatched supporting troops to assist us in our battle to encircle and annihilate the imperialist's forces at Kham Duc. One battalion of 'long-barrelled' artillery [Soviet 85 mm] and the 23 mm anti-aircraft guns will be our comrades in this victory.

The commanders kept stony-faced when told of the extra forces; such promises had been made before. (The attack would be delayed when the promised heavy weapons support did not arrive on time.) One of the battalion commanders muttered, to no one in particular, that if they came, the 21st Regiment would get the best. They do not like to give us southerners too much; their northern cousins complain too loudly, he moaned. Nguyen Van Tri then took Major Mai aside. Major Mai was a native of Hoa Vang village on the outskirts of Danang. Colonel Tri told Mai:

> For your Ngok Tavak duty, take the flame-throwers and the gas and tell your scouts to find a way into the fort that does not get you caught in the old French Foreign Legion minefield. The Montagnard, who was a scout for the Legion's 1st Battalion, 2nd Regiment, told me that it is there.

One week later, the final plans were given. The scouts had been around the positions now for three weeks; they were able to overlook Ngok Tavak from the high ground to the west and southwest with little interference. The 1st VC Regiment was instructed to move from the old French track (vicinity YB 950 814) and move east to the Dak Mi River, from there they would be guided north and then west again along a valley pass to the confluence of the stream Dak Tiang and the river Dak Se. They were to cross here where the 40th Battalion was to hide in the valley to the west of Ngok Tavak until the attack signal was given. The regiment would move only by night and it was to be in position before 4 May 1968. It would be difficult, but it would be done. Battalions of the 21st Regiment had moved off and were last seen going further to the east, but among the soldiers no one knew where the regiment was told to go. Tran Ngoc Hoang from the 40th Battalion said that his cousin, who was a corporal in the 11th Battalion, 21st Regiment, had told him that they would not go too far away from the lazy Nam Bo (southern) soldiers. This comment attracted vigorous verbal rebuttal by the southerners in a manner common to soldiers across the centuries, some of it light-hearted, but most unprintable, especially comments about parentage and water buffaloes.

The officers said their goodbyes. Captain Le Van Can, Commander, GK.33 Mortar Battalion, produced a small bottle of whisky that he said had been obtained from the PX in Danang, which caused some laughter. They all stood and saluted their good fortune; several gripped their friends in a final parting. They knew they would not meet again. It was 28 April, and a message had been received by the 2nd NVA Division that 'scouts' (traitors) inside the camp Strike Force at Kham Duc were ready to cause confusion and disrupt the puppet troops' defensive plans.[1]

Special Forces, Danang

During April 1968, a close watch was maintained on the new road that came in from Laos. Although Route 14 had been classified as nothing more than a trail that was not capable of supporting vehicles, the 5th SFGA was concerned by the possible use of armour in an attack upon Kham Duc. There were eight bridges between the new road and Ngok Tavak. Four of these could be bypassed, but getting around the others was considered not possible, or extremely difficult for vehicles. Although there was no indication of any troop movement north along Route 14, the amount of anti-aircraft fire around the intersection and signs of movement across Route 14 towards the Dak Mi River worried the Special Forces officers. Even though aerial photography was keeping a close watch on the NVA's road development, Lieutenant Colonel Daniel Schungel wanted to increase ground patrols into the area. General Westmoreland questioned him after the May battles on why Ngok Tavak was occupied, and why we had artillery there and what was the mission of the FOB. Schungel replied:

> I told him that we had occupied it [Ngok Tavak] as a patrol base as it (a) enabled us to extend our patrol coverage further south along route #14 and (b) provided early warning of major enemy movement from the south. I directed that it be established as an FOB when we learned of the new road into SVN from Laos. The artillery was there (as opposed to Kham Duc) because it could support that much further south and from Ngok Tavak, could also cover the area of Kham Duc's AO [Area of Operations] NE of Ngok Tavak anticipated more contacts. The mission of the FOB was as already stated: patrol base, interdict route #14, and provide early warning.[2]

Not only did these answers contradict Captain John White's recollection of why 11th Company was on the Ngok Tavak position, the deployment of artillery in such a manner went against tactical lessons learned as well as common battle sense for operations in the western mountains.[3] John White said in a 1995 interview and again in 2006 that he knew nothing of the plan to move artillery into his location. A 5th SFGA Comparative Study of the battles at Lang Vei–Kham Duc, signed off in July 1968, released the following information about the deployment of the guns.

> After enemy road construction was discovered, two 155 mm howitzers and two 105 mm howitzers were requested from III MAF for deployment at Kham Duc and FOB Ngok Tavak. The 105 mm howitzers were to be placed at Kham Duc to support their operations and also provide close in fire support for FOB Ngok Tavak. The 155 mm howitzers were to be placed on Ngok Tavak to give them the capability of placing interdiction fire on the southern limits of

the TAOR [Tactical Area of Responsibility] and supporting their patrolling operations. Only two 105 mm howitzers were received and they were to be placed on Ngok Tavak. The southern limits of the TAOR were not within 105 mm howitzer range and as the contacts occurred closer to the FOB, the 105s became incapable of offering fire support for the patrols. The contacts were then occurring within the minimum fire range of the guns. Camp [Kham] Duc had no artillery capability with which to support Ngok Tavak.[4]

The howitzers came from Battery D, 2nd Battalion, 13th Marines. Captain Conrad Kinsey, commander of Battery D, said that he had argued against sending just two guns.

I was briefed about the mission, as going through Kham Duc to Ngok Tavak for two guns to fire on a bridge building effort by the enemy. I remember this since I made a strong argument at the time to send the entire battery with two 155 mm howitzers (towed) to Kham Duc and to detach two guns to Ngok Tavak. My thought being that the situation as I saw it was very hazardous for two guns at Ngok Tavak without any other support. My Battalion Commander Lt Col Rhys J. Phillips was sympathetic to my plan, but was later overruled by higher headquarters.[5]

What were they thinking? First, the firepower weight of two 105 mm howitzers was inadequate for the task considering that daily bombing raids, which used 750-pound (340-kilogram) bombs, had damaged the NVA roadworks, but not stopped them, nor deterred the NVA troop movement. As a comparison, a 105 mm high explosive projectile weighed less than 20 kilograms. Major General Ott wrote in his Vietnam study on field artillery that 105 mm fire was ineffectual in jungle; this was a task for the heavier 155 mm guns. General Ott also highlighted the need for interlocking battery-fire for mutual protection, as well as troops, other than the battery personnel, to defend the firing location, which the 11th Mike Force Company should not have done; its task was to patrol well away from the base. The general's study on field artillery also said that the demand by infantry for 'tubes' to support their operations outstripped supply.

Despite the amount of artillery in Vietnam, the old cry that there were not enough artillery units to support the manoeuvre elements, was heard again and again. The creation of a fourth firing battery in some artillery battalions, particularly with the division artillery direct support battalions, dramatized the requirements and response.[6]

Ngok Tavak was lucky, or perhaps more correctly unlucky, to get two howitzers.

The cannoneers

Captain Billy L. Whitley, the 2nd Battalion, 13th Marines Logistics Officer, moved the two 105 mm Marine howitzers, ammunition and supplies to Kham Duc and then on to Ngok Tavak. This took place between 16 April, when the warning order was issued, and 4 May 1968, which, as luck would have it, was the date that the NVA had selected for their attack on the camps, but the attack was postponed because their heavy weapons had not arrived.[7] The 2nd/13th Marines Command Chronologies for April listed this sequence of events for the deployment of the howitzers.

> S-3 [Operations Officer] 161900H [Date 16/Time 1900/Group H = South Vietnam] Rec'd warning order from 11th Marines to be prepared to displace one platoon from 'D' in support of Special Forces. [They would be designated 'Delta X-Ray'.]

> S-4. [Logistics Officer] 250930H Attended conference at G-4 III Marine Amphibious Force regarding possible movement of a 105 mm howitzer platoon to Ngok Tavak.

> 260800H Departed via helicopter for recon of Kham Duc and Ngok Tavak for possible 105 mm howitzer platoon site. [There is no mention of a reconnaissance by the operations staff.]

Lieutenant Bob Adams, however, remembered doing a reconnaissance by helicopter with Staff Sergeant Thomas Schriver on 26 April 1968.

This is the date on which Captain Whitley went to Kham Duc, therefore it's possible they were all in the same aircraft. Adams wrote:

> I don't remember if we stopped at Kham Duc, but we met with Capt White and he showed us where we were to put the guns. [Captain White said he knew nothing about the deployment of the guns prior to their arrival on the hill.] That area needed considerable work in order to be able to fire. Trees needed to be knocked down, etc. We flew back to Da Nang the same day. About two days later we started the airlift to Kham Duc. The weather was a big factor and it took several tries to get everyone and our equipment to Kham Duc. I arrived with the two howitzers and a complement of Marines about 28 April.[8]

The Command Chronology for the 2nd Battalion, 13th Marines, continued:

> 261600H. Submitted embark plans for fixed wing lift to Kham Duc and the helicopter to Ngok Tavak. [That included] 47 personnel, two 105 mm howitzers and 1240 HE [high explosive], 60 Ill [illumination], 80 WP [white phosphorus], 40 HC [smoke], and 90 Beehive [Fleschette-finned small darts in the master shell]. Total weight to be lifted 135 000 lbs [61,235 kilograms].
>
> 270730H. Movement of 'D' X-Ray commenced by fixed wing aircraft to Kham Duc.
>
> 270830H. One C-123 departed with one USMC [Marine] and 105 mm ammunition for Kham Duc.
>
> 281215H. One C-130 departed with 18 000 lbs [8160 kilograms] of ammunition for Kham Duc.
>
> 281515H. One C-130 departed with two 105 mm howitzers and 45 troops.
>
> 281600H. One C-130 departed with 12 000 lbs [5440 kilograms] of ammunition and one M37 with driver for Kham Duc [Dodge ¾-ton cargo truck]. This aircraft returned, as the weather was bad.

There were a further five, weather-interrupted, C-130 loads, mainly of ammunition, on 29 and 30 April. The lifts were completed into Kham Duc on 30 April at 1300 hours, with a little bit of humour along the way.[9]

> When we landed the aircraft kept their motors running and we spilled out the back and ran over to the side of the airstrip. This disembarkation was rather uneventful except when the second aircraft arrived and the howitzer in that C-130 was pushed down the ramp. The crew forgot to put the brakes on the howitzer and they of course went running to the edge of the strip with the rest of us. When the aircraft took off the back blast from the props pushed the howitzer and it went rolling down the runway much to the amusement of the Special Forces people who were laughing at the big bad Marines who had landed and here was their howitzer taking off down the airfield.[10]

Although the 2nd Battalion's diary showed when the Marines, guns and ammunition supposedly arrived, that was the neat and tidy record. In reality, the deliveries were erratic, which Bob Adams and Tim Brown remembered when they fired a mission at Kham Duc under most unusual circumstances.

> We arrived at Kham Duc with the howitzers, but we had no ammo or firing equipment. We laid the guns in the southeast corner of the compound . . . we were told of a Special Forces patrol that had made heavy contact and were requesting 'the big guns'. I was asked if we could fire for them. We had no ammunition or fire control equipment at this time. The SF captain said he had a 'whole pile' of rounds, could we use those. I told him we would have to improvise but would give it our best shot. We discovered the rounds were 106 recoilless rifle rounds, not 105 so they wouldn't work. Then he said he had some others in a storage shed. From a rice storage area we obtained fourteen HE rounds and six illuminating rounds. They were in the fibers and the tape was still good. On inspection we saw that they were very old. The powder bags simply disintegrated when we tried to pick them up. Because the tape was still good we felt the rounds were good but we would have to fire a charge

seven (using all of the powder that came with the round). The SF captain produced an M-10 plotting board from a mortar. With some adjustments we were able to use it for the 105s. Not trusting fully in the condition of the ammunition and the plotting board, I plotted a target on a bald spot atop one of the hills. To our great joy (and amazement) we were right on target. The patrol was asking for rounds to be delivered within 50 meters of them, I elected to fire 300 meters from them. After each round was fired, we crept back 50 meters at a time until the rounds were just where the patrol wanted them to be. We expended all fourteen rounds. The enemy broke contact.[11]

Kham Duc was a staging area for the Marines; they remained there only until the detachment was complete and on the ground ready for their lift over to Ngok Tavak, which was planned for 4 May 1968. Prior to this, Adams sent an advance party over at an unknown date late in April to prepare for the detachment's arrival. Greg Rose was one of the group, which was under the command of Sergeant Schriver, as he recalled:

> When the recon party first landed we asked where Captain White was and after a few oriental people telling us and pointing we saw him filling sandbags without a shirt on. Few American officers would fill a sandbag much less be working without a shirt. I ran up to him with the rest of the Marines (three or four of us), saluted and said, Private Rose reporting as ordered, sir! His response, don't fucking salute me, you'll get me shot![12]

Tim Brown remembered that the advance party landed on Route 14 where the trail had been widened at the foot of the path that led up to Captain White's position. He thought that there were around twelve in the group and that they had flown over about 28 April. He continued:

> Captain White spoke with Sergeant Schriver and the initial decision was to set up the gun position right there on Route 14. We then made the decision to dig and build a fire direction control bunker and to clear some trees using C4 [an explosive] and detonating cord

that had been provided by Captain White's forces. The trees needed to be cut down to create fields of fire for the howitzers when they came in. It seemed to be a totally illogical place to put howitzers that had limitations when it came to angles of fire. Nonetheless, this advance party went about the business of digging the bunker, filling sandbags and cutting trees and using the timber for the bunker and the heads [latrines]. The heat and the humidity were difficult to deal with and we were eating C rations. Although it was hot during the day, rain showers started in the evening and it would pretty much rain all night. One of the more unpleasant things about being there were the ground leeches that tended to find their way through your boot eyelets and get on you. They were painless, but disgusting. Of course with the weather being cloudy and foggy in the morning, even at that point we were having trouble in getting supplies flown over to us in the form of drinking water and rations. It was rather hard work and routine, although there was a special occasion one day. I remember a helicopter coming in with some iced water in old beer cans from the Special Forces camp where they had equipment, as amazing as it may seem, to make ice and ice cream. It was very welcome. Prior to its arrival we had to resort to going down to the river to get our drinking water.[13]

Private First Class William H. Loman, Jr, also remembered going down to the stream to collect water. 'After we had been there long enough to run short on water [we] did a water patrol to the stream down the hill. Several tracks were present; I knew they [the enemy] were close by.'[14]

Detachment X-Ray's guns and the remainder of the platoon were lifted into the 'vehicle park' by helicopter on 4 May. The redeployment task was completed at 1700 hours and Captain Whitley noted that the loads totalled 78,000 pounds (35,380 kilograms), which included a vehicle, personnel, rations, communication equipment and ammunition. Lieutenant Bob Adams listed the quantities and types of ammunition taken over to Ngok Tavak in his personal notebook. The numbers were: 120 rounds of high-explosive point detonating fuse; 30 high-explosive rounds without fuses; 30 white phosphorus rounds; twenty illumination rounds; 26 Beehive rounds; ten smoke rounds; 24 variable time fuses; and sixteen timed fuses.[15]

The amount and type of ammunition delivered and the method of getting more would cause some angst in the next few days, and continued to be a strong topic of discussion over the coming 40 years. John White's 11th Company was an army unit; the Marine howitzers had the task to support White, but he was not required to resupply them. Bob Adams understood this because he submitted daily reports to his headquarters and he also requested additional ammunition from Captain Whitley, the Marine Logistics Officer.

> As far as orders, I had no written orders. My Battery CO, Capt Kinsey told me to report to Capt White at NT [Ngok Tavak] with my guns, men, and equipment. While I was on the hill I took orders from Capt White. I was to provide artillery support for his unit that was running long range Recon patrols between NT [Ngok Tavak] and the Laotian border. I was required to send all reports to the 2nd Bn 13th Marines, however. As far as resupply of ammunition, I requested it from the S-4 2/13. He thought it had been sent to us. It was sitting back at KD [Kham Duc].[16]

The weak link in the resupply chain was how to get the ammunition from Kham Duc, where there was plenty, to Ngok Tavak, just 7 map kilometres away. There was only one option: it had to be lifted by helicopter of a type that could do a heavy lift in the conditions that prevailed in the mountains. Marine helicopters were scarce, and their task demands were great. For instance, the 1st Marine Aircraft Wing had slightly more than 300 helicopters to support the two US Marine divisions, ARVN units and the Korean Marines in I Corps. An indigenous rifle company supported by two howitzers in the western wilds of I Corps, doing reconnaissance for the army, would not have rated highly on the 'things-to-do-today list', especially when the Marine system of control over their helicopters was centralised at the Air Wing with no flexibility down at unit level. On top of that, Marine heavy-lift aircraft availability was down to a miserable 31 per cent.

The movement of heavy loads of ammunition by road was discussed in the latter half of April 1968, as this interview with Captain Daniel Waldo, Jr of the 70th Engineer Battalion will attest. Captain Waldo's company was in Kham Duc to repair and upgrade the airfield.

There is a road, but can't drive it. In fact, they were putting in a request through channels at the time . . . to build the road, from Kham Duc to Ngok Tavak because they had, I forget how many rounds a day had to be gotten to Ngok Tavak and they didn't have the air availability to do it.[17]

Captain Waldo's company of engineers had been flown up from Pleiku with heavy equipment and supplies. Their fly-in started on 9 April and it took 'somewhere around 50–60 [C-130 Hercules] sorties' over more than seven days, and at least one C-124 (Globemaster) flight was used to bring in a bulldozer. Pleiku is almost 160 kilometres due south of Kham Duc with a possible approach path almost over the top of Ngok Tavak. These flights were followed by the C-130 insertions of the Marine howitzers from Danang, which was to the northeast. This much air activity around a previously sleepy-hollow, backwoods airstrip would not have gone unnoticed, even by an illiterate Montagnard VC scout. The NVA commander must have cast a worried eye over it all and wondered if they had been discovered, but the poor weather conditions in late April and the dependence on the airstrip for reinforcement/resupply probably convinced him that their attack plan would succeed. Perhaps they all had the same sentiments as Jim Garlitz, one of the Marines, who thought when he arrived, 'What the hell are we doing here?'

The fort

The pathway to failure at Ngok Tavak had been paved with good intentions, and John White was worried. He now had 43 Marines and a Navy Corpsman and two artillery pieces on his doorstep. Some said there were 45 Marines in the detachment—the C-130 manifest listed 47 personnel—but no one had a definite roster. Captain White wanted to sort it out.

I borrowed a helicopter and flew back to Danang where I pointed out that Mike Force was a mobile, irregular unit whose safety lay in having a low profile and not fighting pitched battles. Our Marine artillery could not support us as it could only fire on high angle in the dense foliage and we were having contacts outside that range.

This was a most pertinent point. Lieutenant Colonel Schungel's plan was to use the guns to extend the patrol range of 11th Company out of Ngok Tavak and to interdict the enemy's activities. The howitzers could do neither. Captain White told the officers in Danang during his impromptu visit:

> Everyone in Danang nodded when I said that the Marines were not jungle fighters and I could not let them outside our perimeter with any confidence. And what we were doing was outside of our role. They said they would look into it, but nothing happened. When I returned to Ngok Tavak, I had the trees cut down around the fort and denuded the top berms. We started building a serious defensive position. For the first couple of days the Marines fired some H&I [harassing and interdiction] down Route 14, as ordered by their HQ. They had arrived with their first-line of ammunition, but they were running out. Bob Adams told me the situation and I told him that I felt they would be leaving soon, but that he had better get some resupply.[18]

What was known about the deployment of the guns, and when it was known, is a major point of contention. If two guns were put at Ngok Tavak without the commander on the ground there knowing about the plan, then it was a stupid oversight. Also, ill feeling and arguments about the ammunition for the artillery were stirred by a lack of knowledge on what was where and how it was to be delivered. As an example, John White said that he asked for some Fleschette rounds, only to be told he could not have any because they were restricted. There were 26 Beehive rounds (Fleschette) at Ngok Tavak. It is possible that his request for Fleschette was confused with the tightly controlled Firecracker, a shell that spread small bomblets, which had been used for the first time in the battle at Lang Vei in February. The shells were fired, however, against different types of targets and Firecracker would not have been of any use close-in against an enemy charging White's perimeter. Even so, the guns had not fired a lot, and the amount of ammunition held on the gun position was not important to the subsequent course of events. While it was prudent to be concerned by the resupply problem and to do something about it, the two guns did not deter the

NVA and neither was manned nor fired during the main assault. The enemy's attack had been planned for 4 May—the day the Marine guns arrived—but it was deferred for five days during which the Marine howitzers only fired light, harassing missions. If anything, should the NVA be able to capture the guns intact, the presence of the guns made the hilltop a more attractive enemy objective.

The 11th Company MSF was well ensconced on the top of the Ngok Tavak hill. They had been there since March and from their arrival had made improvements to the fort and its surrounds to defend themselves more effectively. One other possible protective advantage around the hilltop was the likely presence of an old minefield left by the French. Some Marines later remembered being told not to go off the main track to the top of the hill because there was a minefield around the outer dirt berm. Captain White's men did not lay a buried minefield. When the howitzers arrived they were placed downhill and outside the 11th Company's perimeter, which was not the best arrangement for defence, although at this stage, it may have been the better site for artillery fire because the hilltop position was still hemmed in by trees.

For most of the Marines, this was their first experience of true jungle. Greg Rose liked the area.

> I actually felt pretty good about the place, didn't stink like Da Nang, was a hell of a lot quieter and was much prettier. I liked the vibes from John White and the Nungs were quite friendly. John White, while being pissed off at some upper echelon 'MF', was still quite congenial even after I'd saluted him.[19]

Private First Class Paul Swenarski felt it was 'remote' and and that they were on their own. Gene Whisman, also a PFC, recalled that it was 'closed in surrounded by dense jungle, no roads, only way in or out by helicopter or by foot, a very small area'. Private First Class Dean Parrett remembered it as 'beautiful, pretty country', and was 'amazed at the thickness and canopy of the jungle'. But this was dangerous territory and their first duty was to establish a protective ring around the guns and provide fighting positions for themselves. As Greg Rose so succinctly said, 'Dig a hole and protect it with your life, private!' John White ordered more defensive stores: 'We flew in more barbed wire, Claymores [mines], grenades etc and tried to set up the best defensive position we could.'

The Marines suffered their first casualty on the day the howitzers arrived. Corporal Henry Schunck was with Lance Corporal Bruce Lindsey when it happened.

He [Lindsey] and I were on a machine gun nest at one end of that 14 road [Route 14]. So we decided that we were going to put a booby trap out there. We got some telephone wire and we tied a grenade on a stake and stuck it on one end of the road that was going down and we put the wire on the pin and we put it across about 6 inches in the grass not being able to see it because the grass was that high and put the other stake on the other side. Well that one was connected and then I proceeded to straighten out the cotter pin on the grenade and we did that together. And we had it just perfect, but Bruce wanted to adjust the wire on his side. I didn't anticipate him to do anything major that would cause this accident. But they called mail call and I was expecting a package from Mum. I said, are you OK and sure? He said, go get your mail. This booby trap was maybe 35 yards in front of our machine gun and I just looked up from opening my package, and I just looked up in time to see Bruce running from his stake to my stake where I tied my grenade. And I can only speculate that he pulled too tight on it and pulled the pin out of the grenade. And instead of just staying down or jumping towards the machine gun nest so he wouldn't get hurt, I guess he thought he could pull it out and throw it but I just saw him get pushed back from the blast and his body just slammed back. I couldn't believe what I just saw. Everybody knew he was my friend and they tried to stop me from looking at him, but I pushed them away and went down there to see for myself.[20]

Tim Brown also remembered Bruce Lindsey's accident:

We heard this tremendous explosion and we all went running down the road. At first we thought it might have been the CIDG who had come over from Kham Duc. As fate would have it, it turned out that this grenade had blown up Lindsey. Many people think that the VC had infiltrated the CIDG and short-fused the grenade. Others speculate that the pin came out of the grenade when Lindsey was trying to rig it. That event marked the first day of the arrival of the guns at Ngok Tavak; I guess an omen of the bad things yet to come.[21]

Although Battery D, 2nd Battalion, 13th Marines, recorded the death in their monthly report, Marine Lance Corporal Bruce Lindsey was not included in a subsequent *In Memoriam* service conducted on 13 May 1968. According to Conrad Kinsey, the then battery commander, Bruce Lindsey was classified as a non-battle casualty. It was as if Lindsey was wiped from the roll without respect because he was killed accidentally.

The noose tightens

The Mike Force patrol program continued, but the arrival of a detachment from Kham Duc to assist with the defence of the position caused a command headache for Captain White. He said:

> Tactically, things were now more dangerous. We had got to the situation where every time we sent out a patrol it came into contact. Captain Chris Silva, the commander of A-105, Kham Duc, did what he thought was the right thing and sent us some reinforcements from Kham Duc a few days before the attack. Apparently, everyone except me knew that this unit had been infiltrated by the local Viet Cong and was very unreliable. When they arrived, I initially put them on the lower perimeter of the fort.[22]

Major Hardy Z. Bogue, US Army (Ret.), wrote an article, 'The Fall of Ngok Tavak', which was reprinted in *The Advisor* in December 2006. In that article Bogue said: 'Lieutenant Colonel Schungel further burdened White by sending a mortar platoon of 35 CIDG . . . from the Kham Duc garrison. The Vietnamese . . . carried two 81 mm mortars. White took the mortars inside the fort, but refused to admit the CIDG.'[23] There was one 4.2 inch (107 mm), one 81 mm mortar—not two—and four 60 mm mortars inside the fort, according to the Ngok Tavak After

Action Report dated 16 May 1968. The heavy mortar and the 81 mm were crewed by the CIDG; Mike Force soldiers handled the others. No one can say for sure when the Vietnamese arrived, but it is most likely that it was in the last few days of April 1968. The concept of operations for the CIDG was for the 30-man platoon of Strikers—as the Camp Strike Force personnel were known—to assist with providing local security while the 11th Company was out from the FOB, and five personnel would man the mortars. Captain White was told by his Nungs not to trust the CIDG. This was perverse advice from the Nungs, the same troops who had run away and left their advisers during an earlier minor contact with the enemy. When wires to the fort's defensive Claymore mines and field telephones were cut, Captain White placed the Vietnamese–CIDG outside the fort but mingled with the Marine gunners, who had very limited infantry experience, if any. The Vietnamese Strikers moved freely through the Marine work party's position during the days prior to and after the arrival of the guns. One Marine questioned why the Marines were not up in the main position.

> We were in somewhat of a sombre mood following the death of Bruce Lindsey. Nonetheless, we set-up and we were on a 50 per cent alert basis, half slept while the other half stayed awake and it was really crazy. We were all bunched in together, none of us was infantry trained and it would not have taken much to wipe out the entire platoon at that time. But none of us gave really much thought to that and for whatever reason we weren't put in Captain White's camp up on top of the position from the very beginning I'll never know.[24]

On 6 May 1968, a platoon-sized patrol from Ngok Tavak contacted an NVA force just 1 kilometre away to the south on a ridgeline that overlooked the Ngok Tavak fort. The NVA element was estimated to be a platoon reconnaissance party. The next night, 7 May, trip flares on the outer perimeter of the fort were set off, which prompted the Nungs to throw grenades at the possible lurking enemy. At about this time, Warrant Officer Don Cameron fired on an enemy reconnaissance party and missed. One of his Nungs told him that he could not kill the NVA, as if they had some mystical power that prevented their death.

Cameron's next shot proved the Nung to be wrong. Nevertheless, this gloomy assessment by a Nung of the allied force's capabilities against the North Vietnamese, when coupled with the Nungs' recent desertion in battle, should have raised some very worrying questions for the Australian commanders.

John White and Bob Adams now decided to move the howitzers up into the fort, with the first gun moved in the night of the 8th and the second on 9 May. This was a very difficult physical task. Bob Adams recalled how tough it was:

> We had spent most of the night of May 8th moving one of the guns into the fort. The ¾-ton truck couldn't begin to tow it up so it was necessary to take it completely apart in order to get it up the hill. The next morning we decided to just manhandle the second gun up the hill intact by using the helicopter slings and some rope. When John White's men saw what we were doing they came out and cheered and clapped, and then joined in with the pushing and pulling, moving that howitzer up, inch by inch.[25]

A cheer squad under these conditions was rather bizarre considering that the enemy was thought to be all around. Private First Class Dean Parrett also remembered the challenge of getting the heavy artillery pieces to the top of the hill.

> Captain John White told Lieutenant Robert L. Adams, 'because of the North Vietnamese Army (NVA) activity, the two 105 howitzer should be taken to the top of the hill. In case of an attack we would be better able to defend our position from the top of the hill'. We tried to pull the guns up the hill with a 4 x 4 truck, but the truck was not strong enough to do the task. All of the Marines then tied cargo straps to the guns and using the brakes on the wheels we duck walked the guns up to the top of the hill one at a time; what a job that was. The Marines are always up to the task. Lieutenant Robert L. Adams was very proud of us, as we all worked together as a team effort. Once we had pulled the two 105s up the hill, we set them before we ate our C-rations. The soldiers then went to

sleep, except for the ones on watch duty. I was on watch duty and used James E. Garlitz's wristwatch so I would know the time.[26]

Trip flares were set off again during the night of the 8th and the Nungs again threw grenades in response. On 9 May, an 11th Company patrol contacted an enemy force of an unknown number at the eastern end of the ridgeline where the two forces had clashed on the 6th, just 1 kilometre away. The contact was a chance encounter and there were no recorded casualties by either side. On the 9th, the CIDG decided to go home to Kham Duc.

> Against our advice—John White wrote—they proceeded along the road to the northwest and were ambushed at coordinates YC 960021, by an unknown size enemy element, from dug in positions. When they returned to our location they asked if they could be brought into the perimeter near the 105 mm howitzer position. I refused them permission and placed them on the outer perimeter where they could defend...but not be an internal part of our overall defense.[27]

Route 14, where it skirted the main 738-metre-high Ngok Tavak feature, had been previously identified as an ambush alley in the 1st Marine Division plan for the relief of Kham Duc in early September 1967. An air force forward air controller also told Bob Adams on the 9th that a trench, which indicated a possible ambush in the same areas as identified in the Marine Division's plan, had cut the road back to Kham Duc.

> An USAF FAC [Forward Air Control aircraft] flew over, contacted us, and shot a mission to register the guns. As he flew away he reported that the road between Ngok Tavak and Kham Duc had been cut with a trench line, indicating a probable ambush for any egress to Kham Duc. We prepared to engage with the howitzers but the trees blocked our direction of fire. We attempted to fire over the trees using high angle but the target was too close for that method of fire. The howitzers would not elevate high enough.[28]

John White and his Nungs believed that the CIDG ambush was a fake, a lot of noise and gunshots, but not a real clash with the enemy. This suspicion strengthened White's resolve to keep the CIDG outside the perimeter, down in the vehicle park area.

The Nungs and Marines were now positioned around the top of the feature, with the Nungs providing the main infantry protection. As Route 14 from the south was identified as the enemy's most likely avenue of approach, two platoons, the 1st and 3rd, covered the western parade ground in a north–south arc. The 2nd platoon was responsible for the eastern end, with the howitzers and the heavy mortar sited behind them in the centre of the fort. The 11th Company headquarters and the headquarters platoon filled the gap between the two topographic divisions of the hill. The chink in Ngok Tavak's armour was the eastern side, where the suspect CIDG held control of the track entrance to the fort. Although the track was covered by some of the Marines on a .50 calibre heavy machine gun and two .30 calibre machine guns manned by Nungs, the dead ground—the space the machine guns could not hit—was not wired or guarded with Claymore mines. Some of the Marines were uncomfortable with what they knew about the possibility of enemy action. Henry Schunck was one who felt that there was a lack of information on how close the enemy was and what was expected of them.

> They didn't tell us how close they were, but they said they were close enough that we still had time to pull the guns up, as we were at a disadvantageous place to defend ourselves. Captain White, mostly, said pull them guns up, we got the drift then that it was his show. By the time we got them both up it was dusk, that's how long it took us, from early morning till night. I took the first watch although we were all tired. If they [the enemy] were that close then we should have been on a minimum 50 per cent [alert] and we weren't on 50 per cent. If I count all of the Marines out of 44, there was Czerwonka and Cook on that machine gun [the .50 calibre]. I was on the gun nearest the command post. Supposedly Captain White heard the noises they made [the enemy] as they were getting into position, but I didn't hear no clanking. First of all nobody told me that anybody was out there and I wasn't looking for it, plus I'm in the artillery anyway. Us artillery guys we don't

wear no earplugs, those are for sissies, you know what I mean? If
I only knew now, I wouldn't be as deaf as I am.[29]

John White did say, in a filmed interview in 1995, that he heard
the enemy moving into position.

> About midnight my people came and woke me up and I went around
> the perimeter. You could hear the [enemy] troops moving into position
> in the jungle; there was just that muffled clatter...and the odd
> grunt as someone fell over a tree. It was pitch black and they were
> moving into position for an attack. So I went around and told Bob
> Adams the Marine Commander and I got my Nungs all organised
> and we went on a 50 per cent stand-to [alert] and we were ready
> for them.[30]

In his article, 'Venison and Valour', however, John White wrote:

> The moon that night was full and visibility was good. There was
> cloud initially but at about 2000 hours it lifted and shortly after
> one of our machine guns opened up. At about 0300 on 9 May the
> moon set. [The ground attack started shortly thereafter.] While this
> was going on, WO Cameron and WO Lucas heard noise on the
> perimeter of the Helicopter Landing Zone (HLZ) on the other side
> of their wire. Claymores were fired and any potential attack was
> apparently stopped there.[31]

Bob Adams, the Marine Detachment Commander, agreed with John
White: 'That night we were on 50 per cent watch because we knew of
the activity going on near us.'

The platoon patrol that had a chance encounter with an enemy
element to the south of Ngok Tavak was withdrawn on the 9th. This
meant that Ngok Tavak did not have any local patrols out that night to
cover the likely avenues of approach to their position, and that meant
a lack of early warning about any enemy movement. A 50 per cent alert
should have had the howitzers manned, loaded with Fleschette and aimed
on pre-determined likely places the enemy might break through. These
shells were designed for battery defence–anti-personnel fire. As a result

of an apparent lack of communication between the commanders on what ammunition the artillery had, the guns were not readied. With an enemy attack thought to be forming up, this was an error, as was going to a 50 per cent alert; 100 per cent would have been a more appropriate decision.

But William Loman disagreed with White and Adams; he believed that they were not prepared for what happened.

> This was not my first encounter with VC and NVA; however, it was my first encounter being caught with my skivvies down. We were totally unprepared and are very fortunate that the good Lord was watching over us. To the best of my knowledge, word was not passed to the Marines, or at least to the general Marine contingent. The morning of the tenth I woke LCPL Long [not listed in the Marine contingent roster] at 0200, I hit the rack, on the ground, and did doze off, I hadn't been given much reason, other than another night in Vietnam, to think there was imminent danger. No Marines that I am aware of, other than CZ [Czerwonka], Long, myself, and possibly one of the radio operators were assigned any watch. A point of interest, when I evacuated back to the North side of the Fort Center, fighting holes lined the outer berm, there were no troops deployed on that line. I ran into our cook, Scuglik. He and I encountered only two Vietnamese in the holes, I assume CIDG and they were talking about the vast number of VC and left the area. If we were on a 50 per cent alert, why wasn't the North perimeter manned? I'll challenge any that say we were on 50 per cent alert. I'll also challenge anyone that tells me the Marines had a clue as to what was happening. From my perspective, concerning the Marines, I didn't have a clue, and still to this day, don't have a clue as to how we really overcame the situation.[32]

Lance Corporal David Fuentes said, 'it was normal; we put up our watch guys . . . we didn't get a message that an attack was coming and to go to 50 per cent, none whatsoever'. Greg Rose thought that Staff Sergeant Schriver had told them about the enemy the previous day.

> I think it was Staff Sergeant [Thomas] Schriver. He was a salt compared to 98 per cent of us whom had never fired a rifle at the

enemy. On the afternoon of 8 May we went to the river and bathed in leeches and collected water. I could 'feel' doom, like the grim reaper was close at hand. That night Schriver told us to hunker down and get ready for the worst.[33]

The worst was to come, but not that night.

4 THE WARRIORS CLASH

Treachery

Major Mai, Commanding Officer of the 40th Battalion, had got his assault troops into position ready for the attack on the fort; it was 0200 hours on 10 May, a delay of five days from their original plan, but the regimental commander had agreed not to go ahead without their support weapons. A Montagnard–Local Force unit assisted the 40th Battalion. The local unit would remain in place when Mai's unit moved to its secondary mission. All was ready; they now waited for the moon to set so that their first moves would be covered by darkness. The official report for the weather listed moonset at 0300 hours; they were prepared with time to spare. Just prior to this, at 0245 hours, Kham Duc came under heavy mortar and recoilless rifle fire, with approximately 68 mortar rounds exploding in the camp area. Special assault squads were assembled to breach the Ngok Tavak defences using explosives, which would allow the second wave, who had flame-throwers, to fan out and destroy the guns.[1] Major Mai probably had about 350 men assembled for the attack. This group would have been a mixture of northerners and South Vietnamese with some Montagnard Local Force Viet Cong as well. Facing them was a conglomerate commanded by Australian Captain John White with Lieutenant Bob Adams, who was White's direct support artillery officer, in command of the Marines. Although it was an allied group, it was not a comfortable bond of fighting men. In the words of Greg Rose, 'Paul Czerwonka hated slant eyes. He did not differentiate between the South, the North, the Nungs, no one; they were all queer and the enemy.' Ngok Tavak's defenders totalled 210, made up of: three AATTV, three US Special Forces, 41 Marines (out of an adjusted total on the hill of 46, two Marines had been evacuated and three were at Kham Duc on the 10th; this figure includes Marines Higgins and Long who are not shown on the roster, but were identified by other Marines as being at Ngok Tavak), 122 Nungs, as well as three interpreters, three South Vietnamese Special Forces, a Vietnamese–CIDG platoon of 30 and a five-man CIDG mortar crew.

When the moon went down, the North Vietnamese force screened by the CIDG at the bottom of the eastern track began their move towards the top of the hill. It was just after three o'clock on 10 May 1968. The camp Strike Force from Kham Duc had turned on the allies, the first double-cross of the battle. Marine Paul Czerwonka was on the .50 calibre machine gun at the top of the track, Joseph Cook was the loader and Greg Rose said he was there as well. He said that they let the first CIDG through the outer defence and into the position:

> We let the first CIDG through saying, don't shoot, don't shoot, friendly, friendly, after looking toward the Nungs on the other side of the road on the .30 calibre machine gun. The second CIDG, doing the same a few seconds later, made us very suspicious. Czerwonka gripped the handles of the 50 and rose up on his knees and leaned forward. Cook was the ammo feeder and moved behind us to put on his flak jacket and gather more grenades. I took my M-16 off safety and lay down pointing it down the road where the CIDG were. As we heard an explosion behind us, the .30 calibre machine gun and two Nungs copped a satchel charge. Within three to four seconds a second deafening explosion erupted to my right. [This explosion caused injuries that killed Paul Czerwonka, according to Greg Rose, but others say that he was shot.] I saw a group of the enemy run by with flamethrowers lighting up the perimeter. Cook stood up and came toward us pointing his M-16 at the enemy now rushing up the road. I whirled around, shot, thinking it was an NVA. A second or so later he caught an enemy round in the chest.[2]

For many years Rose thought that he had shot Cook.

The two sides were now mixed in a combat melee. Explosions, flame, rifle fire and running soldiers of both allegiances made it extremely difficult to recognise friend from foe. The fight started 'when the guys came up and shot Czerwonka and Cook', Corporal Henry Schunck said:

At the same time, Boom, Boom, Boom, the first three mortars, Lieutenant Adams got it and Sergeant Schriver who was sleeping next to him, he got it. Then Dale Scott got it. And they were moaning and stumbling up towards my gun [105 mm], my gun was nearest the command bunker and people were helping them and I said, take them to the command bunker. And that's how it all started. Then Captain Silva came, but he got hurt, we were just shooting at everything, they were coming in you didn't have to shout out any orders 'cause you know where they were, so you just keep shooting. Conklin went to the .50 [calibre machine gun] and he started messing them up. [Paul Swenarski and Bob Adams said that Conklin was on the .30 calibre machine gun at that time.] So we were all defending our positions and here they come again and their bodies are at the front gate, which was the only area they were coming in. The enemy was taking the bodies and putting them in the bunkers at the front, but they kept coming in there. He [Conklin] took an RPG round, I remember it, but he was still shooting, and I said good he didn't get all that fucked up, but I guess he did. Then I heard another explosion going his way and I saw somebody dragging him to the command bunker. Then I saw [Raymond] Heyne got shot in the head at the front berm. I have to say [Corporal Gerald] King; he held his ground because he killed a whole bunch of them because they didn't know he was in that hole that they had to pass.[3]

Lieutenant Bob Adams had finished his watch at two o'clock and had tried to grab some sleep.

After making my rounds to check on the men, I was relieved by SSgt Schriver (the platoon sergeant). I lay down near gun 2, to try to get some sleep. About three o'clock I was awakened by the sound of the attacking force. I got into my flak jacket I'd been using as a pillow, and was immediately hit in the head and back of my shoulder, probably by shrapnel from a mortar. I lost consciousness momentarily.

Then I looked up and saw an enemy soldier jump the berm, throw a grenade, and run towards the guns spraying fire with an AK. Shortly afterwards, SSgt Schriver came to me. I asked if he was okay. He held out his hands and I could see his hands and arms were bleeding badly. I started to give first aid when another round exploded. I was hit in the hand. I never saw SSgt Schriver again. I saw two more NVA jump the berm, silhouetted by the burning ¾-ton truck. I was able to shoot at them. I could see that the attack was coming through the CIDG position.[4]

The assault crumbled the fort's eastern defences and the Nung platoon and the Marines fragmented into individual fighting pits. Some men were alone; others scrambled together into small groups of two or three, but not in contact with each other. Corporal Raymond Scuglik, the artillery detachment's cook, learned quickly why all Marines are trained to fight and adapt.

The attack started around two or three in the morning. I was outside the [inner] fort on perimeter watching the road leading down to the Marines old position and also into the fort. I'm not sure but I think the CIDG were down at the lower position as a stopping force. When the attack began the NVA came right up the road (no defensive fire or warning from below) yelling and firing as if there had been nothing to stop them. I started returning fire and had grenades and bullets fired at me. Since they knew where I was I moved more around to the side of the fort and new cover. Basically I was alone. All hell was breaking loose in the fort. I could only hear what was going on and did not see much.[5]

Private First Class Paul Swenarski had pulled an early watch and was asleep in the fort when the fight started. He grabbed his M-16 and ammunition and took a position at the fort's wall.

I had two magazine belts [cloth belts that held rifle magazines in pouches], 25 clips [magazines] in all and four hand grenades. I made a recon run with the Australian sergeant [warrant officer who was not named] to the front of the fort [east], he sent me back to send the rest of the Marines to that position. When I reported to Marine Sergeant Roger Matye I was told, we are the rest, take a position and hold it. Due to heavy incoming we got scattered and I ended up in a hole in the wall with Corporal Richard Conklin and a .30 calibre machine gun. We were overlooking Captain White's bunker and facing the 105s [looking east]. I covered our flank while Corporal Conklin fired at the NVA trying to get to the guns. We got their attention and they started throwing grenades and automatic weapons fire at us. We threw back what we could and dived away from the others. We were both hit several times. They fired an RPG into our hole and that put us out of business.[6]

Richard Conklin and Paul Swenarski had grabbed one of the .30 calibre machine guns that had been sited to cover the angles to the northwest and southwest of the fort. One of the ammunition storage areas had exploded and the truck was on fire, which, paradoxically, assisted the defenders by silhouetting the North Vietnamese as they clambered over the earthen walls. Bob Adams, who had been wounded, got himself to Corporal Gerald King's fighting position where there was an M-60 machine gun. Adams wanted King to fire in the direction of the road coming in from the CIDG position, but before he could swing the gun around a grenade fell into the pit with them. Adams thought that it was the CIDG interpreter who had dropped the grenade in with them. He told King to get out. Corporal King didn't; he pushed his commander to safety.

With that shove and then the explosion from the grenade, I was thrown from the hole. [Adams said] I feel sure that shove by Corporal King saved me from even more serious injuries, or possibly even death. I crawled back to the hole; Corporal King was so badly injured I was certain he was dead. It was not until I went back to Vietnam in 1995 that I learned he did not die until later.[7]

Adams then crawled to the adjacent bunker where Richard Conklin and Paul Swenarski had taken over the .30 calibre machine gun. By this time, fire had engulfed the truck and the ammunition pit. Conklin fired some bursts that knocked down several NVA. Adams told Richard

Conklin that they needed help and that he was going for a radio. Adams said, 'I told him to be careful not to shoot any of our men since he was having to fire in their direction.' Lieutenant Adams's next memory was being in Captain White's bunker where White was coordinating the arrival of 'Spooky', a fixed-wing DC-3 gunship with flares and miniguns. At one point, Adams heard White say that 'there were only two of us left', and Adams wondered at the time if he was one of the two.

Fight for your life

Major Mai's battalion continued to rush up the track and spread into the fort throwing grenades and firing rapidly with AK-47s, although some carbines were also heard. These belonged to the CIDG traitors. At the same time, secondary assaults were used to test the strength of the defences in the southern and western quadrants held by 11th Company's 1st and 3rd platoons. Accurate enemy 60 mm mortar fire hit the camp; this was fired from the ridgeline to the south where the Nungs had made contact on 6 and 9 May. Rocket-propelled grenades (RPG) struck the areas around the AATTV and US Special Forces positions. These positions had obviously been spied by the 1st Regiment's reconnaissance parties in the weeks preceding the attack and marked accordingly. The battle strength of the assault soon concentrated on the track up from the old vehicle park, and it became the main conduit that funnelled the NVA into the position. This is when the scattered and uncoordinated artillerymen probably destroyed the North Vietnamese momentum. There was no centre of gravity, no fixed line on which the attackers could concentrate. Pockets of defiance flared in front, alongside and behind the assaulting troops. These were Marines. The Mike Force platoon withdrew—or 'ran on us', to censor the more salty language of some of the Marines, to the old parade ground at the western end of the feature when their platoon commander, Sergeant First Class Swicegood, was wounded. During the battle, Specialist Fourth Class Blomgren, the Mike Force medic, went to check on why the heavy— 4.2 inch—mortar was not firing and he found that the CIDG crew had left the position. Captain Silva went to take over the firing of the mortar. Silva commanded the CIDG at Kham Duc and he had come over to Ngok Tavak to discuss the reliability of his troops with John White, only to be caught there by inclement weather. He was badly wounded in the arm and abdomen and returned to the command post. Even the Naval Corpsman (Marine medic), Scott 'Doc' Thomas, was found later in the battle with a Colt .45 in his hand, although he doesn't recall firing at the enemy. Jim Garlitz found him unconscious in the early morning; Garlitz had thought he was dead. Doc Thomas's story is similar to those of most of the Marine artillerymen. They were exhausted by the physical demands of moving the guns that day and as soon as 'chow' was finished and an alert roster established, the remainder hit the rack. He was awake as soon as the first explosions sounded across the hill.

> I grabbed my A-1 (medical kit) and started for the fire control centre. On the way, I ran into two wounded, not too bad as I remember, put battle dressings on them and got up to run. Explosions—grenades, mortars—don't know which, ended up in an open pit that had rice and other stores. Met [Henry] Schunck there [and] Sergeant Glenn Miller jumped in also. As he [Miller] got up he was hit in the head and killed immediately. I remember Schunck holding him—lots of foggy memories after that.[8]

Corporal Schunck believed that Sergeant Miller's leadership and gallantry gave him the strength to fight on.

> Sergeant Miller came to me and he saw me giving out orders so he instructed me on how best to defend my position and what to do. From time to time he would check with me and we would meet at about the point where he got killed because that was where a lot of the small arms ammo was and he would confer with me and as the battle progressed he would advise me on how to regroup. Sergeant Miller made me fearless because of his fearless attitude and I think that Sergeant Miller had a lot to do with us making an effective defence and I believe he should have been awarded a Medal of Honor.[9]

David Fuentes, who was a young lance corporal during the battle, likened the defence against the first attack to a turkey shoot.

When we finally got the guns up the hill [on 9 May] that was a perfect time to attack us because we were dead tired and they caught us with our pants down. That was the first time in a week that I had taken my boots off, as I hadn't slept much when we were down below. We got orders from Lieutenant Adams to go ahead and put our aiming sticks out and put our scopes up. The most important thing to us, I was a gunner, a shooter, and the most important thing was to get the guns ready to fire. So if my mind served me pretty good we fired a couple of rounds just to co-ordinate them [on the 9th]. I had just got done on my shift, oh, I don't know about one o'clock in the morning and they hit us around three o'clock. I was just lying there when I heard all of the concussions going off and that's when all the helter skelter broke loose, massed confusion that's all I can tell you it was. We got up and starting firing at whatever we could, as a matter of fact I didn't put my boots on until daylight. I've often said that's what saved my life because me being Mexican I resembled a Vietnamese . . . I had 'em running by me, I was the one the fellows laughed at, as there was claims that I was in my underwear. I wasn't, I was in my green utility trousers that I'd cut the legs off, so I was standing there bare-chest with no shoes on and the NVA and whoever else was attacking us were just running right by me. And this was like a turkey shoot, so I was shooting them anywhere I could. And when they came in with the satchel to blow up my gun that really pissed me off. Everything was concentrated to get into the guns, but they were running right by the Mexican.[10]

The initial charge by the assaulting NVA was one of the very dangerous periods of the battle. It was a dagger-thrust at the combat heart of Ngok Tavak that struck down and scattered the defenders. It was a fight to the death that would have tested well-trained grunts (infantrymen); the Marines were not infantry, they were 'cannon-cockers', or '9-mile snipers'. And they were a mixed bunch—some were cannoneers, others worked the fire direction control centre for the guns. There were also radio operators, ammunition technicians, a truck driver and a cook, which was a normal make-up for an artillery detachment whose task is to get rounds on the ground, quickly and accurately. Their ad-hoc

THE WARRIORS CLASH ■ 77

personal equipment, as well as the accessories for the weapons they carried, proved their inexperience for an operation of this type. It was a mixed bag that may have got by at a fire support base or more established position, but it was unsatisfactory for deployment to the remote Ngok Tavak. Marines and armies worldwide pride themselves in saying their first priority is to know how to fight as infantry. It is a solid maxim, but in reality, training time for infantry tasks by other specialists is always limited. Detachment Delta X-Ray was not prepared for this. They would have been very comfortable pounding the enemy at a distance. Fighting charging infantry with machine guns, rifles and pistols amid screams, explosions and the blood and guts of warfare when it is up close and personal is a demanding mental and physical test. Some can shoot and fight and some cannot. The Nungs, for example, fled from the overrun eastern end to the hectic western part of the hill. Marines were forced back around the perimeters, and some had to fight their way to a more protected part of the compound, while others, bewildered and leaderless, got to the area of the command post. A few others fought on and made an effort to fill the void of the killed and wounded commanders and their Marine brothers. There were no cowards; each did what his training and his mind would permit.

Jim Garlitz recalled the shock of killing somebody in the combat action that suddenly exploded before him.

When the attack started I was sleeping next to my gun [105 mm], I had already stood my watch. This was directly adjacent to the opening of the berm where the road came up from the truck parking lot. Once I got into my fighting position almost immediately three NVA soldiers came running through the hole in the berm towards my gun. The first one I shot, I hit him in the side of the head and it was quite obvious that I had killed him. It was a shock to me that I had killed somebody, but there was no time to really dwell on the matter because his two buddies knew where I was at so their attention was directed at me. So, I very quickly had to dispose of them. My fighting hole being located right near the opening to the berm was a very strategic location because the initial NVA thrust came straight up the hill towards that opening. I then looked over the top of my fighting hole and there was a large number of NVA coming up the hill towards me. I went back down and put my M-16 on full automatic, I had a full magazine at that time and I sprayed it into them, probably two or three bursts. I could hear people screaming and moaning and everything else. When I went back down into that hole, I'd emptied the magazine. I put a fresh one on and we exchanged gunfire back and forth, they knew where I was at and they were directing some pretty heavy fire against me. I actually think they did get a recoilless rifle into position and were firing against the berm where my fighting hole was at, but it wasn't doing any good. Then they deployed a flamethrower, and things got pretty hairy for a while, flames were rolling up over the top of my fighting hole and I did receive second-degree burns. I think that I did kill him, or I believe that I did. An AK-47 round hit my M-16, but it was still operational. Boy that was close! I did end having to pull back into what would have been the northeast corner of the berm behind the mound of dirt. And that would be where I spent the rest of the evening [morning of the 10th]. There were several other Marines there, probably six of us; I think Greg Rose and [Private First Class Michael] Moore were with me. Going back to when I left my position I did come across another Marine, [Thomas] Blackman, he had been hit. I tried to help him and when I was trying to help him he was shot in the side of the head. He was gone, so I had to leave him. When I was in the position behind the mound of dirt, my fellow Marines and me were in such a position that we could still lay down fire towards the opening in the berm. And they continued to come through there throughout the night. They did get to my gun [105 mm].[11]

At this stage, an unknown Marine reported to Captain White in the command bunker that 'the enemy were now holding the gun position'.

•

The recorded times for the start of the assault to a report of the 'breakthrough' of the Ngok Tavak perimeter were 0315 hours to 0328 hours. The 2nd Nung Platoon had deserted its position, which left a few Marines and the command element pushed up into the western and northwestern corner of the floor of the fort where they held the bunker and protected the wounded. Some Marines were now in enemy territory;

for example, there was no contact between the group that Jim Garlitz was with, in the top eastern corner, and those at the western end. Marines Schunck, Brewster, Rose, Parrett and Fuentes, to name a few, were still out there somewhere as well. All of the Nung platoons, which were now located around the old parade ground, were held in place by enemy fire and the continuing possibility of a two-pronged assault. The two Australian warrant officers, Don Cameron and Frank Lucas, were in contact with Captain White by telephone, but there was little they could get their troops to do at this stage. The Nungs had no stomach for the main battle going on around the howitzers. Enemy action inside the fort now appeared to be stalled—although they held the greater part of the eastern lobe—and the battle became one of isolated fire-fights and the tossing of grenades between the combatants. The 2nd NVA Division's record of this attack told of the troubles they had in trying to take the Ngok Tavak base:

Our forces began the attack on Ngok Tavak during the evening of 9 May. The battle did not go well for us right from the start. The force assaulting the helicopter-landing zone ran into a minefield and was unable to advance. [It is not clear if this was the old French field, or Claymores.] The force assaulting the lower portion of the command post area was unable to get through the enemy's defensive obstacles. Only the force assaulting the command post itself was able to penetrate to its objective, taking complete control of the upper portion of the position after eight minutes of fighting. Faced with this situation, the commander of the 40th Battalion of the Ba Gia Regiment [1st VC Regiment, 2nd NVA Division] immediately sent his 3rd company into the fray. Our forces quickly overran the lower portion of the command post area but were unable to advance onwards to the helicopter-landing zone. The enemy in that location, using bunkers and underground fortifications that we had not detected during our attack preparations, conducted a ferocious battle. Even when the reserve company was committed to the battle, we were still unable to take control of the battlefield.[12]

Private First Class Dean Parrett was one of the Marines who helped to prevent Major Mai's men from achieving their objective:

We repulsed their attack up the front of the hill. More of the NVA came up the road towards our guns. We killed as many as we could at the time. I did not know what the body count was, but there were dead NVA lying all over the position. What a wakeup call for a bunch of young Marines.

He also remembered a Marine who was happy to have earned a Purple Heart.

I found Robert Lopez on the dirt berm in front of me. I pulled him off the berm and saw that he had died. I crawled back down along the dirt berm to get more M-16 ammunition and talked to one of the Marines; he stated that he had been shot through both legs. I can't remember which one of our Marines he was. He was happy that he was still alive and earned his Purple Heart.[13]

Private First Class Charles Reeder had thought that all the talk of a possible attack was just bullshit.

I slept like a baby until [Private First Class Thomas] Blackman woke me and said we were being attacked, but it didn't really soak in at first. Blackman, [Private First Class Barry] Hempel and I were about 75 yards [70 metres] to the right of the helipad and the ammo bunker was to our right. We were pretty close together in front and to the right of the [Marine] command bunker. Blackman went to the berm to the right and began shooting. Hempel called to me that I should hurry up, and then the mortars starting coming in. I saw Blackman get shot. About halfway across the compound and to the left a mortar hit and killed another one or two of us and still another was yelling for help of a corpsman. This was near one of the 105s. Our sergeant told me to fill in on the berm where Blackman had been killed. I had just gotten over there and a rocket or mortar hit just in front of command post. I thought it had gotten Hempel and maybe someone else as there were two or three others there. About that time I saw the flame from a flame thrower and they set off our ammo bunker. The explosions sent fragments all around and I felt some burns on my arms but they were minor. The hand grenades were flying all over the place. There was firing from the right and I returned fire and it stopped. There were guys firing mortars for a while just to my rear. It didn't sound like they really knew what they were doing but they didn't blow us up so they did good. Sometime later a man came toward me from the direction of where the ammo bunker had been and I held him in my sights but did not pull the trigger. It turned out to be one of ours. We stayed together there until it started getting light. He started firing into the blackness at first but I asked him to wait until we had a target and he did. We at first thought we were the only ones left but soon found that we weren't. The planes came with daylight and I never saw anything so pretty and welcome in my life.[14]

At 0420 hours, Spooky was recorded as being on station over Ngok Tavak. A typical load for these gunships was three mini-guns, with each gun capable of firing at a selected 3000 or 6000 rounds per minute. The aircraft generally carried 21,000 rounds of 7.62 mm ammunition, which were fired in short bursts of three to nine seconds that have been described as the best fart ever heard. Spooky also carried flares with a light equivalent of two million candlepower, which could illuminate a battlefield for three minutes at a time. Captain White directed the aircraft to spray the perimeter. He then approved the aircraft to strike the area of the 105 mm howitzers after shouted warnings to the Marines and the Nungs, even though the Nungs had abandoned their posts around the eastern end of the fort.

> There was no alternative, but to have Spooky fire on the friendly 105 mm howitzer positions, despite the fact that there may have been friendly wounded in the position. This proved later to have been profitable, because the dead NVA and abandoned weapons found in the area indicated that this fire had cleared the area temporarily.[15]

According to John White, the later discovery of the enemy's casualties justified firing into the gun position. He also admitted that he had 'no doubt that some of our own people were killed by that fire', which he regretted. There was no explanation, however, about how the casualties were differentiated between Spooky's mini-guns and the small-arms fire on the ground. Marines who were in the vicinity of the 105 mm howitzers said that Spooky did not fire into that area. Others, around the perimeter, agreed that there was no firing at their position, and the shouted warnings that Spooky was going to fire among them were lost in the cacophony of battle. As one Marine replied, 'You're kidding me, have you ever seen one of those things in action? We'd all have been dead!' The 7th Air Force report, 'Kham Duc' also said in 1968, 'A Spooky AC-47 was overhead [Ngok Tavak] firing extremely close to friendly positions.'[16] In addition, Major Mai replied to a question in 1995 that he had attacked again between 0330 and 0400, but the assault was stopped by the machine guns 'firing in different directions before a helicopter arrived'—although not a helicopter, Spooky got there at 0420 hours. Mai confirmed this in an interview conducted in 1999 when he said that he occupied a command position during the battle that was approximately 20 metres away from Captain White's command post. He stated that there were many explosions and small-arms exchanges, but he was not certain what direction the firing was coming from. He did not know the location of the Americans firing in his direction.[17] Bearing in mind the capabilities of the AC-47's mini-guns, it is unlikely that the centre of the fort could have been targeted without the enemy commander knowing that the fire came from a gunship.

Another name for Spooky was 'Dragon Ship', so called because of the red flames that appeared to spew forth from the 'dragon's mouth'. Tracer rounds, which made up one round in every five, created the 'flame' that made the direction of fire very apparent. Also, the deadliness of mini-guns is explained in this example. During a development test phase that married a 7.62 mm Gatling gun to a DC-3, the gun fired at 6000 rounds per minute for three seconds against 25 mannequins. The mannequins were scattered in different positions over three-quarters of an acre—60 yards by 60 yards, approximately 55 by 55 metres—and the burst hit nineteen of the targets, ten of which were considered to have been killed.[18] The Ngok Tavak inner-fort area was no bigger than 33 by 50 yards—30 by 45 metres.[19] There are other statistics for one gun firing, or three, at slow or fast rate, but they are all deadly, and this would have been especially so against the open space of the Ngok Tavak inner fort. Furthermore, the guns on a Spooky were aimed and fired by the pilot without the assistance of technology; he did not have a night observation device, or radar assistance, for example. Under the battle conditions in the early morning of 10 May, this was a 'spray-the-area' defence weapon that would have also hit John White's command bunker and the American troops that had made their way back to the berm defence line at the fort's northwestern corner.

Owing to the scarcity of gunships, the Direct Air Support Center, which approved support requests, had a standard operating procedure that said that aircraft would only be diverted to support troops in contact with the enemy. The 4th Air Commando Squadron's records for May 1968 showed the following aircraft availability:

> There were four flights that totalled 16 AC-47D aircraft. Five gunships were in 'A' Flight at the Danang forward operating location. [Danang would have been the most likely location to provide an aircraft to support Ngok Tavak.] Pleiku had four [two were destroyed by ground fire during the night of 4–5 May], Phu Cat also had four and there were three at Nha Trang. [20]

As a consequence of the limited number of aircraft, and the travel distance to Ngok Tavak (DC-3s were slow), the gunship arrived at the end of the enemy's assault phase. By now, the more vulnerable enemy targets were more likely to have been around the outer perimeter and on the move. Even though this was difficult territory for the 7.62 mm mini-guns, which lacked hitting power through the dense jungle foliage, this assumption is supported by where the 1st VC Regiment's battlefield clearance team found most of their casualties after the battle. An approval to fire into the fort would have been recorded by the cockpit tape recorder because it was a contentious request due to friendly troops still being in the strike area. No record of that request-cum-command was found, and conversations with ex-crew members of the 4th Squadron revealed that their memories of missions were blurred not only by time, but also by the total number of sorties crews undertook during their tour of duty. As at 24 September 1967, there were 24 crews allocated to the sixteen aircraft, with each AC-47 flying with a seven-man crew: two pilots, a navigator, two gunners, a loadmaster and a flight engineer. The 4th Air Commando Squadron missions in April, May and June 1968 are a good illustration of the crews' workload.

> Sorties flown numbered 1118; Combat hours flown was 4497; Rounds of ammunition fired was over seven million with 11,848 flares dropped. These actions protected 38 outposts and/or Special Forces camps and provided support to troops in contact 316 times in the three months.

The specific actions recorded for May 1968 were:

> The Squadron flew a total of 419 sorties of which 153 were in support of troops in contact. Twenty-one of those were flown to protect an outpost, Special Forces camp or other fixed friendly position. These sorties resulted in 65 confirmed enemy killed. [This is the total for 14 aircraft (two destroyed), but the mission to assist Ngok Tavak did not rate a mention in the squadron's monthly report, which provided an amazing statistic of 110,000 rounds for each enemy soldier killed.] [21]

While this study of whether Spooky fired into the fort's inner sanctum may appear to be overly pedantic, it does provide an answer as to how the enemy's main assault was defeated. Forty Marines were still scattered around the inner fort area—some were wounded, some were dead and some were fighting. The omni-directional ground fire that came from the scattered Marines who could continue to fight was the action that stopped the enemy taking the fort. As a consequence, the enemy's casualties inside the fort that were credited to the Spooky gunship by Captain White were in fact caused by the Marines' small-arms fire. Also, a gunship attack on the fort's interior at this stage in the fight— after 0420 hours—would have shattered the Marines' resistance at a time when the tide of battle had turned in their favour. This would have probably caused the total collapse of the hill's defence because the Nungs had already run away to the western side, which should have been obvious but their action may not have been known by those in the command bunker at the time. This was the second time on this operation that they had deserted their allies when they smelt defeat.

The Australian commander, therefore, did not know who and what numbers of personnel were alive and outside his now compressed defensive line. Captain White did believe that the situation was critical and the loss of the position was imminent. An order to fire then would have been justified, even though the 'friendly fire' may have been to the detriment of an unknown number of allies who were still out among the enemy. Nevertheless, a different conclusion is made here. The gunship fired close to, but not inside the fort's inner perimeter. This conclusion is based upon the information gathered from latter-day conversations with the Marine survivors, as well as the technical data of a Spooky's capabilities and the enemy commander's memories. It is agreed that some rounds may have hit inside the fort, and that, plus the closeness of the strike, gave the impression the centre of the fort was hit by Spooky's guns. Even so, the fire from the AC-47 made sure that the enemy would not reassemble to attack again if they were so inclined, which they were not.

Following the defeat of the 40th Battalion's last charge, and the arrival of Spooky, a dangerous game of death or survival lasted until morning twilight, which was around 0530 hours. It was now a more indiscriminate, indirect fight through hurled grenades, and haphazard shooting at movement that might have been an enemy. During the latter part of the battle the NVA set off tear gas, but the tear gas was of such low density it did not affect the friendly troops. Charles Reeder remembered the gas:

> Pretty soon someone yelled tear gas and I put on my mask, but it was hot and it felt like I couldn't see so I tested the air and found the gas was weak and not even close to being as strong as the gas chamber we experienced back in training. So I took it off. Seems like this was about then that the Special Forces people came in to reinforce our position and after only a few minutes some of the people who were calling out that they were friendly were declared enemy and shot.[22]

One of the Marines believed the gas came from their own ammunition dump rather than the enemy. In either case, 'the wind carried the gas towards the enemy troops ... so after three attempts they gave up [using the gas]'. Several Marines believed that if they survived until daylight they would live and win what was now seen as a battle of retaliation. Lance Corporal David Fuentes was one of the believers. He said he felt that the new day would bring them victory:

> I was waiting for daylight. I felt if I could make it to daylight I'll live. Then we would be ready to fight on if we would have had reinforcements, we were scared shitless and everything too, but at that time the revenge factor in our mind [was high].[23]

Escape

First light—between twilight and sunrise—brought with it several unexpected events. First, the regimental commander had ordered the 40th Battalion: 'To leave only a blocking force behind to hold the captured positions while the rest of the battalion, in accordance with our combat plan, was to prepare to deal with an enemy relief force.'[24] Major Mai, the battalion commander, and Major General (Ret.) Phan Thanh Du, both said in 1995 that the Main Force had moved on and that only local guerrillas were left at Ngok Tavak. Major Mai also said in another interview that he had been wounded and carried from the battlefield and did not know what happened after that. Whatever the force was that remained, they had 75 mm recoilless rifles in support. The NVA force had either gone, or was moving away from the hill when a counterattack was launched to retake the fort. Australian warrant officers Don Cameron and Frank Lucas led this attack. Although termed a counterattack, it was an act of courage by the Australians to move into the battle zone inside the fort, an act that shamed, or at least goaded, some of the Nungs to go with them. The majority were reluctant and at best Cameron and Lucas had a handful of Nungs with them, but when they moved across the berm into the fort some Marines also joined in, which forced any remaining enemy to withdraw beyond the perimeter wire. During this part of the battle, a small group of Marines, who had been isolated throughout the night, decided they were going to go down fighting and take as many of the enemy with them as they could. Jim Garlitz and Greg Rose both had similar memories of a cigarette that saved their lives.

We had that discussion back and forth about what happens if we were it, were we going to surrender. It was pretty much a consensus of everybody that we were not going to surrender; we would go down fighting. And as the battle continued, the sunlight came up and more air support arrived and some of the guys decided, let's just go ahead and charge them and get it over with. And I remembered, I said ok but before I do that I'm going to have my last cigarette. And I rolled over on to my back and lit up one of those nasty C-rat cigarettes. About that time Captain White and the remaining survivors, we had no idea anyone else was alive, came charging up over the berm and at the same time we charged from where we were. Had I not stopped and had that cigarette I'm sure if we had have made our charge before the others, we would have been cut down and not survived.[25]

Prior to this, urgent messages had been sent to the 5th Special Forces Company C Headquarters in Danang, as well as to the Americal Division, warning of Ngok Tavak's grim circumstance and requesting help. Captain Eugene Makowski was roused at 0400 hours on 10 May with the directive, 'You are to fly to Kham Duc and assume command of the 12th Mobile Strike Force Company in basic training there and reinforce the 11th Company at Ngok Tavak.' Captain Makowski wrote after the battle:

I departed Danang in the C & C chopper at 0630 for Kham Duc/Ngok Tavak; we arrived at 0730 and briefly touched down at Kham Duc to pick up an AN/PRC-74 radio [high-frequency radio capable of communications in difficult terrain] for Ngok Tavak. We proceeded to Ngok Tavak where SSGT [*sic* Specialist Fourth Class] Perry, SGT Matheney and SP/4 Pound got off. I briefly talked to a Marine concerning the situation at Ngok Tavak. We put aboard some medevac [Captain Silva was one of these] and then [I] returned to Kham Duc to pick up the reaction force.[26]

Sergeant 'Jack' Matheney's introduction to Ngok Tavak was via a rude awakening in the early hours of 10 May when Lieutenant Melvin told him, 'Get your shit; Ngok Tavak has been overrun!' His immediate reaction was the thought, 'Knock what?' By the time he arrived with Captain Makowski, Spooky had run out of ammunition, but remained on-station to provide a communications link as well as to advise other aircraft about the situation on the ground. Jet ground-attack aircraft were guided initially by Spooky to attack near the camp's perimeter and also on to possible enemy mortar and other fire-support positions, but the fort continued to receive sporadic mortar, RPG and small-arms fire. A helicopter (Dustoff) also flew in to lift some of the casualties out. The North Vietnamese did not fire upon the medevac helicopter. According to the Vietnamese officers interviewed in 1995, this was a divisional policy. There are several recorded non-firing incidents that involved Dustoff flights in the 2nd NVA area of operations, but such conditions could not be relied upon and all extractions were flown with the possibility of enemy fire in mind. Major Patrick Brady, who flew 'Dustoff 55' into Ngok Tavak, recalled:

> We did not take fire even though I could see fire from the surrounding terrain going into NT. As I have noted, sometimes the disciplined NVA respected the Red Cross but you could not count on it (this same NVA unit shot up several of our birds in the next 2 days).[27]

Except for the evacuation of Captain Silva in the aircraft that brought in Captain Makowski, Major Brady and his crew flew all of the Dustoff missions for the Ngok Tavak camp and took out approximately 70 wounded personnel. This was an outstanding feat, but one that did not surpass the January 1968 mission in which Brady and his crew used three helicopters to rescue 51 American and South Vietnamese soldiers from a fog-bound and heavily defended site in enemy-held territory near Chu Lai. Brady was awarded the Medal of Honor for those earlier flights-of-bravery. He had previously been awarded the Distinguished Service Cross.

Major Brady's Dustoff flights had followed the counterattack, which allowed the Marines and Nungs to reconsolidate their position. Almost simultaneously, Captain Makowski and 12th Company were flying in from Kham Duc to reinforce the hill. Prior to their landing, however, the stress of this fragmented battle began to take another toll: there was a breakdown of trust between the Marines, Nungs and any remaining

CIDG. Following the double-cross by the CIDG at the beginning of the battle, the Marines trusted no one. Anything or anyone that looked suspicious was shot. Specific details and the number of men killed are not known, but it was not a lot. Personal admissions in 2006 provided compelling anecdotal evidence that a few enemy and possibly one or two Nungs were killed during the 'mopping up' phase. There was no order given, but among the men who had remained scattered around the fort there was almost a tacit understanding that they were not going to be tricked again. This was action up close and personal and the niceties of the Geneva Convention were thrust aside by a very strong desire to live. Nungs also took aside a number of surviving CIDG traitors and shot them, an action that was not prevented from happening (in all probability it could not have been stopped anyway). Nevertheless, this was ruthless punishment handed out by troops who, themselves, had been disloyal during this deployment, and unreliable when they did not contest the NVA thrust through the fort's eastern sector during the main attack.

The killing of Corporal Gerald King, USMC, by deliberate friendly fire, was more upsetting. While the efforts to consolidate the position and to clear the battleground of wounded and the debris of a fire-fight continued, some of the defenders came upon the badly wounded Corporal King, who refused to give in, firing upon anyone who approached his foxhole. An effort to calm Corporal King failed, and as Captain White said, 'We had to kill him.'[28] A friendly grenade killed Gerald King, but it is not clear who did the killing. However, this action did cause a bitter, albeit hidden, reaction among several of Corporal King's Marine brothers. They discussed killing Captain White in retaliation. Their anger dissolved, however, and they did not act. Whether, at the time, that decision was influenced by their training and discipline, or an understanding that the killing of Corporal King may have been necessary is blurred. In 2006, there was some understanding by those Marines that a difficult command decision was made, one that they accepted as the responsibility of command but did not like. As one Marine explained, 'the area was a mess. We were all nervous and not in any mood to let any "gook" come near, whether he looked friendly or not. We shot at things and asked questions after. If that's why King was killed, then we should all have been shot.'

Although Captain White expected a further assault by the 40th Battalion later in the morning, the enemy's principal attack had been defeated and the 'Main Force' unit had moved off towards Kham Duc. Most of the wounded had been lifted out and, with the 12th Company MSF reinforcements on their way on board Marine CH-46 helicopters, things perhaps were looking a little brighter. Sergeant Robert Mascharka was a crewman in one of the helicopters in a flight of four that carried 12th Company into battle. They made their approach as Dustoff 55 lifted away and cleared the landing zone; this was recorded at 0930 hours. Bob Mascharka recalled, as he said as accurate as any 40-year-old memory may be:

> Our flight of four was doing a radial around the hill while the Army Medevac was loading up on the side of the berm to the raised fort. As soon as the Huey cleared the hill, our first 46 made the approach to the LZ and I could see them taking fire from a variety of places. They made it in and out without taking any hits. We were in trail to them so we were next on the dance card and continued onto the LZ.

The number of helicopters that made it into the landing zone and their sequence of landing was made clear by pilots and crew who flew that day. Robert Basye, who was co-pilot to Major John McCabe, flight lead, confirmed what Major McCabe had said at a press interview back in 1968 that he was first into the Ngok Tavak LZ. Bill Cihak and Fred Guerton followed. They were number two and this is the helicopter that Bob Mascharka saw taking fire. Lieutenant H. ('Bud') Fleming with George Bunda piloted the helicopter on which Bob Mascharka was a crewman—this was number three into the zone, and Mascharka recalled:

> We were taking fire but no hits and discharged our load of Mike Force into the zone. We were taking off and in hover check when several rounds impacted to the side of us and right where our main struts had been on the ground, really fine shooting by the bad guys, and we took damage to the aft section of the aircraft. It really looked like a waterfall with fuel, oil and hydraulics pouring down from the

aft pylon. We radioed an emergency distress call and ran from the chopper. I don't know whether it was then or later that I took a piece of shrapnel to my left leg, which Jack Matheney bandaged later. Bill Cihak and Fred Guerton came back into the zone in answer to our mayday call since they were the nearest and it took a direct hit just before touchdown. [Le Huu Thoi, commander of a 75 mm recoilless rifle team, was credited by the 2nd NVA Division with destroying two 'CH-47' helicopters—*sic* CH-46—just as they touched down.] The engines and the rotors were still turning as the crew ran from the burning aircraft; it was obvious one of them was injured. We were all taking fire and practicing how to be moles. I was in an ammo bunker thinking that I was not in the most desirable spot but with all the incoming I was not ready to look for a new home. The fixed-wing jets [F-4 Phantom] were coming in so low over the hill that I could see the faces of the pilots and the bomb shrapnel was knocking branches out of the trees all around us.[29]

Three aircraft had made it in with their troops, the third one was disabled on the pad when number two, which was empty, came back to rescue the crew and it was destroyed by enemy fire. The two downed Sea Knight helicopters now blocked the Ngok Tavak landing zone, which prevented the remaining aircraft in the flight to land; but approximately 45 men from the 12th Company got in to reinforce the position. Captain Makowski wrote in 1968:

I contacted Captain White and asked him where he wanted the troops deployed. He stated that he wanted them deployed around the helipad. During this time I was talking with Captain White and some Marine concerning the situation. I was told that both 105s were operable but one sight was broken and they were out of ammo. A situation report was given to Kham Duc.[30]

Captain Makowski placed his company under Captain White's command, which meant the Australian captain was now in charge of all of the allied forces on the hill. This was a frenetic and worrying time and it was when John White's military ability came to the fore.

On his own admission, he had previously been seduced by the 'superior' experience and knowledge of the officers in his headquarters:

> I shudder now to think how ill-prepared we were but I naively thought that these people knew what they were doing, that my activities were part of a big plan. The whole concept was a disaster in the making from the beginning. If I had been older than 25 and had some experience, I may have had the nerve to refuse to do the operation; or, at least, withdrawn before we got clobbered. In my naivety, I really believed that there was a grand plan by more competent people than myself.[31]

John White was worried that the Nungs 'were tired and becoming nervous, their ammunition was almost expended and water was running low'. The two officers, White and Makowski, provided the steadying influence needed to calm the Mike Force soldiers, as well as being the command centre for the Marines when Lieutenant Bob Adams was evacuated. John White was on the radio frequently, communicating with Danang, Kham Duc and the medevac helicopter. Major Brady, Dustoff 55, acknowledged, 'John's demeanour gave me great confidence.' Lieutenant Colonel William F. Smith, the Executive Officer of Company C, 5th Special Forces Danang, was now airborne in the Kham Duc–Ngok Tavak area to provide a command and control contact; it was approximately 1030 hours. Although the assault against Ngok Tavak had stopped much earlier in the morning, the position remained under sporadic fire from enemy mortars, 75 mm recoilless rifles, rocket-propelled grenades and a variety of small arms. The defenders continued to consolidate their position and make sure the wounded were evacuated and the dead identified. At this stage, Captain White believed that they could not hold the position should it be assaulted again and he requested permission at 1045 hours to evacuate the hill, but he was told, 'to hold on, reinforcements were on their way'.[32] Both White and Makowski knew there was little chance that reinforcements would be sent to Ngok Tavak. The road from Kham Duc to Ngok Tavak was an invitation to be ambushed, the Ngok Tavak airstrip would surely be covered by the enemy, making it too dangerous to risk insertion there, and the Ngok Tavak LZ was blocked by the destroyed helicopters.

Operational plan *Golden Valley*, the Americal Division's proposal for the relief of Kham Duc, did not include reinforcing the Ngok Tavak position if it was under threat. At 0912 hours, the Americal Division's Duty Officer's log recorded: 'Americal force will be used to reinforce Kham Duc and possibly aid the FOB', but that was the only mention of sending a force to Ngok Tavak. *Golden Valley* was initiated at approximately 0830 hours. At 0845 hours the Americal Division requested approval from III MAF for a change in the reaction force so that the 2nd Battalion, 1st Infantry, would provide the reinforcements instead of the 1st Battalion, 46th Infantry, which would provide a company and a command group until the 2nd/1st was in position. Lieutenant Bobby Thompson, who was the commander of the relief unit, A Company, said:

> The initial discussion about Ngok Tavak did not concern my company at all. Never was 'A' Company included in the thought of relieving Ngok Tavak. The comments initially made were about Ngok Tavak and their possible dilemma. I knew from the morning my company was alerted that we would be at Kham Duc to assist in defending the base.[33]

Lieutenant Colonel Garland L. Owens headed the command group, and A Company, 1st/46th, closed on Kham Duc at 1050 hours. They were immediately assigned to tasks around the Kham Duc camp. This was five minutes after Captain White had been told that reinforcements were on the way to Ngok Tavak. Elements of the 2nd Battalion would not arrive at Kham Duc for a further six hours, a delay that had been forecast in reports on reinforcing the camp. It must have been obvious that a company was not going to help both Kham Duc and Ngok Tavak, which meant John White had every reason to be sceptical about remaining on the hill. I was told, White said, that we would be reinforced by Americal:

> I don't believe there was any misunderstanding, because they would say, reinforcements are going to come and I would say the chopper pad is blocked and the airstrip is fully ambushed, and they would say don't worry stay there. And that's what happened in the end . . . I was given specific times that they would arrive. At eleven o'clock

I said, we couldn't hold any longer it wouldn't matter who had a go at us we would have fallen over. We were just about out of ammo; the guys were getting very twitchy and at twelve o'clock I said, we are leaving here at 1300 and I told everyone to get ready. At 1300 [Lieutenant Colonel] Smith was overhead, I just said OK, I got on the radio and said we're moving out and I was told no, you are to remain there. I just handed the radio back to Makowski; he didn't hear the order or anything. If he had, he probably would have insisted that we stay there.[34]

Eugene Makowski, nevertheless, wrote in 2006:

There was no discussion among us if we wanted to vacate NT or not. Nor did Capt White ask for our opinions. It was; this is what we are going to do. Left unsaid was, if you want to stay and take your chances, it's up to you. Although I knew from monitoring the radio that Capt White had been ordered to stay, I did not question his decision to leave. Prior to the decision, I was resigned to remain without additional reinforcement and would probably be killed. Up until the evacuation began, I was uncertain if I would stay or evacuate. When I saw everyone forming to evacuate, I made the decision to join the group.[35]

From the arrival of Captain Makowski and the 12th Company reinforcements, the position had been secured and many wounded had been evacuated. Sergeant Jack Matheney, who had treated some of the Mike Force wounded when he arrived with Captain Makowski earlier in the morning, also saw the second Marine CH-46 that was hit by enemy fire:

I saw the explosive round hit the second chopper . . . all personnel . . . escaped without serious injury except one of the Marine air crewmen. He was seriously wounded and I did the best I could for him and gave him morphine. A medevac was called for him but it was unable to land on the chopper pad . . . so [it] hovered over the camp [the northern side of the fort] as I assisted lifting him on a litter into the helicopter.[36]

That crewman was Corporal Jon J. Davis. Sergeant Bob Mascharka had taken the stretcher on which Davis was treated from under one of the dead Marines who had been respectfully laid out just slightly to the northern side of John White's command bunker. There were five bodies here. Not only did he confirm that some of those who had been killed had been collected and identified, but he also remembered the loss of Lieutenant 'Bud' Fleming.

> Davis was bandaged and given morphine since he was in a lot of pain. John White had been on the radio and told us that there was a medevac on the way for him and some of the other wounded. At that time he said that since the chopper would be lightly loaded that he wanted as many of us Marine aviators to get out on it as possible. We Marines that were around Davis all wanted to stay on the ground but it was decided that one of the pilots and a crew chief were going to go out with Davis in order to report in with our squadron and to see that Davis got to some medical attention. At this time Fleming was not with the group but over in a trench line further to the east of our location and directly north of the raised fort where the guns were located. I am convinced that Fleming never got the word about the offer to evacuate.
>
> A while later, probably about 20 to 30 minutes, John White gave us the word that the medevac was on final coming up the valley and to get ready. I was one of the four who picked up the stretcher and we went up to the top of the old fort to wait for the chopper and immediately came under a lot of sniper fire from the east and had to move off of the raised fort. At this time the chopper came into a hover right off of the northeast perimeter directly above the northern edge of the fort and almost right in front of where Fleming was in a trench line. We brought the stretcher out to the chopper that was about 7 feet [2 metres] off the ground in hover just above a downed tree and used the tree as a ladder to get the ends of stretcher up to the medevac crewmen in the cargo area. As I was getting off the tree and moving back to the trench line, Fleming asked me what was going on and I told him that Davis and some of the crew were going out on the chopper and I turned away to move further down the line. At this time there were Davis and about 2 or 3 wounded

Nungs and the Marine crewmen on the chopper. As it started to raise up to clear the trees, 2 more Nungs ran out and grabbed onto the skids and then Fleming also ran out and grabbed onto the skid. The chopper continued to rise and cleared the trees and moved off to the north and east out of my view. From where I was on the ground and not far from main group I could hear the chopper and we were taking incoming fire on the perimeter from across the valley. I did not actually see the people fall off the skids but I also did not see anyone firing at the chopper to knock them off of the skids.[37]

Pat Brady recalled:

We were not full the last load and could easily have taken the three who grabbed our skids. One US, Fleming and two Asians. We got to the ground almost immediately but not before two fell. For years I wondered why the other two could not hang on for such a short time. We got the third on board and went back to look for the others. I asked the troops to help but they were on the way out and in fact said, fuck them they were supposed to go out with us, or words to that effect.[38]

Jon Davis, the wounded crewman, remembered it well nearly 40 years later:

We went in and dropped off our load and we got out without being hit. When the next helicopter went down, our pilot did a 180 and we went back thinking we might be able to get in and out quickly. Our luck ran out and we got hit. Luckily, I suppose, I was the only one that was wounded and I remember the pilot telling me to shut up, as I was screaming loudly from the pain of my wounds. I was put on a stretcher and carried over to the other side [fort] where a Huey came in to medevac me. I remember 'Bud' Fleming getting on, but I don't know what happened to him. I was stuck halfway out of the Huey on the stretcher and I was in pain and also watching the crew chief to make sure that he kept a good hold on me.[39]

Lieutenant Bill Cihak was in the medevac when Lieutenant Fleming got on the skid. As the helicopter lifted off, over the trees, and flew towards Kham Duc, Lieutenant Cihak had linked his fingertips with Bud Fleming's, but they could not make a stronger grasp and Fleming fell. Bill Cihak said he just couldn't watch him fall all the way to the ground. They landed soon after, near the Ngok Tavak airstrip and quickly pulled the Nung aboard before flying back towards the hill in a hopeless attempt to find Fleming. There was some discussion on the ground when the Nungs and Fleming ran and jumped aboard the medevac. John White resolved that runaways would be shot. In this case, contrary to previous statements and scuttlebutt, Fleming and the Nungs were not shot off the aircraft, and this was the last flight out of the position.

Spooky, the AC-47 gunship, and then 30 sorties of tactical air, continued to protect Ngok Tavak throughout the morning, and they made doubly sure that the enemy would not assault the position again. John White now set in action his plan to evacuate the hill and withdraw his forces to safety. The Marines were ordered to fire their remaining rounds of 105 mm—some said seven shells remained following the fires in the ammunition dumps, others said nine—and then the howitzers were disabled.

In 1995, during a return-to-the-battlefield visit, the discussion on what had happened in 1968 was badly interpreted, which caused John White and others to believe that the final firing of the howitzers had wounded Major Mai, CO of the 40th Battalion. It did not. Major Mai had asked if the Americans had begun to run away after being hit by the NVA's two DK 75 (75 mm recoilless rifles). Bob Adams and John White thought the question was: Did you fire the big cannons at us, the NVA? Both sides nodded with satisfaction when Adams and White answered yes. White and Adams thought that the 105 mm fire had wounded Mai, and Mai thought the DK 75 had caused them to run away. Each party was happy with their thoughts that their action had harmed the other.[40]

Tasks were then allocated to the groups that remained on Ngok Tavak to ensure as much equipment as possible, or anything considered to be of value to the enemy, was destroyed. Captain White also directed an order-of-march off the hill that would protect any walking wounded and those with little infantry experience. He now had to make an extremely challenging choice: should they take the dead with them, or not? John White decided that they would not, and as Captain Makowski said:

> There was no attempt to take the dead with us. We expected we would have to fight our way off NT and trying to carry the dead with us would have been suicide. After the earlier incident with the mobbing of the helicopter, this was not an option. Additionally, risking helicopters to pick up the dead after two helicopters already shot up would have been foolish.[41]

Leaving the dead Marines behind brought forth a spectrum of emotions. James Garlitz thought it total betrayal—Marines did not leave their dead behind—but looking back he could understand. William Loman said:

> The convincing blow that caused us to leave the hill without them, [was] they will be recovered as soon as the area is secure. It didn't happen; we along with those Marines who remained for 37 years were betrayed. I personally don't care what branch of the military was in charge of the operation, we were screwed, someone has to live with that and I hope that he has lived with the same taste in his mouth that I have had over CZ [Czerwonka] being killed as he was. [This alludes to a belief by some Marines that Czerwonka was tortured to death.] [42]

Sergeant Roger Matye did not feel good about the decision either; it was not something that the Marines were trained to do. Greg Rose carried the emotions for many years after. 'Wow!' he said. 'There were too many emotions. I was numb by this time and didn't give a shit! Within a few days the nightmares and the horrific memories began to gnaw at me.'[43] Paul Swenarski felt that it was a bad situation to leave the bodies, but he understood that the first obligation was to keep as many people alive as possible. Raymond Scuglik recalled, 'I felt relief and sadness when we lifted out. Glad to have survived and sorrow for those that didn't. It was my first time experiencing a life or death situation.'[44] A Marine colonel confronted Captain White in Danang several days after the evacuation. Apparently the colonel had been looking for Captain White and found him at the Australian headquarters building known as Australia House.

> He came looking for me [White said] and he came to me and he was really upset and started abusing me for not bringing back the bodies of his dead Marines. He wasn't from that unit; he wasn't the commander of this unit. He just happened to be a Marine colonel who felt strongly about this issue. He even suggested that the dead Marines should have been evacuated before the wounded Nungs. That angered me. So in the end I got a map and told him that is where they are and if he is so brave he can get off his arse and get out of Danang go out there and become a KIA [killed in action] himself and then he can get Marines to go out and recover his body.[45]

Although a very emotional issue, it was not the first time that Marines had left bodies behind in Vietnam under dire tactical circumstances to protect the living. Likewise, the Australian battalion that served with the US 173rd Airborne Brigade in 1965–66 also had to leave two of their dead behind in action near Bien Hoa on 8 November 1965. The Australian commander ordered they be left, as it was too dangerous to risk the lives of others to recover them. That decision also created acrimonious feelings through the ranks of Australians in Vietnam.

At 1300 hours, Ngok Tavak reported that the force there was 'evading back to Kham Duc at this time'. Sergeant Jack Matheney remembered:

> John White . . . called a formation near the command bunker of all the round eyes. He informed us that we were going to escape and evade out of Ngok Tavak, pointed out the place in the wire through which we were to leave, prescribed the order of march and assigned each of us certain duties to perform before the commencement of the evacuation. We were to carry only our weapons, ammo, grenades and a canteen of water. Everything else, especially anything the enemy could use, was to be packed into the command bunker to be destroyed with C-4 explosives. I looked over at Tom Perry who was standing about 20 feet away and gave him a wink and a smile. The last time I saw him was when we all dispersed to perform our

assigned duties. I shot up several radios and stowed them with other
material into the command bunker. After everything was collected
in and around the bunker we blew it up. The disabled but intact
CH-46 on the landing pad was shot with a Light Anti-Tank Weapon
and began to burn. The order of march from the position was as
follows: approximately one half of the indigenous personnel would
lead off in single file, all the round eyes would follow, and the
remainder of the indigenous troops would take up the rear.[46]

Warrant Officer Don Cameron fired two M-72 light anti-tank weapons
(LAW) at the Sea Knight—the first went straight through without
exploding, but the second set the aircraft on fire and destroyed it
completely. The destruction of the Marine CH-46 created a piece of
humour some days later in Danang. Don was having a drink in the
Special Forces' club when Lieutenant Colonel Daniel Schungel, the
Commanding Officer of Company C, and the senior SF officer in I
Corps, approached him. Schungel presented Cameron with a very official
looking piece of paper, which Cameron said, 'frightened the living
daylights out of me'. It was a request for payment to replace the destroyed
helicopter. Don Cameron went white, and probably wished that he
were back on Ngok Tavak until he saw the emerging laughter on the
faces of the officers around him. Much to his relief, it was a joke.

'I knew that we had to get off that position,' John White explained
in a filmed interview in 1995.

We were very low on ammunition and couldn't get resupplied; we
were shell-shocked and probably couldn't have taken another serious
attack. It was time to go . . . [and] . . . I organised our withdrawal.
So, we put all of the weapons, we had killed the two guys with the
flame throwers so we got those and they had a lot of fuel left in
them and we put them in my bunker, which had all the spare
ammunition and a couple of cases of beer that I remember and my
Scotch whisky [!]. And just as we were leaving we blew it up. But
choosing the route presented obvious problems. The enemy were
all around, but I think that they left this open [indicated in the
filmed interview was the road to Kham Duc] to encourage us to
head off back this way so that they could ambush us. I figured that

the only way to get out of there alive was to cut back the way that they would least expect, which was the way they came from. I arranged six to eight aircraft, Phantoms I think they were, and we brought them in one at a time and they dropped their Napalm [with] the first one right on our perimeter. Then we dropped them in a line one after the other and while it was still burning we followed it out hoping the effect of the aircraft's weapons would leave us free to withdraw. My Nung Commandos led the withdrawal, then after them came myself and then the Marines, and then a tail end of more Nungs. What happened then, a mortar bomb landed right in the middle of the people at the tail end and killed and wounded a few of the rearguard. A Special Forces medic, a fellow called Perry, who was a very fine soldier, he stopped back to look after the wounded and he was captured, but we don't know what happened to him.[47]

The Ngok Tavak defenders got away without detection and it wasn't until John White met up with the enemy commanders in Vietnam in 1995 that they realised that the Australian-led force did get away. Major Mai and Major General Phan Thanh Du both expressed surprise that the Mike Force and the Marines had evaded the ambush set for them on the road to Kham Duc.

The escape down the mountain was surprisingly uneventful, Sergeant Jack Matheney wrote in 2006:

We encountered no enemy soldiers nor received any fire. At the bottom of the mountain we crossed a small mountain stream. On the opposite side was a small, maybe 6 by 6 sandbar. I stopped there to wait on Tom Perry. I could see perhaps a half dozen people at a time coming down the hillside through the jungle. Captain White was at or near the end of the round eye portion of the column and when he reached my position I could see that there were no more round eyes uphill behind him. I informed him that we had a man [Perry] missing from the column. We climbed the next mountain and, upon reaching a ridgeline, cut out an LZ for extraction by helicopter. CH-47 Chinooks [Matheney misidentified the extracting aircraft as Chinooks; they were Sea Knights] soon landed to pick us up. The first chopper was quickly overloaded with Mike Force soldiers and was too heavy to lift off. We had to force several of them off the aircraft and I had to throw several off the chopper before we could take off. These were Nungs. We were airlifted back to Kham Duc where I remained until its evacuation on May 12th.[48]

Eugene Makowski recalled how the equipment was destroyed using the fuel in an enemy flame-thrower and a Claymore mine as a demolition charge as well as the LAW being fired at the helicopter to set it on fire. He also remembered that they had moved in a southeasterly direction and made no contact after leaving Ngok Tavak. He said:

> I told the demo man to blow the bunker after the group was a safe distance; left unsaid was for them to join the group. I then followed the group's trail. Since I could not then see the bunker I did not know to what degree the equipment was destroyed. After a couple of hours Captain White said we needed to make an LZ for extraction . . . [which] . . . we cleared using our knives and anything else we may have had. Captain White determined the order of extraction. Each CH-46 could carry around 10 troops . . . they shuttled back and forth until there were thirteen left. On the last lift we all piled into the helicopter. The crew chief said it was overloaded and some would have to get off. Captain White said no; all would stay. At that point the pilot said ok but we would have to get rid of excess weight. Thrown overboard were the two machine guns, cans of ammunition, helmets, protective vests, fire extinguishers, floor-boards, and even the co-pilot's helmet. Somehow the pilot got the helicopter to raise enough to clear the jungle and fly to Kham Duc.[49]

All of those aboard the last lift recounted the almost feverish activity of dumping anything that may have lightened the load. Dave Fuentes's efforts provided some humour over the years, as it was said that he had stripped to his skivvies. Dave, however, strenuously denied that when he told his story.

> No, I didn't have any [skivvies] on, all I had was my green shorts and my boots and a bandana and an M-60 I found that I picked

and whatever I could shoot with, I took with me. We also had tomahawks to clear the area; the others may have had knives, but us gunners had tomahawks.[50]

Lieutenant M.E. Rhett Flater, USMC, was the pilot of the last flight. He wrote:

Basically, to get out the 20-odd remaining survivors at the landing site on the hill near Ngoc Tavak, I had to take my first load of survivors back to Kham Duc, offload them, then take off and return to Ngok Tavak [where I made] . . . a two-wheel landing with the forward mount held in the air, with the ramp down. We didn't know how many survivors there were. When my crew chief saw how many (John White, his top officers, and the Nungs) and tried to hold off the final ones to avoid an overload, I told him to load everyone since no one was coming back. I dumped nearly all-remaining fuel to lighten the aircraft. We threw off all extra .50 cal shells, supplies plus some radios we didn't need. When everyone was aboard, I pulled the collective up and we lifted off. Due to the excessive weight, the rotor turns drooped below 80 per cent—we lost generators, SAS, ATS and the radios. The warning lights in the control panel flashed repeatedly. I dropped collective slightly, edged the cyclic forward, and we descended down the hill, gaining speed and recovering our turns. I was relieved. We were going to be fine. In the back, several knocked out the cabin windows to better defend us should the need arise. Now we had another problem. We lacked sufficient fuel for the return flight to Marble Mountain. We decided to land on the airstrip at Kham Duc and take on fuel from the drums on the south end. Finally refuelled, we departed through clouds and returned to Danang.[51]

When General Phan Thanh Du was asked in 1995 if they had followed the Americans in an effort to attack them at the extraction point, he laughed and said no. We chased them with our bullets, he said, gesticulating as if firing an AK-47. Major Mai, who was listening to that conversation, added an interesting observation; he said, 'The NVA regular forces could not move as fast in the jungle as the local forces [Montagnards] could.' The northerners needed to adjust to the techniques of fighting in the jungle as much as any new soldiers did. They were experienced at protecting themselves against air attack, but now they had to contend with 'enemy formations' on the ground as well. He also repeated that the 40th Battalion had left the area and a VC Local Force unit continued to fire upon Ngok Tavak, but no further assault was planned for that day.

John White's manoeuvre had tricked the enemy, who continued to mortar the position long after the allied force had gone. The final evacuation, however, was a case of going from the frying pan into the fire. Ngok Tavak was lost and the attacking force now concentrated upon Kham Duc, which was where the helicopters took the Ngok Tavak survivors. Although it was only a brief stopover for the Marines and the Australians, elements of the 2nd NVA Division were making their presence felt and it was obvious that an attack was imminent. Captain Eugene Makowski was left in command of the Nungs when John White and the two Australian warrant officers flew on to Danang. There was an air of confusion at this stage because troops of the Americal Division were flying in to boost the defences and the Nungs were thought to have been backloaded on those aircraft. When he was asked why he was left to command the 11th Company Nungs, Gene Makowski said that he felt abandoned.

> At the time it happened all I knew was that the Australians were gone; someone said they flew back to Da Nang. I never really knew why they left. One explanation was that they were ordered to return [for a debriefing] but I did not believe that was accurate (it was too fast after arriving back at Kham Duc for such a decision to be made, especially when many of the details of the battle were not yet reported). At that time I felt abandoned and that they abandoned their unit when the battle was still going on. Although I felt safer at Kham Duc than at Ngok Tavak, I, and others from the camp, felt that more fighting was sure to come, possibly that night. That night I knew of no intention that the Mike Force would return to Da Nang the next day. I expected we would stay to reinforce the camp.[52]

Command intentions were obviously confused in the jumble of activity at Kham Duc. John White thought that they were all to be returned to

Danang that day, or very soon thereafter, and that he was required back in Danang to be debriefed on the Ngok Tavak battle. He also wanted to make it very clearly understood that the CIDG force sent to him from Kham Duc was not reliable, which had implications for the current defences of the Kham Duc camp. The 5th Special Forces After Action Report of 31 May 1968 recorded the evacuation to Danang thus:

> 101830: all evading elements from Ngok Tavak extracted by chopper to Kham Duc. MSF troops will remain at Kham Duc while all USMC personnel and downed air crewmen continue evacuation to Da Nang. LTC Smith finished the extraction then departed for Da Nang with AATTV personnel for debriefing.[53]

Furthermore, Captain White maintained his outrage at what he considered to be a shambles of resupply efforts into Ngok Tavak, especially the ammunition for the howitzers that he erroneously thought had been denied because of an argument between Army and the Marines. Also, Lieutenant Colonel Daniel Schungel was not very happy with White's disobedience in withdrawing from the Ngok Tavak position. He was also critical of the patrolling methods used at Ngok Tavak and Kham Duc, a concern that surfaced later in a comparative study conducted by the 5th Special Forces Group:

> Even though patrols from FOB Ngok Tavak and Kham Duc were experiencing contacts more frequently and increasingly closer to their base camp . . . these patrols were generally platoon size or larger and were not primarily reconnaissance patrols. Smaller recon patrols could have more easily avoided contact and conceivably could have collected the desired intelligence.[54]

Several strong conversations would take place in the coming days, one of which allegedly involved a physical altercation between John White and the Special Forces' Logistics Officer. But for now, everyone's attention was fixed on the battle for Kham Duc, which was to end with the camp being abandoned by the allied forces on 12 May 1968, two days after the evacuation of Ngok Tavak.

5 AFTERMATH

The victors

There is a difference of opinion in the North Vietnamese accounts as to who attacked Kham Duc. Senior General Chu Huy Man said, 'In Kham Duc, from 9 to 12 May 1968 [the] 21st Regiment/2nd Division, reinforced . . . attacked and liberated . . . Kham Duc.' This account is substantiated in a film made by the (North) Vietnamese about the attack. The commentary on a fifteen-minute segment of very poor quality film said the 'Regiment of Steel' (probably the 21st Regiment), which was reinforced with a battalion of 85 mm artillery and 23 mm anti-aircraft guns, attacked Kham Duc.[1] There is no mention of the 1st VC Regiment, elements of which are known to have been involved in the attacks on Ngok Tavak and Kham Duc. It is possible that the division (minus) referred to in Lieutenant General Nguyen Huy Chuon's *Second Division* publication (see page 29) was two regiments, the 1st and the 21st. That would mean an attacking force of around 2500, a ratio of approximately 5:1 in favour of the NVA. This would mean that the NVA had a battle strength that was more than sufficient to deal with the two separated Special Forces locations. Some of the CIDG at Kham Duc were no more than recruits and an arc of high ground around the base made its defence difficult, especially with resupply having to come by air. Ngok Tavak was isolated and there was no supporting artillery at Kham Duc, so it could easily be contained or destroyed. Although it was not stated in the NVA after action publications, additional combat power may have been gathered in the Ngok Tavak–Kham Duc region to trap American reinforcements in the mountains under conditions that were favourable to the North Vietnamese, and annihilate them. When Senior

General Chu Huy Man had served as the commander of the Central Highlands Front he participated in the drafting of the 1967 campaign battle plan for Dak To, in the Central Highlands, during which he posed the question, 'How to lure large enemy formations out far from their bases so that we could destroy them?' In 1968, General Man took command of Military Region 5, which included the 2nd NVA Division and he may have carried that combat desire with him.[2] The *Second Division* publication said, however, that the Military Region Headquarters had made it clear that 'aggressive efforts' were needed to 'tie down' the enemy and prevent reinforcements being sent to Kham Duc, or at least keep the size of any relief 'to an insignificant level'. The North Vietnamese officers who were interviewed in 1995 anticipated that more than an insignificant number of reinforcements would be sent to the camp. Major General (Ret.) Phan Thanh Du, who was a senior operations officer—tactical watch officer—during the battle, said in 1995 that he had two battalions and some 'special commandos' for the attack on Kham Duc in 1968. This is supported by a message from the CO of Company C, 5th Special Forces Danang, to the CO of the 5th Special Forces Group in August 1968. The message said:

> The 1st Regt, 2nd NVA Div had the mission to attack Kham Duc. There is no other info available to confirm the presence of other units at Kham Duc during the attack. Strength: it is estimated that between 1000 to 1500 men took part in the attack, and one battalion plus rear service elements were held in reserve.[3]

There is a lack of clear information on where the third regiment of the division was located during the battle. It is assumed that the 'missing' regiment was the 21st and that it was either waiting in ambush to deal with any further American support that may have been ordered to bolster Kham Duc's defences, or it was deployed ready to create a diversion by attacking another camp, perhaps Tien Phuoc.

The good, the bad and the ugly

Lieutenant Colonel Ray Burnard, Commanding Officer, the Australian Army Training Team Vietnam, heard a brief description of the action at Ngok Tavak some time on Saturday, 11 May 1968. He said:

My memories of almost 40 years ago are somewhat hazy but are jogged by my diary and the records I kept. [When] Tony Danilenko was killed... I was very concerned to hear his Montagnards had run away and literally left him for dead. I already had a flight booked for Danang and on to Quang Tri on the Monday and it was Wednesday [15 May 1968] before I was able to speak to John White. My diary entry on 16 May was: Torrid time with [Lieutenant Colonel] Schungel and [Major] Hasa [sic Husar—OC MSF] with the result that White, Lucas and Cameron to be moved and no Australians to serve with Mike Force Nung companies. Lt Col Schungel was unhappy with John White's decision to evacuate Ngok Tavak while he was planning to reinforce.

Colonel Burnard continued:

I believe White's assessment was sound. He delayed the withdrawal until 1300 hours and conducted it in a very competent manner. Lt Col Smith, the Deputy Commander of Company C, coordinated the extraction and withdrawal of all personnel at Ngok Tavak, and I would have liked to have heard his views on the decision... but unfortunately I never met him. [When] Smith and the three AATTV members returned to Danang for a debriefing, I assumed that when they left they knew the remnants of 11 and 12 companies would be flown back the following morning. My decision to move all of the Australians out of Company C [5th Special Forces] came two weeks later after Hamersley and Durrington were killed [near Thuong Duc SF camp on 30 May 1968] on what I thought was an ill-conceived operation.[4]

Colonel Burnard believed he had a good understanding with Colonel Ladd when he arranged for the Australians to be moved out of Special Forces in I Corps. Professional suspicions and jealousies, however, obviously ran deep and in 1984 Colonel Ladd spoke disparagingly of the Australians deployed in the Special Forces teams.

The Australians simply couldn't get over that 'abo' complex of theirs, of aborigines, and that's what these people were [Montagnards], a lot of them, and they [the Australians] treated them like dirt. Whereas the way we did it, they had their own officers and sergeants and whatnot. So it became apparent that that wasn't going to work [with the Australians] so I talked to the Australian in Saigon . . . and then later General [Thomas] Daly . . . came up and stayed with me and I explained to him—what we did then, we'd put like two of them, so there'd be at least two with one of our teams of twelve or fourteen, so that our guy was always the commander, the U.S. Special Forces guy ran the thing.[5]

This is an extremely provocative statement and the reality of the day does not match Colonel Ladd's words. As has been mentioned in this book, Australians held influential positions during the formative years of the CIDG. Also, during Colonel Ladd's tenure as Commander, 5th Special Forces Group, Australians commanded Mike Force companies in the two northern Corps Tactical Zones of South Vietnam. John White commanded 11th Company at Ngok Tavak and Captain Eugene Makowski, US Special Forces, deferred to his command during the battle. Captain Geoff Skardon, who commanded Detachment A-107, Tra Bong, in 1965 was incensed by Ladd's remarks.

To state that Australians treated the Montagnards like dirt is a shabby lie and a stupid ill-considered statement. The evidence provided by the SF in numerous reports and commendations over many years describe the professionalism and leadership of those who served as being of the highest order. From a personal point of view I recall that the officers and warrant officers who served with the Montagnards did so with enormous pride. My own observation was that the Montagnards were never so happy as when Australians, particularly when action was imminent, led them.[6]

Ray Burnard felt that the quote from Colonel Ladd was startling and grossly inaccurate, but he believed it stemmed from a problem in Danang's Mike Force. The Vietnamese Special Forces, who, in theory, commanded the Montagnard and Nung soldiers, raised serious allegations about the behaviour of several Australians. Captain Nguyen Ky, who was the Joint Commanding Officer of the Mobile Strike Force Danang, wrote a letter dated 22 February 1968, which was addressed to Major Truong, the Vietnamese Commanding Officer of the Special Forces C Detachment, with a copy to Lieutenant Colonel Schungel, who was his adviser. Captain Nguyen Ky complained of illegal punishment and violent treatment of the Vietnamese and Montagnards by Australians, and he also intimated Australian cowardice through the words of an unnamed American NCO, who supposedly said, 'I'm the only American there if a firefight happens; it's hard to save my life.' The letter also threatened 'squaring away' with an Australian scoundrel and that 'they couldn't care less whatever happens to them'. Nguyen Ky went on to request:

> your Headquarters check on this and release all of the Australians out of the MSF [Mike Force] unit. Fighting and revenging with each other might happen in the very near future and when that happens we are not going to be responsible for it.[7]

Lieutenant Colonel Schungel backed the Vietnamese Special Forces against the Australians and made it quite clear there was no room for mediation. This was a very menacing warning—just over two months prior to Ngok Tavak—and it must raise a question with reference to Schungel's military wisdom and command responsibility. Why did he send three Australians with a Mike Force company, albeit in this case Nungs, to Ngok Tavak in May, with a latent threat of internal fighting and revenge hanging over Australian heads? Did he believe that the Chinese–Nungs were unaffected by the Vietnamese bickering? Even if this were so, there were three Vietnamese Special Forces personnel with 11th Company, and the nearby friendly force and immediate assistance base at Kham Duc was Vietnamese–Montagnard. Perhaps the instant action taken by Lieutenant Colonel Burnard defused the anger in February, but the relationship lacked harmony and it would fragment soon after.

> This was the first of my confrontations with Schungel [Ray Burnard said] and it ended three months later when all AATTV men in his command were withdrawn. I feel sure that Colonel Ladd's quote was not based on his first-hand knowledge, but on Schungel's view.[8]

Lieutenant Colonel Burnard recommended John White for a Military Cross (US Silver Star equivalent) for his actions during the Ngok Tavak battle. When the awards were promulgated he was astounded to find that Captain White had received a Mention-in-Despatches (US Bronze Star equivalent) yet the two warrant officers with him were given medals for bravery. Burnard confronted Major General A.L. MacDonald, Commander, Australian Force Vietnam, only to be told that John White's brother, Peter, who was also serving in Vietnam, had been recommended for a Military Cross too. The general told Colonel Burnard that he was not going to approve two brothers getting an MC in the same list and he decided to give it to the elder brother, Peter! Ray Burnard was furious.[9]

Two Marines, Henry Schunck and Richard Conklin, were awarded Navy Crosses for extraordinary heroism at Ngok Tavak—'double-crosses' of the more courageous kind.

Numerous reports on the battle flowed immediately from the time of the first attacks on the two camps. Some of the information was accurate and some was guesswork that needed correction, but some of the false information was never put right. For example, Brigadier-General Jacob Glick, Assistant Chief of Staff G-3, III MAF, said at a press conference—date unknown, but given soon after the battles—that Captain White was badly wounded, which was why he was not at Kham Duc when it was attacked. That statement was incorrect and it should have been known to be wrong.[10]

•

What really happened to the Nungs coming out of Ngok Tavak? How many made it out, how many were killed in action and how many just disappeared? Which enemy unit attacked Ngok Tavak and subsequently Kham Duc? What was their casualty figure versus those of the allied force? How had the Marines got on following their extraction from Ngok Tavak?

First, the Nungs. Captain White's after action report for the 11th Company recorded that sixteen were killed, 33 were wounded and that twelve went missing. His report continued with figures for the 12th Company that showed they had thirteen missing, but no other casualties. A III Marine Amphibious Force signal dated 11 May listed the casualties as 29 Mobile Strike Force members wounded and 64 missing, but associated figures contained in the same message are inaccurate, which would challenge the correctness of the total report. Thereafter, other than their proposed place in the order-of-march out of the besieged camp, there is no mention of the number of Nungs extracted from Kham Duc.

Figures for the attacking enemy and their identification are listed in the reports from the 5th Special Forces, the Americal Division and III Marine Amphibious Force. A prisoner and captured documents confirmed that the 40th Battalion of the 1st Regiment (VC Main Force), 2nd NVA Division, had attacked Ngok Tavak. Captain White reported that 'the enemy left 31 dead on the position', and he also recorded a total of 50 weapons collected, which included six machine guns, 30 AK-47s, five RPGs, two flame-throwers and two pistols. He also reported that the allied force had not lost any weapons. This last statement placed great faith in the destructive powers of the improvised explosives rigged with the enemy's flame-throwers to destroy the weapons left on the battle-field. Allied weapons *were* lost; the type and number cannot be identified, or quantified, but, for example, there was no trace of the spiked 105 mm howitzers in photographs of the position taken the next day. The remains of the destroyed CH-46 helicopters, however, can be seen in the same photographs. The 5th Special Forces report also added that a further 200 NVA were probably killed by air; this figure is questionable. The number is challenged on the basis of a killed-to-wounded ratio mentioned previously in this book, which would mean the enemy force would have suffered around 700 wounded. The report did not compare the suggested number of casualties with the possible size of the enemy formation; neither did it comment on the battle capabilities of a unit that may have suffered such a number of casualties. There is no record in the allied after action papers of any enemy prisoners taken, which in some respects supports anecdotal evidence that a few of the incapacitated, or those who had stopped fighting, were shot by the defenders after the main battle. In 2006, John White stated that two wounded enemy soldiers had been left inside the fort, and that he arranged, under the cover of a white flag, for these soldiers to be returned to their comrades. This could not be confirmed. The Marines who were asked about this act said they were shooting at anything that looked like an enemy and they did not recall seeing a white flag. The only mention of wounded NVA is in the unsigned after action report—attributed to

Captain White—which stated: 'The two wounded NVA in the position tried to throw grenades rather than surrender. Two NVA pulled the pins out of grenades and lay on them before they died, thus booby-trapping their own bodies.'[11]

The total number of enemy allegedly killed in the battles of Ngok Tavak and Kham Duc was recorded as 576, and the principal attack force was identified as the 1st VC Regiment (reinforced), which had an approximate strength of 1500. The regiment may have been reinforced with the 11th Battalion of the 21st Regiment and the 10th Sapper Battalion of the 2nd NVA Division for its attack on Kham Duc. This meant that the claimed casualties against the 2nd NVA Division—killed and wounded—over two days would have numbered approximately one-third of the division's strength. These figures did not take into account any killed or injured that divisional elements deployed elsewhere, away from the Kham Duc area, may have suffered. This extraordinary number of casualties appeared to have had no effect on the 2nd NVA Division; it fought on as if nothing had happened. In comparison, in heavy fighting in the latter half of 1967 near Dak To, in Kontum Province, 362 members of the US 4th Infantry Division, the 173rd Airborne Brigade and ARVN airborne troops were killed in action. As a result, elements of the American force were rendered combat ineffective during the battle.[12]

Of the American casualties, eleven Marine bodies and the remains of Special Forces Sergeant Glenn Miller were left on Ngok Tavak. Captain Makowski remembered that he had directed the collection of their identity discs:

> Although some bodies were moved, SGT Miller's body was moved to the side of CAPT White's bunker, there was no organized attempt that I remember, of moving bodies to a central location. I do remember seeing at least some of the Marines' bodies still in the locations where they fell dead. Since we were still under periodic small arms and mortar attack and since we knew evacuation of bodies would not occur unless our situation greatly improved (which was doubtful with the LZ being closed), there was no organized attempt to collect the dead for evacuation. There might have been some moving of bodies out of fighting position so the positions

could be reused. My order to collect the dog tags was to ensure
we could account for all the dead.[13]

John White said:

> The American bodies were gathered and put together in the area
> in the fort behind my bunker. The location was: from my bunker
> looking towards the LZ, on the right and in the top tier of the fort.
> This was done by the Marines and not on my instruction. I do not
> know if they got all the bodies [but] I do know that Miller was
> there with them. In relation to identification, I asked Eugene
> Makowski to gather the dog tags, which he did. Some Marines gave
> me a couple of sets of dog tags and I gave them to Makowski. The
> Marines are a tight bunch and they look after their own. They
> identified their buddies' bodies. I did not really know numbers of
> killed and wounded until afterwards. We had the medevac chopper
> coming and going and wounded were just gathered and thrown on
> board with no one really trying to sort out who was Nung, US or
> Vietnamese. Initially, I focused on the evacuation of the wounded
> and, after that seemed to be going well, I concentrated on tightening
> the defence in case we were attacked again and then on getting to
> hell out of there.[14]

Jim Garlitz, Dean Parrett, Greg Rose, Henry Schunck, William Loman
and Dave Fuentes all identified Marines who had been killed. Many
years later, in 1994, Dave Fuentes was able to draw a diagram that showed
the different locations of the Marine warriors' bodies inside the fort.

Delta X-Ray, 2nd Battalion, 13th Marines, was severely scarred by
the battle. Not only had they lost fourteen killed, but the detachment
also had twenty wounded; eighteen had been evacuated and two wounded
walked out when the hill was abandoned. The number killed included
Lance Corporal Bruce Lindsey, who was accidentally killed prior to the
battle, and Thomas Schriver and Verle Skidmore, who died of wounds
after their evacuation. This was from a detachment strength of 46; the
official roster listed 44, but whichever total is used it should be reduced
by three, as Sergeant Harry Fade and two others were stuck at Kham
Duc on 10 May. Delta X-Ray's return to Danang and on to their battery,

located just to the southwest of the Danang airfield, was a dispassionate affair wrapped in what some thought was an air of irrelevance. These Marines had just fought for their lives, escaped by the skin of their teeth and now some said they were told not to talk about the battle. Sergeant Roger Matye said, 'I was debriefed and told not to talk to anyone about what happened. That was a specific order.' James Garlitz remembered, 'They came in the hospital and asked about the dead.' He, also, was ordered not to discuss the battle. William Loman said that he was not debriefed when he got back to Danang. When he was asked if he was given a specific order not to discuss the battle, he replied, 'Not while I remained in Delta. I was told to forget it when I had been with HQ 1/11 for about three weeks. I was also told the Marines had been retrieved and sent home.'[15]

Greg Rose said:

I remember getting into Danang in the night and being taken to the battery area at first light in a six by six. We were immediately whisked off to the Administration Hooch and told to give the admin sergeant a brief rundown and to mention anyone who deserved to be decorated. I remember signing papers swearing to whom we could confirm dead. I was told . . . not to discuss [the operation] with anyone.[16]

When Ray Scuglik and Paul Swenarski were debriefed, Ray got the impression something was being covered up or that someone was going to take the blame 'big time'. Paul Swenarski was told not to discuss the battle and that they would be told when the mission was declassified. Gene Whisman was not debriefed and did not remember being ordered not to talk, but being ordered not to say anything seemed to be the talk on Hill 34, when he got back there. Navy Corpsman Scott 'Doc' Thomas did not recall a specific debriefing; however, he remembered that statements were taken regarding the actions of some of the men. He wrote in 2006:

I remember making a statement that when I returned to Massachusetts I wanted to visit the parents of Cook and Czerwonka. I remember a USMC officer—don't know who—telling me that it wouldn't be good to discuss the battle when I got home, too many people would be upset, and since the bodies were not recovered it would bring heartaches to the families. I never did look them up. After hearing the different stories that were told, and all of the heartache the families did go through I wish I had contacted them. At least I could have set the story right 38 years earlier.[17]

'Set the story right' is a reference to a seriously flawed tale that was told to some of the relatives about a search party going back to look for Specialist Fourth Class Perry, the Special Forces medic. According to this story, the Marines who were known to have been killed during the battle and now lay on the hill had been members of this search party, and had disappeared after coming under a subsequent attack. It was a dreadful piece of misinformation that persisted for many years. The most basic piece of research by those responsible for propagating this tale would have, or should have, quashed any speculation that any of these Marines may have been taken into captivity. Eleventh Marines was the superior headquarters for the 2nd Battalion, 13th Marines, and their Command Chronology for May 1968 is clear: there were no members under its command missing in action. The S-1 (Personnel Officer) Report listed eleven enlisted but unnamed personnel from D-2/13 KIA 'while in def posit' (while in defensive position) with a supplementary note against each that said, 'remains believed to have been destroyed by friendly airstrikes'.[18] This assumption was based on the fact that 30 sorties of attack air had been used on 10 May. Furthermore, at 0545 hours on 11 May, five B-52 target boxes were allocated around Ngok Tavak, three in the immediate vicinity of the hill and two further south. Thirty B-52 bombers struck the targets. To read the words of a Viet Cong who was bombed by B-52 strikes elsewhere, is to understand what that meant.

There was nothing left. It was as if an enormous scythe had swept through the jungle, felling the giant teak and go trees like grass in its way, shredding them into billions of scattered splinters. On these occasions ... the complex would be utterly destroyed: food, clothes, supplies, documents, everything ... in some awesome way they ceased to exist ... there would simply be nothing there, just an unrecognisable landscape gouged by immense craters.[19]

The 2nd Battalion, 13th Marines, Command Chronology also listed the men as killed, not missing, and that conclusion was carried forward in a recommendation for the award of the Meritorious Unit Commendation for Delta X-Ray, which was subsequently approved. Why did staff officers on the Headquarters of the United States Marine Corps write the following in May 1993, which was repeated in a Joint Task Force-Full Accounting document dated April 1994?

> A search team was sent out to locate Specialist Four Perry and recover Sergeant Miller's remains. The search team consisted of Lance Corporal James R. Sargent, Corporal Gerald E. King, Lance Corporal Raymond T. Heyne, Private First Class Robert C. Lopez, Private First Class William D. McGonigle, Lance Corporal Donald W. Mitchell, Lance Corporal Thomas W. Fritsch, Lance Corporal Paul S. Czerwonka, Lance Corporal Joseph F. Cook, Private First Class Barry L. Hempel and Lance Corporal Thomas J. Blackman. During the search operations, the team was attacked by a large PAVN [NVA] force and all the individuals were killed. Their remains were never recovered.[20]

The Marines named were killed during the battle for the Ngok Tavak fort. It was correct to say that their remains were not recovered back to a 1st Marine Division enclave, but to provide a form of false hope to families that any of these Marines may have been taken captive during a subsequent battle after the force had left Little Ngok Tavak, was shameful. Battle conditions at the time, which included the immediate subsequent fall of Kham Duc, prevented any action to be initiated for the recovery of the remains to an American base. The next major allied action in the Kham Duc area did not happen until July 1970, just over two years after the battle.

Why was so little attention paid at the time to this bedraggled band of brothers from Ngok Tavak? Was it, as some have suggested, a silence instigated by planned negotiations between Hanoi and Washington that were to start on or about 10 May in Paris? No, it wasn't. Colonel Jonathan F. Ladd, Commander, 5th Special Forces, expressed a mild reservation about the Kham Duc 'relocation' in a meeting at III MAF on 11 May 1968 where he 'alluded to the current peace talks and the possible propaganda score the abandonment might provide the enemy'. Similar concerns were also expressed about the Ben Het Special Forces camp in II Corps that was attacked in late June 1968. The Paris Peace Talks, however, stalled for five months over such matters as the bombing of North Vietnam, what parties could be included in the discussions and the lamentable arguments over the shape of the tables to be used during the talks. Kham Duc–Ngok Tavak was nothing more than an embarrassing tactical defeat that was brought about by an unnerved high command. General Westmoreland, General Abrams and Lieutenant General Cushman saw Kham Duc as a mini Khe Sanh. The Khe Sanh battle carried scars caused not only by a clash of operational thinking between General Westmoreland and senior Marine generals, but it was also a media nightmare with its never-ending comparison with Dien Bien Phu. Kham Duc, and by association Ngok Tavak, was too difficult to defend and it was just not worth the effort to retake the base after its loss, even though the area provided a logistical springboard for enemy attacks down on to the coastal plains. The explanation provided by III MAF at a press conference in May that the allied forces were withdrawn from the area to allow airpower to attack and decimate a concentrated enemy force was an attempt to put a brave face upon a very dismal circumstance. As General Abrams reflected, 'Kham Duc [and Ngok Tavak] was a minor disaster.' Brigadier-General John R. Chaisson, USMC, who headed the Combat Operations Center, Headquarters, MACV, wrote to his wife and said, 'This is an ugly one and I expect some repercussions.'[21] But, other than expressions of dissatisfaction, nothing happened.

Ngok Tavak was just a small ripple on the surface of a very big battle pond; it was noticed, briefly, which this record in the MACV Review of Events for May 1968 illustrated:

> In southern I Corps, the VC 1st Regiment, NVA 2nd Division, after a period of refitting in the Quang Tin Province–Laos Border area, attacked the Kham Duc Special Forces camp and a nearby [Ngok Tavak] CIDG camp in eastern [sic western] Quang Tin Province on 10, 11 and 12 May.[22]

But attention was quickly diverted as more battles flared in the cockpit that was I Corps. The 1st Marine Division, to which the 13th Marines reported via the 11th Marines, suffered 2380 casualties during the month of May, which included 350 killed in action, as well as seventeen who died of wounds and thirteen who were killed in accidents. III Marine Amphibious Force, the over-arching US command in I Corps, listed the USMC and Army casualties for May 1968, as: killed 1056, wounded 4169, missing 78, died of wounds 73, and killed in accidents 27; a further 180 were injured out of battle. Ngok Tavak was overshadowed by operations such as *Ballard Valley, Allen Brook, Mameluke Thrust* and *Houston*. The uninjured survivors from Delta X-Ray were pushed immediately into service again on *Operation Allen Brook* in the area of Go Noi Island, the 2nd NVA Division's old stomping grounds. A small ripple of interest in a hilltop out in the wilds of western Quang Tin Province had quickly washed away. Delta X-Ray was now back in the artillery business, firing 20,016 shells in support of *Allen Brook*, with a claimed enemy killed figure of 300. However, the Marines who came away from the battle at the fort would not, or perhaps more correctly, could not, forget 10 May 1968, and the Marines they had to leave behind. Their fighting spirit was fittingly recorded as this final paragraph to the award of the Meritorious Unit Commendation illustrated:

> By their effective teamwork, aggressive fighting spirit and individual acts of heroism and daring, the artillerymen of Delta Detachment achieved an illustrious record of courage and skill in keeping with the highest tradition of the United States Naval Service. The bronze letter 'V' is authorized.

The Marines of Delta Detachment who walked out in the final evacuation from Ngok Tavak provided a consensus of opinion, which was one of admiration, as well as appreciation, for Captain John White, who they said, saved their lives. This sentiment was supported by Lieutenant Colonel William F. Smith, the Executive Officer of Company C, 5th Special Forces Danang, who had flown cover in the command and control helicopter on 10 May 1968. He said the move out of the surrounded camp at Ngok Tavak was due to Captain White's professional competence and the large part the Air Force played in keeping the enemy off their backs.

6 AN AFTER-ACTION ANALYSIS

Those who cannot remember the past are condemned to repeat it.
George Santayana, *The Life of Reason, Volume 1*, 1905

Twenty–twenty vision, in hindsight

Santayana's words may be considered too grand to be applied to tactics, the gut feel of battle. What some have done in fire-fights with astounding tactical success, others have attempted to do and failed, miserably. There is a tale, perhaps apocryphal, of a British officer who, during a course at Staff College, was asked to plan an attack on a bridge in Germany. He did and was tongue-lashed by the staff for an inept effort. The officer pointed to his Military Cross and replied, 'That's strange. That is what I did in World War II at this bridge, and for which I was awarded this medal.' But there are some basic rules, which, when followed, will generally provide a sound base for battle success. To look back now on what happened at Ngok Tavak, 40 years after the event, may be seen to be hyper-critical of decisions made under very trying circumstances. Nevertheless, both sides are considered to have made tactical mistakes and they are highlighted here.

The NVA

There was no need for the NVA to assault Ngok Tavak. They could have pinned down the troops there simply through the threat of assault and the use of indirect fire. The Viet Cong and the North Vietnamese Army were known to be meticulous in planning their ground assaults, and prior to this battle they had been watching the allied force for several weeks.

The 40th Battalion, however, stumbled badly in their efforts to break through the 11th Company's perimeter. On their own admission, their initial thrusts against the hill failed because they hit defences that they had not found in their reconnaissance. When they did find a weakness that got them inside the defenders' location, they failed to exploit their advantage. The assault's momentum was lost after the Nungs ran, leaving a fragmented perimeter manned by Marines. The return fire by some of those Marines, coming as it did from many directions, confused the enemy commander and most probably disoriented his assault troops. The standard geometric lines of defence upon which they most likely had practised prior to the battle had disappeared. The attackers lacked the flexibility to break down their assault so that the defenders' weakness could be exploited. They also diluted the strength of their assault on Ngok Tavak by moving the Main Force unit away to prepare for an attack upon Kham Duc and/or any relief forces that might come from that direction. It is possible that the plan was to suck a force out of Kham Duc, which would weaken its defence and thereby make that camp an easier target for the remainder of the regiment to attack. It is also possible that an attack on the main Special Forces camp would bring reinforcements from the Americal Division that would be hit by a lurking 21st Regiment, which may have been the real total plan from the beginning.

The risks for the NVA were high, especially if attack air could join the battle. They were aware of this risk and after scavenging the battle-field for any useable equipment, as well as collecting whatever numbers of their dead and wounded that they could, they moved away from the area quickly. The piece of ground at Ngok Tavak had no significance and a full attack on it was not necessary to create a diversion for the pending assault on Kham Duc. All that was needed was to fix the Ngok Tavak force in a place where they could be dealt with at the attackers' leisure. Pretending to strike by firing mortars and making other attack-like manoeuvres would have been enough to unnerve the defenders and have them ask for support, which would have sucked any reinforcements from Kham Duc into an ambush, if the commander there was so unwise as to dispatch a relief force. Ngok Tavak was isolated by a tactically silly plan by the allied force; consequently, the casualties suffered by the 40th Battalion in an assault on the position were needless.

The allied force

From an allied force point of view, Ngok Tavak was a well-known and well-used campsite. It had been occupied by ARVN gunners and US Special Forces in 1963 and manned on and off between then and 1968. The hilltop was bare and an airstrip was nearby. It was an obvious satellite post for the Kham Duc camp. However, Ngok Tavak was easily watched over from the surrounding hills and to occupy the fort for an extended period was a tactical mistake. It was just too obvious, and its use by an allied force was made more apparent by the frequent helicopter flights to and fro and flights by Caribou aircraft dropping supplies by parachute.

Mike Force Nung companies were not trained to reconnoitre in small teams by stealth, nor were they established to conduct mobile guerrilla warfare. Moreover, the quality of the Nung troops was suspect, and they lacked stamina for battle. These shortcomings became apparent when the Nungs deserted their Australian advisers during a contact with the enemy on 18 April 1968—an ominous warning—and when they ran from their eastern sector post at the height of the attack on Ngok Tavak. Too often, senior Special Forces commanders overlooked the suspect determination of indigenous Mike Force soldiers to fight when they placed them in far-flung regions. They expected their weakness to be overcome by more resilient American and/or Australian advisers-cum-commanders. In this operation, senior command also placed artillerymen in the group's midst, men who had little or no infantry experience, let alone much understanding of jungle warfare. When the Vietnamese–CIDG arrived to be absorbed into a Nung (Chinese) force supported by Americans, the mix became volatile and the group lacked combat integrity.

To put, in such an isolated position, two howitzers that were not capable of performing the task required of them was reckless. This decision should have attracted greater objection than it did. The artillery was placed on a position that was not protected by interlocked arcs of fire from other indirect support weapons, which defied good sense and was contrary to the tactical standard operating procedures of the day. Neither of the guns was set to fire Fleschette rounds in defence of the position; with an enemy force thought to be near and preparing for an attack, that was a bad oversight. The howitzers not only became potential

Ngok Tavak, April 1968. Sergeant Ledbetter (left), Captain White, Specialist Fourth Class Benway, Warrant Officer Lucas, Sergeant Blomgren, Sergeant Miller, Warrant Officer Cameron. PHOTO COURTESY OF KEN BENWAY

Mike Force 'baseball', Ngok Tavak, April 1968. PHOTO COURTESY OF KEN BENWAY

Caribou resupply run, with the parachute-covered command bunker in the middle distance, Ngok Tavak, April 1968. PHOTO COURTESY OF KEN BENWAY

Captain White (left) farewells Ken Benway, April 1968. The parachute-covered command bunker is in the background. PHOTO COURTESY OF KEN BENWAY

Sergeant Ledbetter (foreground) and Captain White inside the rudimentary command bunker, Ngok Tavak 1968. PHOTO COURTESY KEN BENWAY

Major Mai, Ngok Tavak, 1995.
PHOTO COURTESY OF HARRY ALBERT

General Du, Ngok Tavak, 1995.
PHOTO COURTESY OF HARRY ALBERT

Captain John White, Ngok Tavak, 1995.
PHOTO COURTESY OF HARRY ALBERT

Lieutenant Bob Adams, Ngok Tavak, 1995.
PHOTO COURTESY OF HARRY ALBERT

Warrant Officer Frank Lucas, 1965.
PHOTO COURTESY OF AWM FILES

Warrant Officer Don Cameron, 1965.
PHOTO COURTESY OF AWM FILES

Corporal Gerald E. King with a 105 mm howitzer prior to deployment to Ngok Tavak, 1968. PHOTO COURTESY OF DENNIS KING

Before Ngok Tavak. Sitting: unknown (left), 'Billy' McGonigle (glasses–KIA), Gene Whisman and Jim Sargent (KIA). Standing Roger Matye (left), Phillip Dulude, unknown, and 'Butch' Heyne (KIA). PHOTO COURTESY OF TIM BROWN

Lance Corporal Thomas W. Fritsch, 1968.
PHOTO COURTESY OF PATRICIA ZAJACK

Lance Corporal Raymond T. Heyne, 1967.
PHOTO COURTESY OF JANICE KOSTELLO

Specialist Fourth Class Thomas H. Perry, Danang, 1968. PHOTO COURTESY OF SHERRY PERRY

Tim Brown and 'Elvis', 1995.
PHOTO COURTESY OF HARRY ALBERT

The spoils of war. Private First Class William H. Loman, Jr. (left) and Lance Corporal James E. Garlitz II with captured weapons from Ngok Tavak, 1968. PHOTO COURTESY OF JIM GARLITZ

Ngok Tavak looking west after the camp was abandoned on 10 May 1968.
PHOTO COURTESY OF TIM BROWN

The Vietnamese commanders, 1995. Major Dang Ngoc Mai, 40th Battalion (left); General Phan Thanh Du, 2nd NVA Div and General Vo Thu, Group 44. Bill Duker rear. PHOTO COURTESY OF HARRY ALBERT

Survivors 2005. Standing: Bob Adams (left), John White, Tim Brown, Dell Scott, Rodney Higgins, Scott Thomas, Jim Garlitz, Greg Rose. Sitting: Dean Parrett (left), Dick Murphy, Henry Schunck, Gene Whisman, Bob Mascharka. PHOTO COURTESY OF JANICE KOSTELLO

Ray Heyne's sister Dawn at the Vietnam Veterans Memorial wall, Washington, D.C. PHOTO COURTESY OF JANICE KOSTELLO

trophies, they also reduced the flexibility of the troops who were supposed to be out looking for the enemy. The mix of Marine artillery with an Army Special Forces unit also created confusion over resupply. Although this did not affect the outcome of the battle, it was a poorly arranged and messy piece of command responsibility. The Marines were not properly resupplied with their basic daily needs, such as water and rations, and the confusion over how to get the artillery ammunition from Kham Duc to Ngok Tavak was also very poor staff work.

At a more senior level, the efforts to consolidate information on what enemy was in the area and what their intention may have been was fragmented. Each formation had its own assessment, which meant that the 'big-picture' remained blurred. The attempt to use aerial photography, or other technology, to detect a force moving in rugged terrain failed. The Special Forces commander in I Corps complained about the patrols employed by 11th Company being too large, which made them easy to avoid, but there was no indication that any corrective action was taken by him, or his staff. This reconnaissance task was beyond the skills of a poorly trained basic Nung company, but nobody at Special Forces Headquarters in Danang would admit that in the wash-up after the event.

In the end, a tactical advantage was handed to the attacking battalion via the sum of many errors committed by the allied force. That a number of the defenders managed to escape was through the steadfastness of a few Marines who broke the momentum of the assault, and the quick arrival of Spooky and other attack aircraft. Captain John White's disobedience and tactical adroitness in sidestepping a waiting ambush on the road to Kham Duc, coupled with the courage of some Marine helicopter pilots who flew the rescue flights, was their final saving grace.

PART 2 WHEN THE CAPTAINS AND THE KINGS DEPART

The tumult and the shouting dies—
The captains and the kings depart—
Still stands Thine ancient sacrifice,
An humble and a contrite heart.
Lord God of Hosts, be with us yet,
Lest we forget, lest we forget!
Rudyard Kipling, *A Victorian Ode*, 1897

7 AGONY

We regret to inform you

In the film *Saving Private Ryan* there is a poignant sequence that portrayed the delivery of three telegrams, which are to tell a mother that three of her sons had been killed in action during World War II. A car is seen to approach a lonely farmhouse along a winding and dusty road. As the mother washes the dishes, she pauses to watch the car momentarily and then goes about her task, but a realisation draws her to look at the car again. One feels the agony when she wipes her hands on her apron and opens the front door to see an officer and a chaplain emerge from the vehicle. It is obviously news of the worst kind and she collapses to the veranda in emotional distress. Although the film is a fictionalised version of a search for Sergeant Frederick Niland, who was not killed, it evoked great emotion that carried with it a thought of immense compassion for those who have suffered this moment.[1]

The King family did suffer that moment, and what follows is Dennis King's memory of their anguish. Dennis was Gerald King's brother.

> On Tuesday 14 May 1968 at 3:30 p.m. a good friend of our family picked me up at school and told me he wanted to give me a ride home and he wanted to talk to me about something important. His girlfriend went to the same school and she was with us. We just talked about school stuff and when he pulled in my driveway and we got out of the car I asked him what it was that was so important. He was not able to look at me and I could see he was holding back his emotions. I knew something bad was about to happen. I could

feel another person's presence on my right side and as I turned to see who it was, it was my Mom. She put her arms around me and told me Jerry [Corporal Gerald King] had been killed in Vietnam. As I dropped my books we went to the ground together as I was so over-come by what I had just heard that I could not stand. I could see that my emotional outburst was making it very hard on Mom and tried to comfort her instead of having her comfort me. I asked where Ken (my younger brother) was and she said he was on his way home from school. He went to a different school since he was in Jr. High. My friend and I went to find Ken and found him about halfway from home. Mom had called his school and asked them to send Ken home because of what had happened. They ended up telling him for some reason and he was an emotional wreck when we found him. All of us were very close brothers and we had a very close family.[2]

Word of Corporal King's death was already being broadcast on the local radio, and the family was afraid that his father would hear the news on his way home from work. When the brothers heard their dad's car coming they all went to their neighbour's house to allow their parents time alone. Dennis recalled the exact time his father heard the news.

He put his face in his hands and began to cry. It was the hardest thing I ever saw. They were so proud of their Marine son and now he was gone. I remember lying down and crying myself to sleep and praying that when I wake up that this was all just a very bad dream.[3]

The Navy and Marine officers who came to the King house told them that the body was in a hot zone and could not be recovered immediately, but that it would be recovered at a time when it was safe to go back to Ngok Tavak. Either on the same day, or soon thereafter, the family received written advice from the government that told them Gerald King had been killed as a result of 'a hostile explosion that had caused fragmentation wounds to the head, arms, legs and body and that recovery was not made at this time'. That was all the family was told. A memorial service was held for Gerald on Friday, 24 May 1968. Dennis King would find out exactly how his brother died eighteen years later at a 1986 League of Families gathering.

The King family dealt with the loss of their son and brother in different ways. The parents grieved, more often than not alone, in a sad detachment intended to protect the others from their inconsolable heartache. Dennis filled himself with hate and anger, as he admitted in 2007.

> I began drinking heavy. Not caring about anything. I was always down and the best way for me to get rid of the anger was to get into fights and unleash all that energy. I was violent when I was mad and hurt people. My drinking and fighting finally landed me in jail. I was arrested for assault and battery and drunk driving in a small town outside of Knoxville. This happened a week before Thanksgiving. I knew then that I could not live at home anymore and have my family see what this was doing to me. I moved to Oakridge and lived there with a friend to hide my problems from Mom and Dad. I finally realized the only way for me to get on with living was to try to finish what he had started. So I joined the Marines. It was the best and worst thing I could have done at the same time. It pointed me in the right direction and helped me get on with my life. It also gave my brothers a reason to look up to me rather than see me falling apart and making life hell for Mom and Dad. It was bad in the sense that Mom and Dad had already lost one son and stood a chance to lose another, but I did what I had to do for me. And it turned out to be the right thing for all of us.[4]

Gerald King's father continued to search for answers about his son's death and to find out if there were plans for the recovery of the bodies left on Ngok Tavak. He asked Congressman John Duncan for his assistance to answer questions to which there never seemed to be an answer. The father's search went on for over four years. Dennis King remembered:

> He could not let it go. Dad constantly called the congressman's office. There were times he would go into a rage and just walk out the door to be alone. I think getting answers would have helped

him. My Dad died on 24 November 1972, at the age of 48, just 4½ years after Jerry. He grieved himself to death over Jerry's death. Mom wasn't far behind. She died 9 months after Dad. She had cancer; she was 42. She would have times during the years that followed Jerry's death when she would stay in her room all day and cry and come out later and cook dinner for Dad and act like everything was fine. They did not grieve together as they just couldn't stand to see the other one hurt, so they grieved separately in their own way. Before Mom died she asked that we never forget Jerry and somehow find a way to bring him home.[5]

Corps Casualty Assistance Officers now carried their burdens of sadness across the States. A dreaded harbinger in the colours of the Marine Corps would be seen to approach homes in California, Connecticut, Kansas, Kentucky, Massachusetts, New Mexico, Tennessee, West Virginia and Wisconsin.

The Fritsch family lived in Connecticut and Patricia, Lance Corporal Thomas Fritsch's sister, remembered that terrible day.

Tommy and I were very close and this tragedy has taken such a toll on our family over the years, it's hard to know how to begin, so I will just go to that horrific day. It was a beautiful sunny day, I was nineteen years old and it was my day off. I was home with my Mom. There was a knock at the door, which would devastate the family. When my Mom first opened the door she first saw the marine major standing there and smiled thinking it must be a friend of Tom's coming to visit, then she saw our parish priest behind him and immediately knew. We both knew. Mom started crying and saying over and over Oh no, Oh no, please God no, she kept backing up and then just sat and cried. My father was on 2nd shift and had just left for work prior to the major and the priest coming. My father's work was called and requested that he be sent home, but not to be told why, just that he was needed at home. As soon as he came around the corner and saw the government car, he said he knew. When he walked in the house and saw the priest, he too almost collapsed. My younger brothers, Bill, who was 16 and Steven who was six, were home as well. My 26-year-old sister, Gloria, who lived in California was notified immediately and caught the next flight home. We were told how very sorry they were to inform us of the death of my brother on 10 May 1968. His body was not recovered, but they were very sure [that he had been killed in action]. The next day we received a telegram that told us the same information given to us by the major. I could never accept the fact that he was gone. Someone knocks on your door and says your brother is dead [and] you are just supposed to take their word for it. The government has lied to us so many times, how am I supposed to believe something like this. This is my brother; he is part of me. You can't just take a piece of me away and not explain it to me. I needed more and I wanted answers, and I would have them no matter how long it took.[6]

An explanation as to why telegrams and letters were received, which may seem to convey a heartless feeling for those killed, can be found in the following account. During the Vietnam War, according to a research officer at the National Museum of the Marine Corps, the official notification to the deceased Marine's next-of-kin was conducted by a personal visit from an official Marine Corps Casualty Assistance Officer. Following this visit, letters were delivered from the deceased Marine's Commanding Officer. This letter was normally very sparse on detail, and then a letter to the primary next-of-kin would be despatched from the Commandant of the Marine Corps. The Casualty Assistance Officer would inform the primary next-of-kin whom the Marine had previously designated as part of his personal administration; any listed secondary next-of-kin would be told of the Marine's death by a telegram. As an example, this meant that it was possible that one parent would be officially advised in person, while the other received a telegram, even though both may have been present during the official notification.

Lance Corporal Raymond Heyne was also killed at Ngok Tavak. Prior to his deployment to Vietnam, Ray, or 'Butch' as his family knew him, had served in the Mediterranean on board the USS *Shadwell*. He wrote frequently to Janice Kostello, one of his older sisters, and sent her many small mementoes from his travels around the ship's European ports of call, a practice he continued in the Pacific when he was deployed to Hawaii. According to Janice, he was proud to be a Marine, although she thought that he was 'not too enthused to go to Vietnam', even though he said 'they had a job to do'. Butch had enlisted in 1966 and went to Vietnam in 1968, which was to be the most deadly year for America in the war. It was there that his sister thought his attitude had changed:

> There were so many young men dead and the war dragged on. From some of the things he had said I don't think he was happy being there, he sounded rather depressed. He wrote about looking forward to coming home and going to college or buying a small farm, or even farming with John [Janice's husband]. He rarely mentioned his future until he wrote from Nam. He asked about the kids at home, if spring seeding was done yet and things like that. He always did, but his other letters, before Nam, mostly talked about things he saw, places he'd been, friends and happier things. It was good that he had gotten to see all the places he had been to in his short lifetime. He was only there two months and a few days before he was killed. Not long enough for me to get a full picture of how he felt, but my thoughts are from some of the things he had said that he didn't really like or trust the Vietnamese.

Once again, the arrival of a casualty officer brought a message of shock and numbness that Janice Kostello explained would never go away.

> I had just froze on the back steps of our home when I saw a vehicle that had US Marine Corps painted on the side door coming down the country road to our farm. I don't even remember going back into the house. John [Kostello] came in the house at some point, I'm not sure just when. These kind men [the casualty officers] helped me call my sisters and presented the scant information they had to me with such kindness and compassion. It was all going over my head at the time; I just couldn't focus intelligently.

The Marine officers remained with the family until the seven Kostello children got home from school. The younger children were puzzled and sad, but the older ones broke down in tears; they had been more like brothers and sisters to 'Uncle Butch'. The officers didn't know where

Ngok Tavak was, or if it had been bombed and they certainly didn't know about the subsequent battle of Kham Duc, or the significance of that battle with regard to the retrieval of the bodies of those killed by hostile action. As Janice Kostello said:

> They tried so hard to console my terrors. Perhaps the Montagnard people had buried the bodies, they assured me the bodies would have been covered by now. I hadn't even known about Kham Duc or how that played into the picture for many, many years, and the casualty officers obviously didn't know anything of what had taken place except the few brief lines they had, no info on any connecting battles whatsoever. Just overcome by a human wave they said, and bodies not recovered.

The scant information provided by the casualty officers to the Heyne family was repeated to others, which ignited a desire among the families of those killed at Ngok Tavak to know more about the battle. The explanation that the attack was a 'human wave' would have conjured up a vision of the Chinese-style frontal assaults used in the Korean War, but it was a misleading description for what was a standard infantry attack upon a defended position. The weak point in the defensive perimeter was the track up from the old car park. When the enemy's assault troops streamed up the track and then began to fan out into the fort, their movement would have been seen as like a human wave.

Some Ngok Tavak families now embarked upon a search to find out what had happened to their loved ones, as well as to obtain a better understanding of what was going on in Vietnam. Janice Kostello's pursuit of knowledge on Vietnam never wavered. She read books, watched movies, talked to those whom she thought could help with pertinent information, but she didn't get any answers to the questions that burned in her mind.

> His last letter came just a few days before we got word of his death, 'they are clearing the area for us now, pray for me, love, your brother Butch'. He had never written that way before. But that is not what instigated my researching; my curiosity after did that. And always

wishing I could contact the other families, hoping that possibly someone would have some information.

I feared that something would happen to him and I had a dream in which I reached for Butch's hand and screamed. That was it . . . just terrified and reaching for his hand. The dream was just a few days before we got word of his death. Indeed it had become a horrible dream come true![7]

No one family's grief can be greater than another's. However, when Grace McGonigle, the mother of Private First Class William McGonigle, wrote to Tim Brown 30 years after her son's death, her words displayed an agony too great for one family to bear. Two of the McGonigle sons had a fight when 'Billy' came home on leave, which resulted in an outburst of angry words from James against his Marine brother with a wish that 'he drop [over] there'. When Billy was killed, his brother took it awfully hard and although the family told him 'those things happen in war', James began to drink heavily and eventually killed himself. The McGonigle family had also been 'told so many stories' they really didn't know what had happened to their Marine son. The last letter they received from Washington told them that 'they think he [is] dead and his body had been [burnt] up'. Mrs McGonigle also referred to the infamous letters that told the families that a search party had been sent off to find Specialist Fourth Class Thomas Hepburn Perry. This prompted the McGonigles to join with the families of known prisoners of war and of those listed as missing in action in the hope that someone would provide that much sought-after piece of information on their loved one. But, for the Ngok Tavak group, there were only the 'same old stories'. Grace McGonigle finished her letter to Tim Brown, 'I just want to know what really happen and for sure he is death [sic]. I don't want him to be over there POW.' She was concerned about what the 'enemy' might do to him. Mrs Sherry Perry, wife of Thomas Perry, would live with that dread for many years to come.

Missing!

There is one common denominator in the story of Perry's disappearance: no one from the Ngok Tavak force knew exactly what happened to him when they evacuated the hill. Sergeant Jack Matheney, who had arrived with Perry on the helicopter that brought Captain Makowski across from Kham Duc for his first look at the situation said, 'The last time I saw him [Perry] was when we all dispersed to perform our assigned duties.' Captain John White also lost track of Perry. He thought that Perry had stopped back to aid some wounded and had been captured. When the force evacuated Ngok Tavak, they crossed a small stream where Jack Matheney said he stopped to wait for Perry, but he could see that there were no more 'round-eyes' to come and he told Captain White that a man was missing. White's reply, according to Matheney, was: 'I know. So, what do we do, go back for him?'[8] It was said in a manner that didn't require an answer and it was obvious that going back for him was completely out of the question. 'We'd all have been killed,' Matheney said. Although the enemy did not follow up the escaping group as it made its way to the east, the remnants of the allied force could not be sure that there was no threat of a further attack against them. Timing was critical. Helicopters were needed, a pad had to be cut and tight control was required over the remainder of this mixed group if they were to survive. Although it may seem like a callous decision, there was no option but to push on and get as many out alive as was possible. Any dead and missing were now on their own.

The second Sunday in May is Mother's Day. In 1968 that Sunday was 12 May, two days after the battle of Ngok Tavak. Perry's son, also named Thomas, was nine months old, and he and his mother Sherry were on their way to Canton Center, Connecticut, from Albuquerque, where Sherry attended university. Sherry was going to a computer workshop near Boston, Massachusetts, and the Perry family were to baby-sit their grandson. That afternoon, her father, Rex Borough, had phoned to tell her that two army officers had been to the house. Sherry asked her father, 'Did they tell you that Tom was dead?' He replied, 'No, Tom was not dead.' It took some time for the casualty notification system to change and to get new officers to the Perry house. At one stage, Robert, one of Tom Perry's brothers, said, 'I hope he's not lying somewhere all shot up and in pain.' Sherry replied, 'I hope he is, considering the alternative.' When the army officers arrived at the Perry house, they asked to speak with Sherry alone. According to Sherry, Scott and Robert, Tom's brothers, were listening through a crack in the sliding doors into the library and Tom's mother, Margaret Hepburn Perry—known to all as 'Peg'—and his father Thomas McFall Perry, strained to hear from the living room. 'The men told me Tom was missing,' Sherry said. 'My reaction was stunned silence. The idea of missing in action had not occurred to any of us during the long wait for the officers to arrive.' The officers had told Sherry's father that her soldier husband was missing, but he had not told his daughter. Sherry's son told her in 2007 that his grandfather had told him more than once that when he had seen the officers through the front window, 'his heart fell through the floor'. Rex Borough had asked the officers, 'Is Tommy dead?' And they had said, 'No, missing.'

> But my father never told me this, not when he phoned me in Connecticut that day or ever after that. I wish he had. My father was not good at dealing with emotionally charged topics. He never spoke of Tom again, and never said he was sorry that Tom was gone until once, just a couple of years ago. My reaction seemed so strange to the men [casualty officers] that they asked me if I was really Tom Perry's wife. I assured them that I was and asked for the rest of the family to come into the parlor.

Now the whole family asked for more information, but the officers could not add any more details about what had happened. Once again, a family got basic information on a battle in some far-flung God-forsaken outpost that was followed by a letter in later years, which told of a Marine 'search party' going back to look for the missing Perry. A feeling of uncertainty was now compounded by a further torment that some members of the search party may also be captured. Sherry Perry remembered:

> The Army was, to say the least, not very forthcoming with information about what had happened to Tom, not during the next few days, or the next several years. I do have some correspondence from them, but it is not very helpful, and some of it is downright deceitful.[9]

The letters from the Marine Corps and the Army that told the families about a search party stung the recipients, and many thought they had been lied to. Snippets of information on the possibility that some men from the Ngok Tavak–Kham Duc battle were held as prisoners of war bubbled to the surface in a pot of information that boiled with rumours, puzzles, pieces of speculation and wild guesses that had been greased with some facts. According to a 1992 US Defense Intelligence Agency report, there were 1919 Americans lost and/or unaccounted for in Vietnam. These figures have been revised by the Joint POW/MIA Accounting Command (JPAC) over the years and, as at 30 August 2007, there were 1754 not accounted for. Whether the officers and officials who were involved in 1993 and 1994 were deliberate in their obfuscation of actions around Ngok Tavak is hard to know. Looking back, there does appear to have been an element of sloppy staff work rather than a deliberate act to misinform people. Those involved in the subsequent lobbying to have the Defense POW/Missing Personnel Office (DPMO) conduct searches through Ngok Tavak and Kham Duc would vehemently disagree with this conclusion. There is, however, a tenuous link in the documentation that can be followed back to what could have been a very poor interpretation of an original 1968 report, which, sadly, perpetuated the error about a search party being sent to find Thomas Perry. Julie Precious, Southeast Asia Analyst with DPMO, wrote much later, in 1996:

> The basic CG 1st MAR DIV document . . . apparently this inaccurate description of US Marine Corps involvement in a purported search for SP4 Perry has been noted in the Bright Light Reports since 1976. The MAR DIV document appears to have been the nominal source for the inaccurate reference to a 'search operation . . . to locate SP4 Perry' that appears in the 9 April 1976 Bright Light report. The inaccuracy was carried forward . . . and was inadvertently included in our Comprehensive Review scrub sheets. There appears to be no factual basis for the statement, however, and our current writes have been corrected to reflect our current understanding.[10]

But the damage had been done and would continue to be done in the years leading up to this admission. It was a poor piece of staff work that should have been detected very early in the POW/MIA investigative process. Also, much of the detail concerning events that surrounded the battle, which in later years appeared in an increasing number of articles on the internet, where it was treated as gospel, was incorrect and unhelpful. Even so, there is little doubt that the loss of so many bodies from the battles of Ngok Tavak and Kham Duc—bodies that were probably located within known broad local boundaries—should have attracted a greater urgency for recovery than it did. That urgency should have been flagged in the files when the Americal Division and the 6th ARVN Regiment went back into Kham Duc in 1970 and found skeletal remains in the old camp area. As an interesting aside, there were several Australian advisers with battalions of the ARVN regiment during this operation. There is no mention, however, in their reports of any activity around Ngok Tavak while they were deployed into the Kham Duc area.

As with grief, no one's loss is greater than another's. Nevertheless, for the great film star Katharine Hepburn's nephew to be listed as missing added an element of fascination to the report. (Not that one would expect that those who may have held him captive could have known that he might have provided them with a great propaganda-cum-bargaining tool.) Thomas Perry was one of Katharine Hepburn's nine nephews, and, according to Sherry, Katharine and Tom were 'fairly close'. Katharine Hepburn was a woman of influence; she was outspoken and possessed an acerbic tongue. She could have caused political headaches for the administration if she had taken Thomas Perry's missing status to heart and demanded answers, not only on his fate but on the conduct of the war as well. Sherry Perry did not feel kindly towards the family's famous aunt, whom she thought 'self-centred, superficial and self-absorbed'.

> She had my father and me over for dinner once in New York, and Katharine was very charming and cordial towards my father. Towards me, she was always a snob; at least that is how I took it. She never once mentioned Tom to me after he became missing-in-action, though they had been fairly close. In both the Hepburn and Perry families, it was unseemly to mention the dead, not polite.

Katharine Hepburn's reluctance to mention Thomas Perry's demise may have stemmed from the death of her older brother, also Tom, whom she found hanged in a house in Greenwich Village in 1921. Hepburn was devastated by his death and became deeply depressed, following which she used her brother's birthday as her own date of birth. No matter the reason, as far as Sherry felt, once Tom Perry was out of the picture, so were Sherry and her son. 'I had only hard feelings towards "Aunt Kate",' Sherry Perry reminisced:

> She never contributed anything to my son and me. I did ask her for $1000, which she gave to me when we went to Europe. In May 1970, I went to London with my sister and her daughter, and then I stayed on for about six months trying to see Madame Nguyen Thi Binh, who was in Paris for the Peace Talks. We'd go to her home outside Paris, make an appointment, for about six weeks later, show up at the appointed time, and be told politely that so sorry she is busy with the peace talks and can't see you right now. Would you like to make another appointment? We did that three times. At the appointed time the third time, we were given the same greeting, so I said no thanks, we'll just wait.

Madame Nguyen Thi Binh had been an active revolutionary in her youth against the French, and then the Americans, and was the chief delegate for the National Liberation Front (Viet Cong) at the peace talks, where she ranked second in the hierarchy behind Le Duc Tho. Tom Perry's wife was adamant she was going to meet Madame Binh and set about 'blockading' her house until Binh met with her. She wrote:

> I had a little Volkswagen, a square back that aunt Kate's money had paid for. So I loaded it up with supplies, contacted two local newspapers and told them that I planned to stay in the little round park in the cul-de-sac outside Binh's house until she saw us. For a couple of days, there was some press interest in the unfolding story, but as far as I know, nothing was ever written about it. We did end up seeing Ms Binh for a very short time, along with three other wives. We were served tea and cookies. Basically, she said that her government was giving all of the information it had about all American prisoners and missing-in-action. She told us how sorrowful her people were to have so many missing personnel [300,000] about whom they knew nothing. [Which was a very

powerful statement.] She spoke briefly, always through an interpreter, whose French must have been better than his English. I don't know who the other wives were; that was just before the League of Families was formed. When I got home, I joined the League when it had an Oregon chapter and I remained an active member until 1973.[11]

The wife of a missing soldier suffers an additional burden over and above the grief of the absolute; it is a dreaded 'maybe'. Much of this is due to the difference between a beloved husband and father being killed and lost forever versus he's still there, perhaps. Missing in action is an ongoing story, and Sherry Perry felt that hers was going on and on:

> I've had to live a lonely life since I was 26 years old. I became a mother with no husband—maybe, with a young child to care for, in a community full of hate and protesters against the war while I was mourning my-probably-dead husband. Even worse, as far as the country was concerned, was the Nixon era, which was so secretive about all of the bad things that happened in Vietnam. It was also the policy of Washington, I believe, towards the wives of missing and prisoners; we were told that talking about our men could cause them additional harm.[12]

The League of Families came about because of a perceived indifference by the federal government of the United States. One wife believed that the American government's policy of keeping a low profile on the POW and MIA issue was unjustified. Her action started an informal linking of families in the 1960s, which culminated in the adoption of a formal incorporation of the League's charter in May 1970. Now, in addition to the government's 'unremarkable silent efforts regarding their lost men', there was a growing number of Americans who wanted the United States out of the war. In particular, those with a more powerful voice added their cry of 'get out' to a rumbling chorus of dissent against America's commitment to South Vietnam. Jane Fonda was one. Her highly publicised visits to North Vietnam, where she was filmed and reported in situations that pandered to the North Vietnamese war effort, was considered to be traitorous by a lot of veterans and their families. For many, this hatred of 'Hanoi Jane' would remain unabated over the years. According to

Sherry Perry, Katharine Hepburn's role in the film *On Golden Pond* with Jane Fonda was an unforgivable slight against her nephew and the families of the Ngok Tavak battle. However, Tom Perry's wife thought: 'She [Katharine Hepburn] probably never gave a thought about what she was doing with Jane Fonda. Jane's father, Henry, who Katharine admired, was the real reason she made the movie.'[13] Regardless of her motive, Hepburn hurt the Perry family, even though her actions may have mirrored the attitudes and actions of so many around the world who had rallied against the 'American War'. A lot of members of the armed forces had returned to their home and into an ungrateful society, which scarred many of them and their families forever. As Janice Kostello said:

> It angered me when people said things like: no wonder they couldn't win that war, they were all druggies, or in World War II we were men, we won our war! People could be so cruel. It bothered me for a long, long time to even see a Vietnamese person on the streets, or in a business place. I didn't want to feel hate . . . but I just couldn't accept them for the longest time.[14]

The missing, those classified killed/body not recovered, and prisoners of war made up an infinitesimal number when measured against the country's population. During the war, more than 50,000 Americans were killed and over 150,000 were hospitalised due to wounds; these figures overshadowed the 1919 unaccounted for Americans. The missing/prisoners of war all but disappeared from the nation's conscience, their memory almost swamped by an emerging 'greater good' that showed itself as a desire for an economic and diplomatic link between the old adversaries. Some of the bureaucrats, politicians, senior defence officers, and a large part of the American public did not count on the resilience of wives, sweethearts, friends, families and military buddies. The lost would not be forgotten, nor left behind, but the motto, 'I will not leave a fallen comrade behind', would demand a great deal of those who believed in this article of faith. It would require stout hearts, Machiavellian political dexterity, a conviction that it should be done and that it could be done, and perseverance. A journey of more than one thousand emotions was about to begin; one path on that journey would reach its end ten years later.

8 FULL ACCOUNTING

A moral compass

The total story of the efforts to recover and account for all Americans lost during the Vietnam War cannot be told here. It is a complex story— a story of many challenges that embraces all of the best and worst of emotions, as well as political and bureaucratic manoeuvres, not only by national governments, but also by ex-service organisations and those who would link themselves to the full-accounting efforts for commercial gain. The official joint prisoner-of-war and missing-in-action efforts by the United States started during the war with endeavours conducted through two mortuaries located in Danang and at Tan Son Nhut airfield on the outskirts of Saigon. In 1973, a US Army Central Identification Laboratory was set up in Thailand with a mission to search for, recover and identify personnel lost as a result of the Vietnam War. That unit location closed in 1976 and the laboratory moved to Hawaii. Over the next three decades the Central Identification Laboratory changed its nomenclature, but kept its mission active to achieve the 'fullest possible accounting of Americans missing during the war in Southeast Asia'. The Joint Task Force-Full Accounting (JTF-FA) organisation was created in January 1992 and in October 2003 the Joint POW/MIA Accounting Command (JPAC) was activated, which merged the duties of the Central Identification Laboratory and the JTF-FA. JPAC is located in Hawaii.

In the telling of the many campaigns to recover the lost, emotions run high. There are commendations for compassionate and valiant activities, as well as charges of skulduggery levelled against politicians, bureaucrats and individuals whose intent was honourable, but not in line with 'the common good'. And there are the bone-sellers—the less said of them the better. Over a two-month period in 1973, 591 American prisoners of war were returned home from Vietnam to Hickam Air Force Base during the aptly named *Operation Homecoming*. According to reports repeated in *The Bright Light*, the JTF-FA publication dated 26 August 1998, 'The initial turnover of prisoners was brief and un-ceremonial.'[1] The story continued:

> On Monday, Feb 12, three medical-evacuation planes landed at Hanoi's Gia Lam airport behind an advance plane bearing a support team and officials. Operation Homecoming, which began as Egress Recap, began shortly after Secretary of Defense Melvin R. Laird raised the prisoner issue in May 1969. For 97 men in the initial group of ex-POW released, Operation Homecoming meant freedom after six or more years in captivity. One, LCDR Everett Alvarez Jr., was captured in 1964. The operation finished on March 27, 1973.[2]

Of the 1919 recorded as lost in Vietnam according to the Defense Intelligence Agency (DIA), 'over 1100 were reported dead at the time of their loss, but their remains could not be recovered at the time due to wartime conditions and circumstances of loss'.[3] The DIA report said that the preponderance of evidence collected indicated that the 'Indochinese governments' (Laos, Cambodia and Vietnam) had released all Americans who were detained at the time of *Operation Homecoming*. Many, however, were sceptical of this conclusion, and reports of Americans still held captive continued to surface. The DIA report went on to say:

'Clearly, there are Americans who did or who may have survived their loss incident and for whom the Indochinese governments can provide answers as to fate. They have not done so.'[4] Many had misgivings about the conclusions drawn by DIA and other agencies that no more Americans were alive and held captive in the region. President Ronald Reagan, in February 1987, appointed General John W. Vessey, Jr, a retired four-star general who had served in World War II, Korea and Vietnam, as his Special Emissary to Hanoi for POW/MIA Affairs. In this position, General Vessey began a program in which the Socialist Republic of Vietnam and the United States of America would jointly investigate 'the cases of 237 missing men who were determined to be among the most likely individuals to have been captured and who conceivably might still be held'. General Vessey believed that the American public 'was not satisfied with answers that were based only on an absence of credible evidence that Americans were held captive'. The two countries conducted ongoing joint investigations to assist each other to account for missing personnel. Although General Vessey's initial attempt was to concentrate upon the likelihood of finding Americans alive and still held as prisoners of war, he subsequently requested studies be undertaken to 'determine the number and type of losses that might be accounted for by remains recoveries as well as those persons whose remains the US and the SRV may never be able to find'.

Once more the misleading letters written by JTF-FA, and repeated by the US Army's POW/MIA affairs, raised false hopes among some of the Ngok Tavak families that their Marine or soldier son could still be alive and held captive somewhere in the region. The JTF–FA, Case 1167-0-01 through 13, which summarised the search party story about going back to Ngok Tavak to look for Specialist Fourth Class Perry, was translated and handed to the Vietnamese government during a technical meeting on 5–6 April 1993. This angered Marines who had survived the battle and had told officials that the search party story was false. Tim Brown was furious and vowed to fight the bureaucracy that he now felt was deliberately, almost conspiratorially, muddying the waters and not doing all within their powers to recover the dead Americans left on Little Ngok Tavak hill in May 1968. To make matters worse, the extension of that battle included the camp of Kham Duc where there were also missing and killed/bodies not recovered, which made this defined location an area that contained the largest number of possible recoverable remains of the Vietnam War. It all seemed to fall on deaf ears.

The JTF-FA publication, *The Bright Light*, Volume 6, Number 8, of 26 August 1998, began with the following headline: '1973's Operation Homecoming: Just the beginning'. Little did the authors of that publication know just how prophetic those words would be. Further success would require moral and physical courage of the many who truly believed in the phrase 'to achieve the fullest possible accounting'.

Semper Fidelis–'Always Faithful'

'Marines die, that's what we're here for. But the Marine Corps lives forever. And that means YOU live forever.'
Gunnery Sergeant Hartman, *Full Metal Jacket*.[5]

It will probably be seen as impertinent by some to take as a heading the Marine Corps motto, but 'Always Faithful' is evocative of all that was to happen over the years to find, recover and bring home those who were faithful not only to the Corps, but their country, too. Army veterans will not be too proud to accept this banner as their cloak of loyalty to their missing soldiers, as the words on the POW*MIA flag certify: 'You Are Not Forgotten.' This flag was and still is the symbol of the National League of Families, but it is now much more than that, as the flag must, by law, be flown on six designated days each year as a national sign of America's commitment to ensure the fullest possible accounting has been achieved for US personnel still missing and unaccounted for from the Vietnam War. In this story, Ngok Tavak is but one major battle among many hundreds of the Vietnam War, and the commitment of many is condensed and told through the eyes of a few. It began with a Vietnam Veterans of America (VVA) initiative, which was approved by the VVA's fifth national convention in Burlingame, California, in 1991. VVA members were asked to assist the POW/MIA issues under discussion between the two governments by returning artefacts and providing information that they may have on the more than 300,000 missing Vietnamese. The reported response to this initiative was recorded as 'nothing short of phenomenal'. Information that included identity cards, military and personal effects, photographs, letters and information of possible grave sites, was sent in and handed over to the Vietnamese. The covering letter to the Vietnam Veterans of America report for February 1995 concluded:

> While the direct results of a program like the Vietnam Veterans Initiative are hard to measure, we do know that it has produced concrete information leading to the possible resolution of the fates of a number of American POW/MIA.[6]

Back to the future

Tim Brown was medically evacuated from Ngok Tavak on the same day as Bruce Lindsey, who had been killed accidentally just prior to the 10 May 1968 battle. What happened on that hill would scar him for life, and over the next 26 years it would drive him with a passion that was fuelled by guilt, anger, shame and outrage. When Brown was interviewed by Tom Berger, a writer for the *VVA Veteran*, Brown's tenacity for getting action to recover the bodies of those left behind was very apparent.

> It was hammered into Marines in particular that we never left our dead on the battlefield, Brown said. I, along with others who were at Ngok Tavak, knew there wasn't anything to be done at the time. It was tactically impossible to do anything. I was Medevaced out well before the rest of them basically got slaughtered. So guilt and a sense of responsibility and a sense of devotion to those guys I served with gave me the drive to do what I could.[7]

Tim Brown's personally assigned duty to find those lost at Ngok Tavak started not long after he returned to the United States from Vietnam when he saw an advertisement in *Leatherneck: Magazine of the Marines* in the early 1970s. The family of a missing Marine sought information on their son. Tim Brown knew this Marine and he knew that he had been killed at Ngok Tavak. The parents of Private First Class William 'Billy' D. McGonigle had placed the advertisement and it caught the attention of Janice Kostello as well, although she did not meet Tim Brown until a few years later. Tim Brown spoke with Billy McGonigle's father, and told him that they had served together in Hawaii and in the platoon that was sent out to Ngok Tavak in 1968. Information that they had received, which indicated that their son might possibly be still alive and a captive, concerned the McGonigles. Brown knew the information was not true, but that sliver of doubt created by 'official information' overrode the details provided by him, even though this truth initially came from a member of the artillery detachment who had fought in the battle.

It would take a few more years before the VVA became a voice of substance devoted to the needs of Vietnam veterans. Following the return of the hostages from Iran in 1981 and the dedication of the Vietnam Veterans Memorial in November 1982, the Vietnam Veterans organisation began to take shape as membership and chapters grew. In 1983, Tim Brown joined a group in Texas to form a VVA chapter and it was here that he developed the fire that got him in contact with the surviving Marines of the Ngok Tavak battle. From that point, he went on to collect as much information as he could gather through after action reports and other official files, as well as the memories of those who fought the battle. This was something of a crucial period, when the warriors would battle through a bureaucratic 'mindfield' and when answers always seemed to spin away from their grasp. Other veterans would join the fray; soldiers, Marines, sailors, airmen would come and give the veterans not only a voice, but also 'a sense of brotherhood'. The veterans soon learned that a new field of battle—politics—awaited them. But they were up to the task and they adjusted to the cut, parry and thrust of the political and diplomatic worlds, with, perhaps, the odd slash, cut and butt-kick thrown in to remind their opponents that they were speaking for a growing organisation that was too significant to ignore. Prisoners of war and the missing in action constituted one of the outstanding issues that the VVA would pursue with legislators and the general public to ensure that these men were not forgotten and that full accounting was not a worthless slogan.

Band of brothers and an initiative

William (Bill) Duker, a Navy Corpsman who served with the Marines in Vietnam, stepped forward; he would be one of a band of brothers that would pursue the fate of the lost Americans. His understanding of the number of Americans who did not return from the war changed markedly in 1981. Bill Duker wrote:

> I met three women who all were missing a loved one from the Vietnam War. Two had husbands still missing and the other had a missing son. Two of them are now dead, not knowing the fate of their loved ones. This chance meeting stunned me, as I was not aware of the magnitude of the number who did not return. I began to study the POW/MIA issue and meeting more and more family

members, fellow veterans and others who provided me with more and more information. Although I met many wonderful individuals who would not give up on finding out what happened to those who did not return, I also discovered the ugly underbelly of those who wanted to either sweep the issue under the rug through disinformation or misinformation, but also those who preyed on the families for profit and self promotion. I became what would be classified as 'an activist'.[8]

Bill Duker's memories highlighted some of the factors that had an influence on the focus of the veterans' investigations: who knew what, what was their authority, where did the information come from, and what was its reliability? Sadly, along the way, some government initiatives and the hopes and prayers of some people were trashed, sometimes inadvertently and sometimes deliberately. In 1991, James L. Brazee, Jr, the National President of the VVA, appointed Bill Duker to chair the VVA's committee on POW/MIA affairs. Thoughts were beginning to crystallise into action, which would be stirred along by men of conviction. Deplorably, a few would ride off into the sunset with a black mark against their name, but their early contributions were significant and very important to the future success of the VVA's efforts at Ngok Tavak.

There are always many unsung heroes in a battle, and unfortunately the same is true of the efforts undertaken by numerous men and women who conducted a continuing and relentless campaign for America's lost in general and for those who lay at Ngok Tavak–Kham Duc in particular. It is easy to name the senior officials of the VVA and government departments, and politicians, too. People such as Tim Brown, Bill Duker, Donnie Waak, Jim Brazee, John Catterson, Vernon Valenzuela, Bob Necci, Tom Mannin, Randy Barnes, Tom Corey, Bob Maras, Dan Carr and Harry Albert from the VVA are easily identified as champions of the cause. But behind each one of those names there are many faces that helped make the VVA campaign possible; they remain the unknown. Regardless of the VVA spirit to energise the issue of the unaccounted for, no private venture could succeed in Vietnam without government support. Governments had to open the doors, no matter what the veterans of both sides felt about helping the other; national agendas set the rules and timetables. In the eyes of some of the veterans, however, both governments were dragging the chain, and the pathway for those searching for the more than one thousand lost Americans was very rocky indeed. The Vietnamese, of course, had an instant and cutting rejoinder— we are searching for more than 300,000! This was one challenge for the American searchers who began to concentrate on the possibility of recovery from the Kham Duc–Ngok Tavak battle, which carried a count of 32 killed/body not recovered, or missing in action. To have this many in a fairly easily defined topographical location, albeit in very difficult to find individual positions, energised the VVA president, Jim Brazee, to authorise a Kham Duc–Ngok Tavak project in 1992.

Following the 1992 decision, the VVA undertook a heavy lobbying effort, which tightened the focus on the potential for body recovery, and to obtain information on the missing from the Ngok Tavak battle. Something was beginning to move in Tim Brown's favour. Having convinced the VVA that the official USMC report on the casualties caused by the fighting at Ngok Tavak was grossly incorrect, now all the VVA had to do was to explain to DPMO what really happened. A retired Air Force brigadier-general, now Deputy Assistant Secretary of Defense, James Wold, then headed the Defense Prisoner of War/Missing Personnel Office. The Office had been recently formed (in 1993), absorbing the Defense Intelligence Agency's POW/MIA Office and its database on personnel missing in Southeast Asia. Bill Duker recalled one of the VVA's early meetings with the general and his staff about Ngok Tavak.

> Shortly thereafter [Brown convincing the VVA to examine his claims about the battle], Tim and members of the Committee (VVA POW/MIA) met with the US Department of Defense POW/MIA Office. In one of our meetings with General Wold and DPMO staff it became apparent that they intended to support the official USMC report of the battle and the aftermath. This was frustrating and disappointing to all of us as we felt this was an injustice that needed correcting; families were being misled.[9]

Tim Brown didn't understand. He was frustrated because, in his mind, uncovering of the truth was a very simple task—just ask the men who were there. He said:

It seemed like they wanted to bury it and they had told lies to the families. They kept going back to the wrong information that these men were organized into a search party to go look for the Special Forces medic Tom Perry and that they were killed during that search and their bodies were not recovered. That did not happen.[10]

But the wheels were turning, and in 1993 Jim Brazee called Bill Duker to tell him that the VVA had been invited to send two representatives on a Congressional delegation to Hanoi and asked if the VVA should accept. The purpose of the delegation would be to assess the cooperation of the Vietnamese government regarding the accounting of US POWs and MIA. Duker wrote later:

I suggested to Brazee that the VVA should send two representatives. He decided that I should attend along with him. Two other veteran organizations sent representatives: Veterans of Foreign Wars and the AMVETS. Although the mission was to grade the Vietnamese, we also heard from the Vietnamese in Hanoi, what is the US doing to account for over 300,000 Vietnamese still missing from the war? It happened that the VVA had a resolution in the National POW/MIA Committee that actually addressed this question. On the final day of our meetings General Tran Van Quang, President of the Veteran Association of Vietnam (VAVN), once again broached this question. We then pledged to go back to the US and ask our veterans to provide any information that could help find missing Vietnamese soldiers through mass gravesite information and maps. We also would ask the vets to return any souvenirs or artefacts to us that were removed from Vietnamese bodies during the war so that they could possibly be returned to their families.[11]

The men travelled with the bipartisan government delegation, which had as its members Senators John Kerry, John McCain and John Glenn, as well as Congress representatives Dana Rohrabacher, Lane Evans and Douglas 'Pete' Peterson. Two members of this party, McCain and Peterson, had been prisoners of war in Vietnam—Peterson later became ambassador to Vietnam—and Kerry and Evans were Vietnam veterans. Senator Kerry's Vietnam service and post-Vietnam activities subsequently attracted a great deal of critical interest when he declared his intention to run for president. The VVA's men, Brazee and Duker, used the stamp of approval obtained from being a part of such a delegation to their advantage and displayed an approach of 'good faith' in discussions with their counterparts that showed they were genuine in helping Vietnam find their missing, too. As Winston Churchill said: 'In War: Resolution. In Defeat: Defiance. In Victory: Magnanimity. In Peace: Goodwill.' Sadly, the war had to come first.

On the return trip to the US, Brazee and Duker discussed what to call the program; they finally agreed on the Veterans' Initiative Task Force (VITF). The initiative got the concurrence of the Defense Department's Joint Task Force-Full Accounting, as it would not compromise government-to-government efforts and any information offered up would be available to both sides. Garnett 'Bill' Bell, an acknowledged Vietnamese specialist and former head of the US POW/MIA office in Hanoi, reportedly said to Jim Brazee that the initiative 'dramatically changed the discussion' on POW/MIA matters with the Vietnamese. This comment was made after Jim Brazee had met with Vietnam's General Secretary Do Muoi, where Brazee said, 'it is not a one-way street'. A genuine feeling of compassion and understanding started to emerge among the veterans of both sides. They also felt that they could contribute something beyond the words of the bureaucrats and the politicians, which just might make a difference and account for some of the missing. Bill Duker noted later:

> The POW/MIA Committee members were enthusiastic in supporting the initiative and the Committee agreed that it was only fair to lead by example in giving Vietnam's veterans the kind of information we are asking their government for. Every worthwhile thing Vietnam veterans have accomplished, we did for ourselves: our memorial, the original vet centers, and sharing information on Agent Orange. It makes sense for Vietnam vets to lead the way toward resolving the POW/MIA issue.[12]

While the heavies had been talking, a JTF-FA team, led by Sergeant First Class Stephen E. Thompson for the US and Mr Pham Quang Nhue on behalf of Vietnam, had arrived in what was now Quang Nam/Danang Province. They travelled to the Phuoc Son District, where

Ngok Tavak is located, to interview Vietnamese who were veterans of the attack of 10 May 1968. The team interviewed Mr Dinh Van Nien, who said:

> About 0300 hours one morning in March [May] 1968 he participated in the initial attack on Ngok Tavak post. After the first 30 minutes his unit retreated. One month later, he came back to Ngok Tavak and observed two pairs of legs at two different locations. He believed the legs were Americans because they were big.[13]

The joint team then travelled to Ngok Tavak where they found old fighting positions, bunkers and trenches around the hilltop, as well as the wreckage of the two CH-46 helicopters that were destroyed during the battle. The team did not find any evidence of remains, nor did they get any information about burials in the area. The team recommended that the case, Reference Number 1167, be placed in the pending category. The search and recovery specialist recommended, 'no further operations for this case'. This was not an encouraging recommendation for the VVA team. And once again, that dreaded piece of misinformation resurfaced: 'The remaining twelve individuals were all killed in action during a search operation.'

Patricia Fritsch Zajack, the sister of Lance Corporal Thomas W. Fritsch, who was killed at Ngok Tavak, mirrored the disquiet and emerging anger that the families were feeling about the new allegations of what happened in the battle. She wrote to the USMC Casualty Officer at Marine Corps HQ with copies to Senators Dodd and Lieberman. Patricia asked for some honest answers. She explained in her letter of 14 October 1993:

> We were told [in May 1968] of the death of my brother on 10 May 1968. His body was not recovered. The major also told us that if they were sure of anyone, they were sure about my brother. [The letter described what they had been told about how Lance Corporal Fritsch had been killed.] This past May, June 1993 my father received information stating that the circumstances of my brother's death was not as originally told. On 10 May 1968, my brother was one of eleven that was sent to look for SGT Perry . . . [Perry was a specialist

fourth class at the time of the battle]...the eleven came under attack and were 'believed' to be dead.[14]

Speculation that perhaps more Americans may be alive in the region rippled almost constantly through the communities searching for the lost, and their questions were: How can we be sure that they were killed? Could some be alive and in captivity? As Patricia Zajack explained:

> On October 2, 1993, a POW/MIA organization held an all day vigil for Vietnam, Korean and World War II veterans POW/MIA. My brother was being honoured...and an account of what happened [in May 1968] was read. The account was the same as the most recent one my father received [in May 1993], except now another piece of information comes into play. It seems that of the eleven that went to search for SGT Perry, four were taken POW, and the remaining seven are still unaccounted for. The names of the four were not released. I really would like to know, was my brother one of the four that was taken POW, and if not, then just exactly what happened to him? I understand that many things have to be classified, but the war has been over for twenty years. Don't you think you have played this out long enough?[15]

A cruel light of hope had been generated by this announcement that challenged the information provided by the surviving Ngok Tavak veterans. The officials, too, had been led on an occasional merry chase by those with tall tales to tell, but they were obliged to analyse every possible lead. In this instance, there was nothing to support the statement made by the organisers of the vigil that four of the 'Ngok Tavak search party' were prisoners of war. Perversely, this newly generated optimism created doubt. Was Tim Brown's information correct? Maybe, just maybe, he was wrong. Also, one other major factor in the Perry story that is seldom mentioned is that Thomas H. Perry, who was now carried on the record as a sergeant first class, was declared: 'presumptive died (hostile)-missing-BNR (body not recovered), 15 May 1978' instead of MIA. This decision was taken in consultation with his now widow.[16]

Something of a wild card was dealt by the Clinton administration on Monday, 13 September 1993, when the president announced that the trade rules for American companies would be eased, which would allow them to bid on projects in Vietnam that were funded by international banks. The more restrictive trade embargo, nonetheless, was to remain in place 'to make it clear to the Vietnamese that more needs to be done'. *USA Today* reported: Clinton waived some restrictions 'to encourage further progress, by Vietnam in providing information on US POW and MIA from the Vietnam War'.[17] The decision received a cautious welcome as well as bitter condemnation, and it divided the loyalties of the veterans' communities, which were recorded by their press releases and *USA Today.*

> The National Alliance of Families said it [the decision] was ... collaborating with the enemy. Some of the POW/MIA 'activists' were living in a bamboo-cage trailer to protest the possibility of lifting the embargo. The head of the National League of POW/MIA Families stated that tangible progress on the outstanding cases had not been met. Jim Brazee, president of the VVA, declared, Vietnam veterans are encouraged by President Clinton's action in retaining the trade embargo with Vietnam in a way that maintains Vietnam's cooperation in resolving the issue of the fullest possible accounting of American POW/MIA. But, Tom Burch, chairman of the National Vietnam Veterans' Coalition announced, if the embargo is lifted, even in part, it will be the final death knell of (POW) left in Southeast Asia. Other prominent veterans, including senators who had served in Vietnam, recommended reconciliation.[18]

Business leaders, however, were more impatient and intimated they wanted the market opened up completely. This fuelled some veterans' thoughts that trade was more important than the missing, and that the trade negotiations had polluted the resolve of some within the administration to achieve 'full accounting'. Ironically, trade, especially the possible isolation of Japan and the potential loss to the access of raw materials and the emerging markets of Southeast Asia, was one of the under-pinning strategic issues that involved America in Indochina in the 1950s.

Fragmentation within

Prior to the efforts of 1994, the VVA had to get their new venture up and running. First, a resolution was adopted in August 1993, which said in part:

> The Veterans Initiative is way of finding the missing, one at a time. It gives veterans something else we can do to help obtain the fullest possible accounting of our POW/MIAs, something that won't get in the way of government-to-government efforts or whatever else you're involved in.[19]

The Veterans' Initiative was advertised to its members with a leaflet headed up: '*Would you search your attic for a POW/MIA?* Would you go down into your basement and look? How about opening that dusty old duffel bag?' The advertisement highlighted how members may help through the provision of any information that a veteran may have in their possession.

> If you have information . . . concerning NVA or VC losses . . . be as specific as you can concerning the number killed, whether or not they were buried, the date and location, and their unit if you know it. If you have letters, photographs or other documents taken from Vietnamese, you may send copies or originals. You may send things anonymously if that is a concern for you.[20]

However, these were difficult times. Arguments raged over whether this was 'aiding the enemy' or helping the search for the American missing; was the effort misguided, should the dead have precedence over those who may still be alive in captivity? Feelings of compassion were mixed with outright hatred, which often clouded what the issue really was: Did anyone really know? Each side of the debate saw the issue in black and white, but in reality it was an argument of infinite shades of grey. Every side had a different point of view about what should, could or could not be achieved. Allegations of unconscionable conduct were levelled against the Department of Defense and its new POW/MIA office. And some politicians copped a good deal of flak as well. Others said the Vietnamese were using the POW/MIA issue as a diplomatic and economic trading tool and that the good offices of the VVA were being duped. In 1995, Bill Bell's association with the VVA was viewed with 'hesitation' because of a concern that he was not in favour with the governments of Vietnam and the US. Bill Bell and George J. Veith wrote later, in a paper delivered at Texas Tech University in 1996:

> Lieutenant General Tran Van Quang, former Deputy Minister of Defence, Political Commissar of Military Region 4 (DMZ) and former head of the Enemy Proselytizing Department, was reassigned as head of the National Veterans Organization of Vietnam. He has been tasked to work with US organizations, such as the Vietnam Veterans of America.[21]

The Bell–Veith paper told of 'guesthouses' being established by the former communist security cadre to cash in on the impending American veteran tourist traffic. They were critical of the 'amount of money spent in Vietnam on visits by VVA leadership and its members, compared to the minimal results achieved in MIA accounting'. Their paper criticised the resolution of 'last known alive cases' based entirely on circumstantial evidence, and the authors disparaged the Veterans' Initiative on this:

> Thus one can easily see why the VCP [Vietnamese Communist Party] is interested in gaining the cooperation of the 'Veterans Initiative', obviously in the hope that untrained veterans, interested primarily in healing their own psychological challenges, will unwittingly serve to increase the weight given to such circumstantial evidence. Ironically, although circumstantial evidence is considered adequate to determine that an American serviceman is dead, it is not considered sufficient to conclude that a man is alive.[22]

Given the tone of the Bell–Veith Texas Tech University paper, it is difficult to reconcile the congratulatory statement allegedly provided to Jim Brazee by Bill Bell following the Brazee–Duker visit to Vietnam in 1993. Bell replied to a direct question on that statement in 2007:

I don't recall ever having said that the VVA Initiative proposal 'dramatically changed the discussion' of the POW/MIA issue with the Vietnamese. Words like 'dramatically' are not in my normal, military-influenced, soldier vocabulary. I recall that when any proposal was made to the Vietnamese communists about exchanging or sharing information with them their general response was 'give us everything you have and we'll get back to you later'. The quote alleged to have come from me appears to be simply another case of wishful thinking, and exaggeration perhaps, on the part of Brazee and his close-knit group of Vietnam vets manipulating the VVA at that time.[23]

In subsequent communication, Bell's displeasure with the 1994 VVA initiative is made very apparent:

I publicly voiced my opposition to VVA sending delegations to Vietnam to hold 'hug and weep' with communist veterans while ignoring our former allies of the RVN. I also voiced concern that so-called 'Veterans Initiatives' might cause more harm than good due to the inexperience in the POW/MIA issues and lack of language skills of the members of the VVA involved in the missions to Vietnam. As examples, I cited the identification media (military and police I.D. cards) of former members of the RVNAF [South Vietnamese forces] depicted in VVA brochures mistakenly handed out as information related to communist MIAs. I noted that some US corporations doing business in Southeast Asia were donating relatively large sums to Brazee's foundations in what appeared to be attempts to influence the Clinton Administration to lift the economic embargo against Vietnam. They were more interested in a political cover to be provided by VVA. This was not in the best interests of the United States because we would in effect be voluntarily giving up our last remaining leverage, almost guaranteeing that we would never achieve the 'fullest possible accounting'. I decided to leave the VVA.[24]

Further efforts at 'disintegrating the enemy' (to erode the resolve of an opponent) are found in the manner in which the government departments of North Vietnam handled prisoners, especially Americans.

The Bell–Veith paper provided detail from the Vietnamese instructions on the usefulness of prisoners of war for propaganda purposes, exploitation for intelligence, and for political expansion of communism. They showed examples of how prisoners of war were to be handled as well as the directives on what was to be done with bodies so that they would be useful at some future stage in negotiations. As Bell–Veith highlight, the policy was developed in the war with the French. 'Live prisoners were used for political concessions, and remains, or information [on remains] was to be used for economic concessions.' The principle was to capture, label and move prisoners up the line. Good records were to be kept of deceased personnel with information on the date of death and burial location.

There are several elements of this policy that are relevant to the Ngok Tavak story. First, US killed in action:

> In the event corpses of US KIA are recovered from a battleground, they should be secretly buried after removing all personal effects. Their graves should be marked for future recognition. The Standing Committee of the southern arm of the Politburo . . . called for all units . . . to hide bodies of Americans killed in action, and to collect all personal documents for forwarding to Hanoi.[25]

As with all armies in war, the grand directives of the upper echelons are not always strictly obeyed in the heat of battle. Bell and Veith acknowledged that the PAVN (NVA)/PLAF policies were not always obeyed and it was possible that the documents that recorded prisoners of war or bodies did not always get through to Hanoi. Furthermore, the 1993 investigation of the Ngok Tavak site by JTF-FA, and their questioning of NVA veterans who were involved in the 1968 battle, did not glean any indication that American bodies were found by the NVA on the battlefield. The common theme of what happened after the battle revolved around how frightened the enemy was of US air attack and the damage caused by the bombing of the position after the battle. No one believed that there would be any recoverable remains on the hill, even though one of the NVA veterans said that he had seen 'two pairs of legs at two different locations', which he believed to be American because they were big. However, there was no mention of finding, burying and documenting the US killed in action for future reference. Another part of the NVA's military proselytising cadre guidebook contained an instruction on celebrity prisoners of war. 'Special treatment was to be granted to US POWs having special social standing, such as those who were the sons or relatives of American celebrities or high ranking officials in the US government.'[26] As mentioned previously in this book, it would have been doubtful that the Local Force around Ngok Tavak during the final phases of the battle would have been aware of the significance of the name Thomas Hepburn Perry. If Perry had survived and if he was moved in strict accordance with NVA POW policy up the chain to an appropriate prison camp, his usefulness would, in all probability, have soon been recognised. The lack of interest in the Ngok Tavak hill by the Vietnamese as a possible site with 'tradeable remains' probably influenced the actions of the Americans as well. The Vietnamese saw nothing there; as a consequence the Americans didn't see anything either. Although some battle relics were obvious during the first JTF-FA 1993 inspection, the pervading opinion of the small number of witnesses that nothing could have survived, or remained recoverable following the American bombing, affected the investigators' thoughts. It was a lost cause, or as some would say, a wild-goose chase.

Tim Brown, Dan Carr and Donnie Waak would display the perseverance necessary to overcome the 1993 setbacks; they would go to Little Ngok Tavak hill to conduct not only a personal pilgrimage on behalf of those who had fought there in a costly battle, but also to provide detailed information to the JTF's investigators on where they may find American remains. They would do that in 1994.

9 ON THE GROUND AGAIN, 1994

'Team Bravo'

In 1994, the VVA sent its first official Veterans' Initiative Task Force delegation to visit Vietnam. Bill Duker had resigned as the chair of the POW/MIA Committee and Vernon Valenzuela was appointed as the first chair of the VITF. Valenzuela was a wounded veteran, and qualified counsellor, who probably understood better than most that finding and bringing home their lost buddies would contribute greatly to the psychological healing of many veterans, even though there would be many emotional challenges along the way. After Jim Brazee had told the Vietnamese during his 1993 trip about the VVA resolution to find as much information that the members may have on Vietnamese casualties, he flew home via California where he attended a state council meeting of the VVA. Brazee explained what had taken place with the Vietnamese and what he and Bill Duker had proposed in line with the previously approved national resolution. Following that briefing, Vernon Valenzuela took Brazee aside and asked him if 'he understood what he was expecting emotionally out of the veterans'. They finally agreed that it could be a healthy and healing action for those who carried emotional wartime distress. Soon after, Valenzuela went to a Yakima Indian sacred ground for a healing education week. While he was there, Valenzuela spoke with an elder and told him what the VVA had intended to achieve with the Veterans' Initiative.

> One night, the elder came back to me and told me that 'it would be a good thing, and that he had thought about it and sweated over

it' and then he gave a quote that we [VVA] used a lot and that was 'Things taken in anger and pain must be returned in order to heal that anger and pain'. When I left there, I went to a National Board Meeting and told Jim [Brazee] about that and that was one of the phrases he gave us permission to use to go out to the vets and talk to them and he asked me to be the chair of the Veterans Initiative Task Force. That felt weird, I didn't know what that would entail and didn't want to go back to Vietnam, there was nothing there that I had left behind, it was just not something that I looked forward to doing, ever. But, I accepted it and it was kind of a good–bad thing. It turned out, after it started, to be such a high-profile program with such possibilities that a lot of the politics that existed within VVA started to raise their heads. It was hard to be the chairman of it when you had the president and the vice-president and other higher-up people actively involved. But we put the word out and started out going around to tell people and we met some initial resistance from some vets, but we were able to calm that down through attending regional meetings and we gained a lot of information. One of those meetings was with Tim Brown who had a large file on Ngok Tavak and his friends that he had lost there. Initially it was one of the things we could get right on to, and everyone said that. And at one of the [VVA] Board Meetings when we were getting ready to make our first trip to Vietnam and where we had gathered a substantial amount of information, Tim came to my room one night and said, in the pack it wasn't stuff on Ngok Tavak it was Kham Duc, and I was shocked. So we had a conversation about it and the next day I went to Brazee and talked to him. There was a lot of mumbling around that Tim had an agenda, and all that sort of stuff.[1]

This was only part of Tim Brown's 'deception' to get others to take an interest in the old battle site. Although he had been a member of the Marine artillery detachment sent to Ngok Tavak in 1968, he did not participate in the battle because he had been medically evacuated several days previously. Some news articles, however, had picked up on his efforts with a byline 'survivor of the battle', or similar, and Brown found it convenient not to correct them. On his own admission, he carried the falsehood into personal meetings and he used it in some of his correspondence as a means of gaining sympathy for his cause. Valenzuela took the information to the VVA Board of Directors, who continued their debate about Brown and his Ngok Tavak–Kham Duc file, as Valenzuela recalled:

> I kept saying it doesn't matter, he has this information that we should take back and what harm can it possibly do? And Jim Brazee interceded against the naysayers and said that we would take it. There was a large group to go to Vietnam, but Tim and his group was not funded to go, so they secured their own funding, which ensured that his hobby about Kham Duc and Ngok Tavak would be dealt with. And we went to Vietnam where Tim and his group would meet up with us in Hanoi.[2]

There were fourteen people in the first VVA delegation to visit Vietnam between 16 and 24 May 1994, but only six were funded by the VVA. Planning to get the two teams into, around and out of Vietnam stumbled through the usual difficulties: visas, flights, accommodation, in-country transportation, more approvals, language and minor illnesses. Perhaps not unexpectedly, JTF-FA declined to assist Tim Brown's team. Colonel William H. Frizell, USMC, Deputy Commander, JTF-FA, explained in an April 1994 letter:

> The Joint Task Force is not resourced to lend support of the nature you request to private organizations conducting their own investigations. Neither are we authorized to intercede on your behalf with foreign governments. During your visit to Hanoi, you are welcome to contact our detachment for a briefing on our current operations in Vietnam.[3]

Nevertheless, something happened behind the scenes. Tim Brown, in his capacity as executive director of the Vietnam Veterans Foundation of Texas, had written to Colonel Joseph Schlatter at DPMO on 4 February 1994. In that letter he referred to JTF-FA Case 1167, Ngok Tavak, and provided a drawing of the old French earthen-works fort, which had marked on it 'the location [based on the best recollections of three surviving veterans] of the bodies of the Marines who were killed and left behind'. The letter also said that Glenn Miller, US Army, was also left near the 105 howitzers, but they could not recall exactly where. This drawing would play an important part in the further investigation of the Ngok Tavak site by the Joint Task Force-Full Accounting.

Brown, Carr and Waak, now designated 'Team Bravo'—they weren't part of the 'A-Team'—started their venture in May 1994. Brown's mind was fixed on one point, Ngok Tavak. Along the way, he would prepare alternative travel plans to get from Danang to the area of Ngok Tavak, one by helicopter, the other a three-day round trip by road. In the end, they went by road. There was also the necessity to meet and greet along the way. Both sides, no doubt, were somewhat apprehensive about meeting former enemies across the table, but they accomplished their 'diplomatic' duties with aplomb. The A-Team had prepared the way during a widely reported ceremony in Hanoi where Jim Brazee handed over a suitcase that held nearly 100 items that may have detailed information on the fates of more than 1800 Vietnamese missing or dead. According to a VVA briefing paper on the trip, the delegation met with high-level members of the Vietnamese government and their defence department. During the visit the members visited six major city locations inside Vietnam and handed out thousands of flyers, printed in Vietnamese, which explained the Veterans' Initiative. The senior officials of the VVA recognised that there would be considerable scepticism on the part of the Vietnamese, and they understood that their credibility would only be established over time. Was it naïve to believe that camaraderie between warriors would overcome any problems, or was Bill Bell's more critical and somewhat cynical view more accurate? Only time would tell, or perhaps the answer would never be known.

The drive out from Danang to Kham Duc was about 160 kilometres in a straight line, but the road-cum-trail, was in poor shape. Tim Brown remembered:

Team Bravo went by Land Rover that we chartered with the help of our interpreter Mr Dao Ngoc Ninh, better known as Elvis. The team was Don Waak, Dan Carr, Elvis and myself. Mr George Esper of The Associated Press and his photographer, Lois Raimondo and their interpreter followed in another vehicle. The trail/road took a long snake type course going around some big mountains to get to Kham Duc. It was a 6–8 hour trip. We arrived at Kham Duc around noon and had to wait an hour or so to meet with the District People's Committee to tell them why we were there, and most importantly to get permission and a guide to Ngok Tavak. This effort very nearly failed because the locals just did not want us up there.[4]

The refusal was for good reason. A recent inspection by a JTF-FA team had discovered not only was the hill a favourite habitat for a lot of snakes, but it also had not been cleared of unexploded ammunition from the time of the battle. It was classified as a very dangerous site.

Don Waak was a 101st Airborne Division trooper from 1969–70 and now a member of the VVA. Tim Brown was his friend—a Marine and an army airborne trooper, friends! Tim's obsession with Ngok Tavak had influenced Don's interest in the battle and in the seeming lack of interest by agencies searching for the remains of those left behind. When the Vietnam Veterans Foundation of Texas gave Tim the funds to return to Vietnam, Don told him he would not let him go alone. Through the generosity of VVA chapters 252, Odessa Texas, and 292, Beaumont Texas, funds were made available for Don Waak to make the trip. He was to return to Vietnam 24 years after he had left. As Don said, 'how exciting, how unreal and how terrifying'. He also remembered what the conditions were like when they left the main road from Danang.

> We went from paved, to rocky, to dirt, to gravel to literally no road. If we went thirty kilometres per hour we were lucky. Then the jungle moved in. Many thoughts and emotions ran through me. What the hell was I doing here? Massive anxiety came over me, but there was no panic. Of course it had only been last night that I had been in the jungle—in my dream. Hell, I had been in the jungle for the last twenty-five years.[5]

The difficulties of obtaining the approval of the People's Committee at Kham Duc for them to go on to Ngok Tavak seemed insurmountable, but after a bit of 'bubble-gum' diplomacy with the children and an impromptu rendition of 'Blue Suede Shoes' with Elvis, the interpreter, they got their guide and authority to go.

> When we got permission [Tim Brown said:] we had to drive another seven to nine kilometres down what was Route 14. Upon arrival at the bottom of the hill, we all proceeded to follow the guide through the bush to a trail up the hill. I could only make it about half way where I broke down mentally and physically. George Esper remained with me, and Don Waak took over.[6]

Don Waak had similar memories to Brown's:

> A few miles and we were at the base and the only way up was through the jungle. Talk about a struggle. Forty-three years old and totally out of shape, but I also knew the techniques that kept me going twenty-five years ago. I don't know what I expected to find at the top of the mountain, but I wasn't prepared for the scene. It was almost like stepping back in time. The top was littered with unexploded 60 mm and 4.2 mortar shells. Various equipment such as rotted boots, ponchos, jerry cans, helmets, even the hood of a ¾ ton truck that the Marines had used in 1968 were laying around. Signs of recent digging by the JTF-FA was evident, they had searched the mountain ten days prior to our arrival. Coincidence?[7]

Was Waak's query about coincidence an exclamation of disbelief in the recovery efforts of DPMO and the JTF-FA, and that there was some hidden, dark and perfidious strategy in play by the two governments and their agencies? Governments have the means; they can make their opportunities and have many capabilities to conduct covert operations to mislead their peoples, as history will certify. But there must be a motive. To examine the many claims made about the aftermath of the Ngok Tavak battle is to uncover many allegations; some are outrageous, some plainly absurd and others disturbing. For every strong accusation of a misdeed by the American government, there is an equally vigorous denial by the government's agencies. What may have influenced people not to tell the whole truth about those left behind at Ngok Tavak? The search party story was a fallacy and it could have been easily exposed very early in the investigative process. It was a staff error that should not have attracted high-level attention to the point of concocting a cover-up. Simply put, some middle-level staff officers could have been castigated—some might say castrated—and the error corrected. Perhaps the fact that the bodies were left behind was a deep embarrassment that caused unease, even years later, but surely not to the point of lying, knowing that such an act might prevent recovery and repatriation of those bodies. There was more praise to be won in the finding than the hiding. Another sticking point for the US government may have been Thomas Hepburn Perry. Everyone knew he was missing, but no one knew for sure whether he was a prisoner or not. If there was some indicator, therefore, that might suggest he was still alive after *Operation Homecoming* in 1973, then that could have shamed the administration, especially when President Clinton had eased trade restrictions in September 1993. Even though Perry had been declared 'a presumptive death' in 1978 it was on circumstantial evidence, the type of evidence challenged by Bill Bell in his statement that said, if circumstantial was good enough to declare a death, then the opposite must also apply— the person could just as well be alive.

Search at Ngok Tavak, 1994

Colonel William H. Frizell, USMC, Deputy Commander, JTF-FA, wrote this letter to Tim Brown in February 1994:

> We are familiar with the cases of the Kham Duc Special Forces camps. And, contrary to what you may have been told, we have investigated the case. Although the case was not a 'Vessey Discrepancy Case' [possible live prisoners, or high priority] it was investigated by one of our teams in May 1993 during the 23rd Joint Field Activity. During the course of the investigation, our team interviewed a witness who had been a participant in the initial attack on the Ngok Tavak post. He led the team to a hilltop and indicated two areas where he has observed human remains approximately one month after the battle. The joint team searched the area for physical evidence and human remains but found none. Because we have depleted all current leads in the case, it has been placed in the

'pending' category. *This means we have nowhere else to go unless we come up with new leads through archival research or a witness presents new information* [emphasis added]. I should emphasize our ambitions are the same as yours. Our desire is to return every possible American—either to reunite him with his family or to lay him to rest with the kind of honor, dignity and respect he deserves. All our efforts are aimed at answering the questions you and the families have been asking for so many years. We intend on pursuing those answers until we achieve the fullest possible accounting.[8]

This is a message from a serving Marine colonel to a Marine veteran about the bodies of Marines left on the battlefield in 1968. These are not the words of a disingenuous officer. It is a frank and open piece of correspondence about the efforts to find and recover those missing in the 1968 battle.

On 3 May 1994, Investigation Element 3 (IE3), led by Major Robert K. West and Mr Vu Viet Dung, returned to Ngok Tavak to reinvestigate the position in an attempt to obtain additional information on American remains. They were to conduct a search of the site using a diagram given to DPMO's Colonel Schlatter by the Vietnam Veterans Foundation of Texas. This was a piece of new information of the type referred to by Colonel Frizell in his February letter to Tim Brown. The commander of JTF-FA reported the results of the May investigation in an immediate priority signal that included such addressees as: White House National Security Council, Secretary of Defense, Secretary of State, Joint Staff, DIA, CIA and CINPAC Honolulu. This signal was sent on 3 June 1994. A summary of that IE3 report said: 'one of the two witnesses interviewed provided limited first-hand information concerning the attack. He claimed that no American bodies were left behind after the battle.'[9] This information clashed with the details that had been provided by the American veterans and it was the major cause of the almost self-destructive difference of opinions between the VVA and government organisations. The bodies had been left on the hill—and the American veterans were correct in saying this—but other than the witness who said that he saw legs that he thought were American, no one else saw American bodies on the hill immediately after the battle. The possibility that the bodies may have been buried elsewhere could not be disproved, but based on witness statements this was improbable. The senior NVA commander thought that the battlefield clearance unit would not have had the time to do that in 1968. The 1994 IE3 report continued:

> Labourers cleared the site of the former compound of thick, overgrown vegetation. The team dug a total of eight test pits in accordance with [the diagram]. The diagram depicted where US veterans who survived the battle last observed the bodies of fallen US servicemen. The search yielded several pieces of military related debris but no remains or personal effects. This is an extremely hazardous area to operate in due to large quantities of unexploded ordnance [and snakes] at the site and a reported uncleared minefield on the outer perimeter. Recommend this case be placed in the pending category.[10]

The team's analyst commented on the battle with a strange observation. He said:

> After the camp was overrun, it was evacuated by all US and ARVN forces [Mike Force] and air strikes were called in. After the air strikes, NVA forces occupied this compound for a short period until it was recaptured by ARVN Rangers. Only a first-hand witness from one of the units that occupied this compound after it was overrun could have any knowledge concerning the disposition of the American bodies. No such witness was provided or identified during this JFA [Joint Field Activity].[11]

This was a flagrant inaccuracy; ARVN Rangers did not recapture the position. The search and recovery specialists recommended that 'no excavation' be conducted at the site, with which the team chief concurred. The team chief also commented on the veterans' diagram, which he noted was an 'extremely valuable tool and their assistance was greatly appreciated'. Major West concluded his report with some sobering comments.

> After 26 years, if the bodies of these thirteen men were left in the open, it is doubtful that they would remain in the same position

and intact after air strikes, occupation by NVA and ARVN forces, and years of scavenging by indigenous personnel. Recommend this case be placed in the pending category.[12]

This was a further setback for the Veterans' Initiative Task Force and Tim Brown in particular. In September 1994, Brown provided a project update on Kham Duc–Ngok Tavak to the VVA. He told them that a map given to the Vietnamese, which would help them recover up to sixteen of their soldiers buried near the old Kham Duc airstrip, played an important part in getting approval for Team Bravo to go to Ngok Tavak. He concluded his report with the sentence, 'The Veterans' Initiative is working, and is providing results thanks to you!' Brown was also required to report to Vernon Valenzuela, the chair of the VITF, which he did in October 1994. Although he reported on the successful recovery of remains, partial remains and other material, it was a positive result for recovery activity only at Kham Duc. Tim Brown worded his report craftily; by connecting Ngok Tavak to the success at Kham Duc he was able to influence the thinking that the accomplishments were connected to the two locations, even though the official reports about Ngok Tavak were negative. It was a simple tactic: the project was named Kham Duc–Ngok Tavak and when the numbers of missing or known dead were added together they had a greater emotional impact. He urged that any future delegations should include *persistent* follow-up with JTF-FA and the Vietnamese on the Kham Duc–Ngok Tavak project. Again, he connected the fate of the dead and missing, from both sides, to the two locations. Brown's concluding paragraph made it clear that he, and other veterans, would not be deterred from finding the bodies of those left behind in 1968. They were planning to return to the area in May 1995, and a VVA press release dated 3 November 1994 confirmed that a delegation would return to Vietnam in 1995. Included in the press release was advice that survivors of the 10–12 May 1968 battles at Kham Duc–Ngok Tavak would gather at the Vietnam Veterans Memorial in Washington on the 219th birthday of the United States Marine Corps to celebrate the return of the remains of men lost in that battle. This, too, was a superb piece of PR; the ground battle at Kham Duc was an army affair. Blending the dirt taken from Ngok Tavak in 1994 with that at the Memorial on the USMC birthday reinvigorated images of the fallen Marines at Ngok Tavak so that they would not be forgotten. The two battle sites had become one, even though they were separated by 7 kilometres.

In the sometimes very subtle manner of public relations battles, Mr Vu Xuan Hong, General Secretary of the Vietnam–USA Friendship Society, declared 'that VVA's upcoming delegation to Vietnam will be received by Vietnam's war veterans as the "Tet Offensive of Friendship"'. There was a very powerful message in that barbed phrase, the interpretation of which depended very much upon what side of the fence the veteran was on in February 1968, but in a propaganda score-line it was Socialist Republic of Vietnam–1, the previous state of South Vietnam and its allies–0.

10 TO HANOI AND BEYOND, 1995

Hanoi

The 1995 VVA delegation planned to arrive in Hanoi in February and, following the usual formalities, would split into three teams—Bravo, Charlie and Delta—with the entire delegation under the control of the VVA national president, Jim Brazee. Team Charlie was to focus on Agent Orange issues in Hanoi and in the southern province of Tay Ninh. Team Delta, led by Vernon Valenzuela, and Team Bravo, Tim Brown, had three-pronged tasks: Agent Orange, post-traumatic stress disorder, and the exchange of information with the Vietnamese war veterans on the dead and missing on both sides. Team Delta was to operate in the area of Ho Chi Minh City (Saigon) and Tay Ninh. Team Bravo would concentrate on the Hue, Danang and Kham Duc areas.

Tim Larimer, a journalist stationed in Hanoi, who wrote for the *Washington Post, Houston Chronicle, New York Newsday* and other US newspapers, was very interested in covering the delegation's visit. Lois Raimondo from Associated Press, who had travelled to Ngok Tavak in 1994, was still in Hanoi and very impressed by Tim Brown's PR talents. Tim had asked Lois if he could bring her anything from the US, to which she replied that she would like a book written by Tim O'Brien, but if he couldn't get hold of it a chocolate bar would do! Raimondo was trying to interest the new AP bureau chief, Kathy Wilhelm, to follow the story 'wholesale'. What made this visit a more attractive story was the make-up of Team Bravo. The team would include Bob Adams, the Marine artillery detachment commander during the battle; John White, the Australian captain who led the force on Ngok Tavak; and Greg Rose, a

Marine who was in the group that escaped from the hill after the battle. From the Vietnamese side, it was possible that Major Mai, the commander of the battalion that attacked Ngok Tavak, would travel out with them, and retired general Phan Thanh Du would also participate. With some luck and diplomacy, the two sides would come together again in 1995 to explain what had happened 27 years previously and, perhaps, with a piece of good fortune, find something that would convince the authorities to excavate the hill.

The nine members of Team Bravo arrived in Hanoi on 8 February 1995. They were: Tim Brown, Don Waak, Harry Albert, Earl Veeder, Bill Duker, David Mann, Bob Adams, John White and Greg Rose, who now lived in Australia. A Vietnamese assistant, Mr Dao Ngoc Ninh (Elvis), who had travelled with the team in 1994, would act as their main guide and interpreter. Jim Brazee's arrival was delayed due to the death of his father-in-law, but Tom Corey, the VVA national secretary, stepped in to the senior position with assistance from John Catterson, who explained to the group the outline information on the schedule of activities for the following days. The next day, 9 February, was a full day and one that Tom Corey reminded the delegation required their polite behaviour, even though some sensitive issues may be raised. Corey told the group that he was aware of the emotional aspects that influenced them all.

> From the first trip to this trip there are a lot of emotions going around, and people are kind of wired and real sensitive (a background interjection–that's a real understatement), but we've got to get beyond that and remember what we're here for and we came as friends and we want to leave as friends. We might say something, or somebody might get a little sensitive about something, but again we've got to get beyond that and help each other get through this trip. And the mission that we're here for is the Veterans' Initiative and the only way we're going to make this work is working together as a team so I ask all of you to please cooperate and work with each other.[1]

The briefing continued with a quick rundown on where they were in Hanoi, which was not far from the Metropole Hotel that had a 'pretty decent bar probably full of American bankers and lawyers', a comment that in Harry Albert's video of the briefing extracted a brief expletive followed by 'well that puts it outside our price range'. Protocol demanded that the entire delegation begin their journeys throughout Vietnam by meeting first, the Vietnam Union of Friendship Organisation and the Vietnam–USA Society. The USA Society was the VVA delegation's sponsor in Vietnam, which meant they were responsible for their visas, and provided the administrative support necessary for the individual groups to move around Vietnam. The delegation was also scheduled to meet with the 'famous General Giap', which was announced in a rather injudicious manner considering the delegation was housed in a hotel arranged by their sponsors. 'We will have a meeting with General Giap,' the delegation was told by John Catterson, 'the famous general who presided over the defeat of the French, and thinks that he presided over the defeat of the Americans.' To a listener, such a statement could have called into question the Americans' open messages of wartime errors, friendship and reconciliation. While they continued to sort through their schedule, a question was asked: What was Ha Long and where was it? Although it was a minor issue it was a little humorous, if not naïve, but no one knew where it was, or what it was. On the wall behind their meeting table hung a picture of the very scenic Ha Long Bay.

Personal tensions did prevail and the group went to its meetings the next day with some feelings of trepidation, but these were not openly admitted. There was a noticeable change in the atmosphere around the table when both sides made their introductions and spoke of genuine assistance and hope in the cause of reconciliation, friendship and success. One of the Vietnamese speakers acknowledged that the VVA delegation's visit, 'marked a huge step in our friendship and I would like to say, our reconciliation. I highly appreciate your activities, especially your initiative because it comes not from a sense of responsibility, but it comes from your heart.' He went on to say that the relationship, although only one year old, had developed very quickly and the documents that the VVA had given to them had been used to find the remains of some of their military men. The spokesman reiterated the Vietnamese government's desire to assist and he hoped it would be helpful to their efforts during this visit. As this was the VVA's third visit, he felt that it should be more successful than the second, or the first one. This feeling of goodwill and helpfulness was followed by a minor harangue on economic matters. Vietnam was one of the poorest countries in the world, the government official explained, and he told them what was needed to improve Vietnam's GDP. Perhaps this was a crude signal that indicated further success in POW/MIA matters would be accelerated if America cancelled her trade embargo against Vietnam.

Tom Corey replied and expressed his excitement at the comments made by the Vietnamese that indicated they were willing to hand over more information during this trip and he agreed with the Vietnamese remark that their visit was from the heart. Corey and others in this delegation wanted to show veterans back home in the United States that the Veterans' Initiative could work and that they, the Americans and the Vietnamese, could function as a team. He also picked up on the use of the term 'Tet Offensive of Friendship' when he said, '31 January 1968 was when I was shot!' Tom Corey was now confined to a wheelchair and he showed personal courage and belief to undertake this trip to assist the Veterans' Initiative. He went on to say:

> We come here, and I cannot emphasize how important this trip is and we want to continue to come back and we are going to play an important role in what happens with the normalizing of relations with Vietnam as far as the United States government is concerned. Because there are many other veterans organizations that oppose it, and we're on record of not supporting it at this time until there is the fullest possible cooperation with full accounting. But things can change and a lot of things can change on this trip.

Corey went on to thank members of the organisations for their assistance, referring to several Vietnamese by name, including Mr Elvis—Mr Dao Ngoc Ninh—which, if it was intentional, was a nice piece of diplomatic ice-breaking, as it brought smiles to the table. Tim Brown also helped with his opening announcement that he was 'born in the year of the pig—1947', which added to the smiles. He went on to explain his thoughts and the efforts of both sides in a voice that was truly diplomatic. In reply, the Vietnamese war veterans acknowledged the good efforts that had been made and they looked forward to meeting again at their headquarters where both sides could talk more about cooperation, and perhaps a little more freely away from the government minders. The 'Tet Offensive of Friendship' also caused a few smiles when it was mentioned again. Men on both sides of the table understood the hidden meaning in the phrase and nodded in agreement, which was linked to looks of wry amusement. The propaganda score now was one all. In closing, the Vietnamese spokesman emphasised how important they saw the relationship between the VVA and Vietnam as being. He added, that although there were some difficulties in arranging a schedule because of the size of the group, it was hoped that the delegation could meet with the agency responsible for solving the American MIA issue so that they could see what was being done and how it was done in Vietnam. Finally, he confirmed that a meeting with the country's vice-president had been approved.

> In order to recognise your great efforts and your contributions to the process of normalisation of relations between our two countries and the process of healing wounds of the war on both sides and the process of reconciliation between the Vietnam and American people this afternoon, our vice-president Madame Nguyen Thi Binh will have a meeting with you. I think that this is a great event for all of us because it is recognition of efforts done by VVA.

Prior to the meeting with the vice-president, the VVA delegation met with the agency responsible for American MIA matters. During the meeting, several difficult and sensitive matters were raised by Tom Corey, which was necessary to convince critics that these delegations were not afraid to ask challenging questions and that they were not lap dogs of the Vietnamese. After acknowledging that the Vietnamese agency had a tough job, he said:

> We also have a tough job with a lot of veterans and other people at home, these veterans and others feel that there are live POWs in Vietnam; they feel that you are still 'warehousing' remains and it is up to us to convince them that you are cooperating with us and that is the message that we have to take back. Unfortunately it is a very strong force out there . . . and we want to convince them that we are working together to resolve this issue.

The Vietnamese official did not answer the questions directly. As expected, he meandered through party-line rhetoric and said that they had worked closely with the official American organisation—Joint Task Force-Full Accounting—but they promised their full cooperation with the VVA efforts.

Following lunch, they moved to the Presidential Palace for a meeting with Madame Nguyen Thi Binh. The Palace was built for the French governor-general in 1906, but now it was used as a venue for government functions. The VVA delegation was being feted in grand style. Madame Binh's expressions of support for their initiative impressed them and to their surprise they heard that the vice-president's birthplace was in the renamed Province of Quang Nam–Danang, which included the Kham Duc–Ngok Tavak camps. Each side spoke of the difficulties that the war imposed on them, both nationally and personally. Some comments from the VVA side of the table, however, were derogatory in their criticism of the American and Australian participation in the war, and conveyed in a manner that was beyond the authority of the person to say what they said to such a high-ranking official in an open forum.

The delegation now had the Hanoi stamp of approval, but would the power of the 'emperor' extend beyond the city's walls? That would be put to the test after they met with the Joint Task Force-Full Accounting personnel for a rundown on their activities in Vietnam. This meeting, which appeared to be the standard show, took place on 10 February 1995. Tim Brown reported that Team Bravo was given a special briefing 'on the cases and situation relevant to the Kham Duc–Ngok Tavak project'. Joint Task Force briefing personnel told the team 'to be cautious of mines, unexploded ordnance, and snakes, which infest the area of operation', and they were warned to beware of bandits due to a gold rush near Kham Duc. John White provided JTF-FA 'with confirmation of the US Army Special Forces medic, Tom Perry's capture by NVA forces on 10 May 1968'. He said, 'This was confirmed by two Nungs who were captured with Perry and subsequently released via a prisoner exchange program in the Dak To area.'[2] This must have come as a surprise for the JTF staff because there had been no previous mention of Perry's capture and an alleged prisoner exchange in an area approximately 100 kilometres south of the May 1968 battle. (Subsequently, in 1996, the Defense

POW/Missing Personnel Office labelled this suggestion 'vague state-ments'.) After the briefing, Team Bravo was given maps and satellite position fixes on where a possible Vietnamese grave site at Kham Duc was thought to be located, and they were on their way.

Old foes gather

They now headed for the sharp end of their mission via some R&R in Hue, which was on their route to Danang. This stopover would help the men relax and prepare for their extremely important meeting with the Vietnamese veterans of the province they were to visit. (A more devilish description of this day in Hue would suggest that a person of ill-repute may make some money from the sale of a film of a group that looked very much like Team Bravo dressed in Vietnamese historical-period robes when they went to dinner that night.) Further down Highway 1, Don Waak went back to Fire Support Base Tomahawk, which used to be at the northern end of the Hai Van Pass and about 40 kilometres south of Hue, where, he said, 'I buried a bracelet and part of my past.' Emotional tensions were obvious when the men got closer to a meeting with their old enemies. In Danang, Ms Nguyen Thuy Anh from the Foreign Economic Relations Department for Quang Nam–Danang Province joined Elvis, their guide and interpreter. Ms Nguyen Thuy Anh was also proficient in English and obviously a government minder. It was now time to finish their preparations in readiness for their meeting with the 'enemy'. John White, as the ranking officer—a retired major—was appointed the group's initial spokesman with the knowledge that rank and standing meant something in Vietnamese culture. In the past, they had girded for battle; they now prepared for peace on Monday, 13 February 1995.

Before the meeting with the Vietnamese veterans, three of the men in the American–Australian delegation were asked how they felt. What was going through their mind and what were they going to ask the Viet-namese veterans? John White replied:

> I don't think I'll be asking very much of them. I'll be thanking them. The thing that's going through my mind is what a special privilege I have. First being here, there were a lot of people who didn't make

it off that hill. The other thing that goes through my mind is the irony that some 25 years ago that the people that we are going to meet today were intent upon killing us and we upon killing them and ensuring there were no survivors on either side and now we're meeting to discuss how it all happened. The question of what I am going to ask of them, absolutely nothing. What I really want to do is meet the commander of the force that opposed us and thank him for his honour. This man did have the opportunity of killing everyone on that hill if he had put his mind to it. As it was, when the medical evacuation helicopters came in, someone, somewhere, gave the order that all firing was to stop and I expect it will be the man I'm meeting today. We got our wounded out and we got ourselves out and his task was to take the hill, and he did and he did it with great honour.

Bob Adams, the commander of the Marine artillery detachment, was asked about how he felt meeting the people who plotted the battle against him in 1968. He replied in a similar vein.

Feelings are really hard to put into words. I don't believe that I hold any judgement [ill feeling] on these people; they are a group of very good warriors, they were doing their job, just as we were doing ours, but it appears they did it a just little better than we did. I think that this is an opportunity that seldom comes to a person like myself. I would like to know how they planned to take the hill and just what their strategy was. I'd like to thank them that every time a medevac chopper came in, they allowed it to come in and stopped firing and I really appreciate that. As we were moving the guns up the hill, one that night and one again the next morning we just manhandled it up there . . . I had a small 8 mm movie camera, it would really be unique and wonderful if they had picked that up and developed that film what a great surprise that would be if they were to say, hey look what we've got to show you.

Tim Brown said that his biggest question, and one to which he would like to get an answer, was: What happened to the American bodies after the allied force left the area? As he explained to the interviewer:

> After we escaped and evaded the area and they then occupied the area, what did they do with the bodies of our fallen comrades? Were they mass buried in a grave somewhere nearby, as I hoped they would be and if so, could they remember, or could they recall, or could they assist us in perhaps finding that location?

Team Bravo had gathered in the meeting room to wait, a little nervously, for the arrival of the Vietnamese veterans. Four retired officers and two officials of the Vietnam Veterans Association for the province attended; the officers were resplendent in their dress uniforms with medals. Lieutenant General Vo Thu was the senior man present. He is often confused with the commander of the 2nd NVA Division in 1968, or a more senior commander responsible for the Kham Duc battle. Vo Thu was neither; as previously mentioned in this book, he was the Commander of Group 44. Although introduced as a general, Phan Thanh Du was wearing the insignia of a major general and he was identified as a senior officer involved in the 1968 Kham Duc battle. A third officer was a senior colonel who was located in Quang Nam Province during the war, and the last officer to be introduced was Major Dang Ngoc Mai who was the 'head of the battalion that attacked Ngok Tavak'. Mai was wearing the rank of a lieutenant colonel. All of the officers were now retired.[3] Following John White's introduction of the VVA delegation, General Vo Thu told them that Hanoi had confirmed their travel and he expressed his pleasure to have them visit. Vo Thu added:

> Previously we have prepared things to reach our target, our common target. Firstly we wish Mr John [White], Adams [Bob Adams], the leaders of the delegation and other members of the delegation good health and we hope you enjoy your visit here.

It was obvious from the general's demeanour and facial expressions that he was genuinely pleased to see the visitors and hopeful that they would enjoy their visit. The general continued:

After thirty years of war, we are now at peace . . . and now we think of you not as enemy as before now we receive you as friends. And we hope that our meeting between and cooperation between veterans in our two countries will develop and that's why we hope in our meeting that we can talk to one another . . . with a feeling of friendship and a feeling of goodwill and we hope that our meeting will be successful.

Vo Thu got to his feet, and spoke briefly of a genuine and open discussion on the issues between them, and this simple act, of standing for that part of his presentation, portrayed sincerity that was reflected in the expressions of the VVA delegation. During several parts of his talk, the general mentioned that 'we can discuss openly'—it was as if he understood that there might have been inhibitions on both sides to address some of the more sensitive issues. But here they were veterans together and they could solve the puzzles that bothered them.

John White responded on behalf of the delegation. He reiterated the feeling of friendship between the groups and also mentioned the task of rebuilding, which needed them to let go of the past and to look to the future. But he added, 'One of the main troubles of letting go of the past is resolving a major issue of the war and that is what happened to your soldiers and our soldiers who are missing, or whose bodies are not recovered.' Both groups continued to stress that their efforts were genuine. General Vo Thu told them of his own family's losses during the war, and it obviously pained him to tell the visitors that their bodies had not yet been recovered. The numbers of B-52 bombing runs were used as an example of how difficult it was, and would continue to be, to find the remains of bodies, with just small pieces here and there. Nevertheless, Vo Thu continued, the Vietnamese veterans would do their best to help. These discussions had proven that they could do much together, and on that note a schedule had been planned for their trip to Kham Duc, which they could review before their travel. Before the meeting broke into individual groups to look over the maps and drawings, Greg Rose, Bob Adams and Tim Brown also expressed their feelings of honour and privilege to meet with the Vietnamese veterans, and that they could now forge a new friendship in peace. Everyone spoke of the conscious effort that was needed to build a bridge between the two groups if they were to obtain any useful information that would assist their quest. Suddenly, an obvious change took place in the meeting room; it was as if subconscious suspicions were washed away and both sides believed that the other was truly here to help.

The old soldiers then gathered for a photograph. First, all together, and then the commanders at Ngok Tavak, John White and Major Mai and Bob Adams and Major Mai. Phan Thanh Du, the officer who had more command influence during the battle, appeared to be ignored. Following this session, they examined the photographs and drawings of Kham Duc in an effort to orientate themselves to where things were and how they may recognise them today. The large airstrip at Kham Duc had all but disappeared and the old camps were also gone. Lieutenant General Vo Thu then told the meeting, General Du and Major Mai would go with them tomorrow. The plan was to meet at the China Beach hotel at 0730. During the trip the visitors could discuss more detail with the veterans, indicating Du and Mai. Phan Thanh Du told them again that Mai was the battalion commander for the attack and that he 'was head of the operations of the division' and all of its activities at that time in 1968. He then said, 'We hope that we can guide you, but the base company—local force—was responsible for the area after they left the battle to go to another one.' Major Mai interjected with a reminder that they had gone from the area after one day. Du continued, 'But after the battle we did not know what happened either.' At this point, Vo Thu re-emphasised the goodwill and sincere effort that they hoped would bring success, and also said that they should meet after their trip for a further exchange of information.

That afternoon, Bill Duker, Don Waak, Harry Albert and Bob Adams, accompanied by Major Mai, took a trip back to Hill 55, which was about an hour's drive to the southwest of Danang. Duker had served there in 1970 and he had conducted medical visits to all of the surrounding hamlets; it was an emotional retracing of his old footsteps. Some of the concrete steps and foundations with markings, one dated 2/15/67, and the scars left by the helicopter pad and some bunkers indicated Marines had once been on Hill 55, but it was now nothing more than a wind-swept hill from where they could look over green rice fields towards Marble and Monkey mountains on the horizon, nearer to Danang.

'D-day'

'D-day' was 14 February 1995, and at 0800, the members of Team Bravo were on their way to Kham Duc. They travelled in a four-vehicle convoy, one of which was marked with the logo of the United Nations Population Fund. Not far into their trip they crossed a river on a rickety wooden pontoon bridge, which, nonetheless, was robust. The road was passable and of reasonable quality as they drove through the valleys that carried the souls of many a battle. Passing Dai Loc, Thuong Duc and An Hoa to the south, the convoy entered the foothills of the awe-inspiring mountains ahead. Along the way, a natural rock-faced waterfall provided a welcome roadside stop for the American–Australian team, as well as for Phan Thanh Du, who was feeling ill; Bill Duker had some medicine that calmed the general's motion sickness. This was the same spot that the group had stopped at in 1994; it was a roadhouse provided by nature. The road continued to be surprisingly solid and in parts had a bitumen surface. As they made their way further uphill, the fringes of the mountains began to show jungle-type growth, although the group had not yet entered the tree canopy area of primary jungle. The region was sparsely populated, as it had been during the war, with a mixture of Montagnard structures around the hills and Vietnamese houses in the villages. When they arrived at Kham Duc the convoy headed immediately to the People's Committee Headquarters, which was a lifeless grey block that brought to mind the term 'Stalinist architecture'. (One of the group thought that the building was their hotel!) Each person had a question as soon as they got out of their vehicle—where was the old camp, where was the airstrip, which way to Ngok Tavak—all speaking at once. At this point, Western impatience almost got the better of them as they made an effort to ask General Du to talk immediately about the battle. Ms Anh rescued the moment by telling them that she needed a short break to recover from the trip. Also, the delegation had not yet met with the People's Committee to ensure that they had approval to conduct their journey through this district.

The first meeting was with the chief of administration, who welcomed them to the district and wished them a successful trip. He then told them the committee was not sure of their time of arrival and they were not ready for a meeting. He made the point:

According to our leaders, we should slow down a little bit, lunch have a short break and then at 2 p.m. have a meeting here with the People's Committee. And we are sorry to inform you that the accommodation here is not as good as Danang and China Beach Hotel. Also is it possible if you could inform us a little bit about your idea of things to do here.

John White replied on behalf of the American–Australian team:

With regard to the things that we would like to do; there are two things, one is to work with our comrades-in-arms here Mr Mai and Mr Du and to visit the battlefield that we all fought on. And for many of us here that will be a very personal trip. But of equal importance, members of this delegation have brought maps and information on the burial grounds of the Vietnamese war dead and we would like to work with you . . . to help your government try and find these graves.

They then went for their lunch break, which began with one of life's superb ironies. Dao Ngoc Ninh explained how he got the name Elvis and was enticed into a rendition of 'Blue Suede Shoes'. As he sang, the Socialist Republic of Vietnam's red flag with yellow star fluttered in the background.

•

The People's Committee meeting began with a formal greeting by the chief of administration in which he again welcomed the VVA delegation and wished them success, especially after their long, 150 kilometres of travel from Danang. He then introduced the People's Committee, beginning with Mr Ho Van Hoa, the chairman, who had a dark and ominous look about him. Mr Lien, a retired colonel who had served in the region, was now the chairman of the Veterans Association in the Phuoc Son District. The third member was an active army lieutenant colonel, the chief of the military service for Phuoc Son, and there was also a member of the administrative staff present. Following their opening speeches, during which both sides expressed very similar sentiments, the VVA team again offered their information on a possible local grave site from the 1968 battle of Kham Duc. Mr Hoa agreed with their itinerary and said: 'It was very smooth and suitable . . . and we also will do every-thing we can to make a favourable environment for you to follow your itinerary.' Suddenly, Mai got to his feet and in a powerful verbal outburst berated the committee chairman, telling him that this visit had been approved all the way from Hanoi and that he and General Du were there as veterans of the battle, and that that was the only reason why they were there, because they had fought in this area during the war. Obviously, something was not as Elvis had translated, or else Mai had detected reluctance on behalf of the chairman to approve their visit to Ngok Tavak. A latter-day independent translation of the tape indicated that the chairman had mumbled something about speaking to Mai about the visit later. This translator said that Mr Hoa was a northerner, probably from the southern area of North Vietnam and he considered him to be a 'dangerous man', although that assessment may have been biased, as the translator was a former member of the South Vietnamese Army.

Following Mai's outburst, a long discussion was conducted in Viet-namese between Elvis and the committee; it was not translated. The chief of administration then asked what time they would like to start their itinerary tomorrow. This concerned the VVA delegation. They only had that day and part of the next to do their searches in both Kham Duc and Ngok Tavak. More discussion followed and it was agreed that they would look around Kham Duc that afternoon.

•

At the site, team members studied maps, photographs and notes and tried to find prominent features and orientate themselves to the 'new' environment of Kham Duc. There was considerable confusion over where old buildings had been, especially the Special Forces camp. The VVA delegation did not have a global positioning system, which meant they had to search the area for some recognisable military ruins or signs of an old military environment such as concertina wire, cement footings or similar items. They found the base of an old flagpole, but uncertainty prevailed as to where and in what direction the old camp had spread. The team were 'lost'; they had no method of checking their position accu-rately against the old camp's position. Not being capable of doing that meant that they could not confirm where the Vietnamese grave site might have been.

Soon after wandering around the area searching for information, General Du and the VVA delegation gathered on part of what was the old runway. A small crowd of locals also watched while the general explained what he had done at Kham Duc. He said:

All of the military men all over the world follow [a certain method of operations]. But, for Vietnamese People's Army we follow another way. That is the very unique [bravery] of the People's Army soldier. We belonged to the Liberation Forces' of Central Vietnam. At the time we attacked this camp with the following target, first to liberate the task force base camp and to make smaller the American occupying area. And this would widen the Liberation forces' area. The second reason to attack the camp would have the American [send or come] other people here to help. In that case we would have more opportunity to destroy them.

This was interesting because it revealed that he, as a senior divisional officer, had a plan to deal with American reinforcements, which probably meant there were more elements of the 2nd NVA Division at his disposal, but which had not been committed in the attack on the camp. Du continued, 'Unfortunately we failed to achieve the second target because the American 196 Brigade refused to land here because they were afraid of being destroyed by the People's Army.' General Du went on to describe why he had attacked the camp from the river approach rather than the hills. Simply, the hills had some small American positions about a platoon size on them, and there was a force at Ngok Tavak, which they knew to be about a company in strength, and he used the river for the main attack route on Kham Duc because no one would expect them to come that way. He told them, 'We had prepared for the attack to the base camp for about two weeks.' When asked what they had planned to attack in that time, he said 'The whole area'. Du said that he personally got close to the airfield to observe and that Major Mai had done the same at Ngok Tavak. This was a rather damning indictment of the effectiveness of the Special Forces' reconnaissance efforts in 1968. Du then told them how they had trained for the attack:

And the way we follow in attacking is different to another country because we had no tank, we had no plane and we had no big cannon. So that is why we trained our soldier to fight in the condition of being in the forest [jungle].

When they had destroyed the hilltop positions they were not worried by what was left in the valley, Du said:

You believed in the defending system and observation posts, so that's why when we wiped out all of the bunkers and observation [posts] outside, all of you in the valley on the inside would be like an orange without skin. We would destroy them like a tiger eats pork.

Phan Thanh Du was interested in how his plan had worked and he asked, 'What do you think of the situation at that time, when we attacked from the river up here? Is it uncertain, or is it a surprise attack?' On the video of this discussion, an unidentified voice in the background replied, 'Well, we don't know.' John White interjected and said, 'But I do know because I talked to the commander who was here at Kham Duc', but he did not answer Du's question. He then went on to ask why General Du had attacked the well-defended Special Forces camp rather than the newly arrived troops who were not as well prepared. Du replied they did it to control and destroy the airstrip. Although the main attack may have been directed at the Special Forces camp—following the attacks against the outposts—the first assaults by the enemy were against the positions of the newly arrived Americal troops. These attacks came from the northwest, south and southeast, north, south, southeast and northwest again in an obvious attempt to take control of the runway. This was confirmed by the Special Forces' report after the action as well as the Americal Division's Tactical Operation Centre's log:

120320 Outpost #7 under attack, both mortar and ground. 120415 Outpost #1 under attack, both mortar and ground. 120936, ground attacks on north and south ends of runway against Americal units. 121006 An attack from the northwest into Americal units on the west side of the runway, which was broken up by airstrikes.[4]

Kham Duc had been mortared on and off from 0245 hours on 10 May. The directive to abandon Kham Duc was received on 12 May at 0030 hours and the first airlifts out took off between 1030 and 1130 hours, which was before the enemy's main assault, which was seen to form up at 1200 hours and then attack at 1400 hours. No one should have been surprised by 12 May, but both sides were; the Americans by their order to withdraw, and the Vietnamese when the Americans began their pull-out.

General Du reminded them that the biggest cannon they had was a 120 mm mortar. There was some laughter when he was reminded that they also had flame-throwers. Du told them he had two battalions for the attack with some special commandos who did the initial assault. He then said the reason there were only two battalions for the attack was that the others were waiting for the American reinforcements to come. Major Mai claimed that he had two companies—about 300 men—for the attack on Ngok Tavak; however, the divisional report said he had used his three companies. Mai said poetically that he called these men ghosts, 'They appear, disappear, appear and disappear.' Du then stated that they waited for one day and when the Americans didn't come they moved away and all of the activity at Kham Duc was given to the local guerrillas.

Putting aside the fact that the two Vietnamese officers played somewhat to the local crowd for effect, it was a very revealing explanation of their activities in May 1968. The decision on whether Du's account is more accurate than the American after action reports will be left to the mind of the reader. This comment by General Du, however, is worth pondering: 'There were many young American kids of the 196th Brigade who were very lucky at that time, but for us we were very sad because we lost the opportunity to destroy them.'

Little Ngok Tavak, 1995

On the way to the Ngok Tavak battleground, the old warriors stopped at what remained of the airstrip, which appeared to have been cratered by bombs. There they discussed how an ambush had been set for the soldiers on the hill, who the attackers thought would come back this way to Kham Duc when they escaped from the attack. Fortunately, General

Du commented, 'You did not come this way otherwise many of you would not have the chance to come [back] here.' Du also explained:

> The guerrillas who were here at the time were minority [Montagnard] and they were very skilled in the fighting in the jungle. Guerrilla forces were also used to attack the observation posts at Kham Duc, so that the Main Force battalions were available to attack the camp. The total number used in the attack on Kham Duc was about 1200, which included Major Mai's battalion that came back from Ngok Tavak to form part of the reserve forces.

In total, the general spoke of a two-battalion attack with commandos and one battalion in reserve and Mai's battalion also coming into the reserve after Ngok Tavak; all of this meant that the total force used in the attacks on Ngok Tavak–Kham Duc was a reinforced regiment. The possibility that the 21st Regiment was also nearby, as the divisional reserve, and available to deal with any American relief force cannot be discounted. It made military sense. Du said the attack against Kham Duc by the two battalions was so successful that he didn't have to use his reserve. When asked what casualties they had suffered, General Du said they had received information about the 'upcoming B-52 bombing and they had to move away quickly'. He then passed all of the battlefield clearance duties to the Local Force, so he did not know the number of casualties. Warnings about B-52 bombing came from Russian intelligence trawlers in the South China Sea. 'The planes' headings and airspeed would be computed and relayed . . . [to] elements in the anticipated target zones [who] were then ordered to move away perpendicularly to the attack trajectory.'5

At the base of Ngok Tavak, the men gathered to talk through the battle, standing on the ground that they had fought over 27 years previously. Du proudly handed over an expanding pointer, which he delightfully identified as the 'commanding stick' from the battle of Kham Duc. John White explained how his force got away, and there was an audible 'Ah', when he said that they went east across the river and not down the road in the direction of Kham Duc and the ambush. At that time, Major Mai replied, the main attack had finished and they had moved away; he had been wounded as well. The local forces were responsible for the battle then and they only chased after the escaping allied force 'with their bullets'. Bob Adams asked how many dead and wounded Mai's force suffered, but this agitated Du, who warned Mai and walked away from the conversation. Mai replied, 'I was wounded at the time and sent to the hospital,' but he gave no further details. They were also told that after the American force had moved out, the hill was bombed and after that one of the Vietnamese reconnaissance teams went up to the hill and they then informed the headquarters that there was nothing there. Elvis explained further: they meant that there were no remains of the bodies. Tim Brown's reaction was one of mild resignation and, in an unspoken manner, he accepted that this might be the end of the search. Bob Adams went on to talk about what he remembered of the attack:

> The first thing I heard, he said, were the mortars, and I put my helmet on and my flack jacket. And I was hit in the head, through the helmet and then in the back. Then they [the enemy] were coming through here [he pointed to the track up from the car park] and there as a small truck that was burning . . . this silhouetted them as they came in. After turning one of the machine-guns to fire at the many enemy coming in, I was thrown out of the hole by a grenade blast . . . I went to my command bunker and I woke up in Mr White's bunker.

From this statement, it is apparent that the Marines were not ready for the attack and were completely surprised by it. Or, if they were aware of an impending attack, why were they at 50 per cent alert only?

Now it was time to go back up the hill, and it was tougher than they expected. The old track up from the car park had been destroyed and it was covered in impenetrable undergrowth, so they had to use a foot-track that came in from the western side of the feature. Not only was the hill heavily overgrown, it was steep and they were no longer twenty-something years of age. The jungle had reclaimed the hill completely; even the inner fort that had been cleared nine months earlier during the 1994 JTF-FA search was now choked with secondary growth. This pointed to how often the feature had been used in the 1960s. The photographs of that time show the central area of the fort completely bare of growth, a state that could only be caused by frequent use. There was some mirth expressed when the two commanders, Mai and White, figured out that they were about 5 metres apart during the battle. Mai, at one stage, nonchalantly, picked up a rusted mortar bomb and waved it around like a harmless firecracker. Perhaps the VVA delegation did not heed the warnings given to them by JTF staff in Hanoi that this was a very dangerous location due to the snakes and unexploded munitions. The old soldiers were unperturbed by the dangers. They had gathered to commemorate the souls of the lost from both sides in this battle of long ago, a battle of no great significance in the history books, but one that burnt in the hearts of all of the men on the hill that day. Tim Brown laid down a flag of Texas, and the Vietnamese burnt joss sticks, which each man was given to place in a place of reverence. General Du conducted a small service of remembrance that was followed by one minute of silence. John White responded with an explanation that the two forces that met here both believed that they were right. What was right or wrong was not the issue of soldiers; nobody won—everybody lost, and it was for the lost lives that they were gathered here. General Du reminded them that the war was one of independence for the Vietnamese people. It was a moment that could have caused some ill feeling, but it was defused by a restatement that the service was to remember those who lost their lives on Ngok Tavak. Bill Duker conducted an American Indian ceremony for the fallen soldiers whose bodies were not buried, so that their spirits could be with their families. On completion of the religious ceremonies, Greg Rose and Bill Duker moved nearer the eastern end of the inner fort where Bill cut Greg's ponytail in memory of Paul Czerwonka's spirit, the Marine who was killed at the start of the battle in 1968. Greg buried the hair on the site.

Following their salute to the fallen, the men emerged from the jungle with an obvious emotional freedom. John White remarked, 'I only have one statement to make: I realise now that I am no longer 25 years old. That is a very steep hill.' Major Mai answered several final questions about the attack, telling Bob Adams that he had some special teams to get in close to the bunkers in advance prior to the battle starting. John White wanted to know how long before the battle Mai's force had been in the area for their reconnaissance. In reply, Mai said 'Oh, some weeks before'; Elvis speculated two to three weeks before. That answer had been corroborated by General Du's talk at Kham Duc, and it confirmed the criticism offered by Colonel Schungel that the patrols out of Ngok Tavak were easily avoided by the enemy. The 1st VC Regiment of the 2nd NVA Division had run rings around the 5th Special Forces and taught them a patrolling lesson that should not be forgotten.

11 PAPERWORK, ANALYSES AND POLITICS

Team Bravo reports

Team Bravo reported to the People's Committee on the way out, high-lighting the importance of the Kham Duc–Ngok Tavak recovery efforts to the officials. The chief of administration emphasised that the committee had made their best efforts to assist all of the high-ranking teams that had come to investigate the recovery in recent times. The chairman did not attend this meeting. The journey back down the mountains was a more joyous affair; one of the vehicles flew an American pennant, and rather loud rock-and-roll music may have helped to cover the rumbling road noises. Their speed away from the old field of battle appeared to be a little faster than on the way up. At one point, the vehicles stopped on a bridge and someone said, 'Coming back with a lighter load, eh.' A subliminal relief, perhaps!

Lieutenant General Vo Thu and the other officers, Du and Mai, met Team Bravo for the final debriefing on their return to Danang. The Vietnamese officers again were resplendent in their dress uniforms and decorations. Each side expressed its satisfaction with the visit and hoped that the efforts of friendship, reconciliation and discovery of the missing would continue into the future. A final lunch together, then some group photos and the teams were on their way, some south, others north. It was a happy time, but it was also time for the VVA delegation to take stock of their efforts and to report to the Board of Directors. Every member of Team Bravo was requested to provide his personal thoughts on the team's achievements. The consensus of opinion rated the visit successful; there were a few administrative concerns that needed to be addressed,

but these were in-house matters that could be fixed by the Veterans'
Inititiative officers. For example, there were too many people in the delegation; the lack of good media coverage was seen as an error; and there
were comments about internal politics detracting from the overall effort.

Several members of Team Bravo had reached a painful conclusion
regarding the remains of the eleven Marines left behind in 1968. Harry
Albert wrote:

> Team Bravo's mission was not only to work on trying to account for
> the Vietnamese gravesite at Kham Duc, but try to determine the
> fate of the eleven Marines left behind at the Battle of Ngoc Tavak
> on 10 May 1968. I feel that this part of Team Bravo's mission was
> successful, in that the fate of those eleven Marines is now known,
> as painful as it may be.[1]

Earl Veeder expressed some pessimism about 'full accounting', considering
'more normalized trade relationship and with, soon expected, full
diplomatic . . . relations to be established'. Veeder also recalled memories
of B-52 bombing and its effects:

> I have seen the damage at Kham Duc and at Ngoc Tavak and realize
> that it is most likely that whatever bodies have not been recovered,
> will not be recovered and that it is probable that at both sites, the
> currently missing bodies were destroyed by the massive bombing
> campaigns after the battles.[2]

Even though the Ngok Tavak hill was shown as being within one of
the B-52 target boxes, the bombs did not hit the inner fort. The hill
area had been struck by 30 sorties of tactical air that had dropped
bombs and napalm from around 0840 hours through to 1430 hours on
10 May 1968 to protect the defenders and assist them with their escape.
Bob Adams, who commanded the Marine detachment, sadly summarised
his thoughts:

> The Marines teach that we are never to leave anyone behind. This
> is a good philosophy but, at times, it is very unrealistic, as it was

that day in May. I am confident in my heart that those remains will not be recovered and I am reconciled to that fact.[3]

Tim Brown commented on the lack of press or media coverage of what was a unique and historic meeting between battlefield commanders. 'As far as is known, this was the first meeting, since the war, between four battlefield commanders who opposed each other in combat.' Although it was a good story and worthy of better press coverage, Brown's claim was not an accurate one. In 1991, Lieutenant General (Ret.) Harold G. Moore, co-author of *We Were Soldiers Once and Young* (Random House, New York, 1992), met with the opposing NVA commanders from the 1965 Ia–Drang Valley battle. Brown went on to highlight the positive outcomes of the meeting with the Vietnamese officers.

> These meetings involved very candid, honest, and thorough discussions, not only between representatives of America and Vietnamese veterans, but also provided Australian forces representation, perspectives and impressions as well. Massive B-52 bombing raids continued in the area for a week. This, of course, created devastating destruction and forced an immediate withdrawal by the 2nd NVA Division. Accounting for the dead on both sides, for the most part, was severely impacted by the bombing raids, and what activity that did occur was left to local liberation forces (VC). The Vietnamese were unable to recover many of their own dead and did not bury any of the following Americans. [Here he named twelve known dead and Fleming who fell from the helicopter.] It is the collective consensus of Team Bravo and the Vietnamese that their remains were destroyed with little hope of recovery.[4]

According to 7th Air Force documents, B-52 bombing took place over a three-day period.

> In the three-day period, a total of 120 B-52 sorties were flown in the Ngoc Tavak–Kham Duc area. Approximately 12,000 bombs were dropped, a total of 3450 tons of ordnance. These caused 130 secondary explosions. One mission flown to the west of Kham Duc on 13 May reported 78 secondaries [explosions], some of which

were ten times the magnitude of bomb bursts; many others were more than three times as large. On 14 May, three US Army personnel . . . were picked up by rescue helicopter. They reported . . . B-52 bombs landed as close as 250 metres from their position. They further stated that no B-52 bombs landed on the Kham Duc runway. The evaders had observed no enemy being killed during the airstrikes.[5]

Lobbying for the hill to be excavated and a search for remains would continue in the face of these pessimistic conclusions. Why?

What reinvigorated VVA action to go back to DPMO and ask again that Little Ngok Tavak be excavated? The answer may be found in the reaction to the release of two films. During their stay in Danang, following Team Bravo's visit to Ngok Tavak, Harry Albert interviewed John White on video about the 1968 battle. Bill Duker believed this interview which was White's detailed account of the battle convinced the US government to do something about the Ngok Tavak site.

I personally hand-delivered videotaped copies of the interview to General Wold upon our return [in 1995] and later to JTF-FA, Detachment 2 in Hanoi. The results of this interview, I believe, turned the tide in terms of convincing the US government, in particular DPMO, to investigate and excavate the battle site.[6]

Logically, the interview should not have made any difference. Team Bravo had just visited Ngok Tavak and there was a strong feeling, which had been expressed in the team's written reports, that the remains would not be recovered due to the results of bombing and/or natural deterioration. Ngok Tavak had been investigated twice in two years by JTF-FA, which recommended the case be placed into the pending category. John White's recollections of the battle did not provide any information that wasn't already known; indeed some of his statements were refutable, although at that time—1995—his statements were taken at face value and not matched to other details such as unit after action reports, MACV analyses and intelligence reports. In April 1996, however, the VVA wrote to Julie Precious, Southeast Asia Analyst, DPMO, and asked: 'Subject: Major White's videotaped Ngoc Tavak battle disposition. What is the DOD [Department of Defense] contemplating doing, if anything, in regard to correcting inaccuracies and/or fabrications in this official case narrative?'[7] Although the John White filmed 1995 interview was useful, such an enquiry must have diluted the film's influence and its importance in getting DPMO and/or JTF-FA to reconsider their actions around Ngok Tavak. An adjunct to that VVA question concerned Thomas Perry. The VVA wished to know what had been done regarding the confirmation of the capture of Perry, a reference to the Nung story provided to JTF by John White.

DPMO provided a detailed reply to the VVA questions, although they tiptoed around the charge of 'inaccuracies and/or fabrications' in the White narrative. In particular, DPMO addressed the question of Camp 'Bravo', which was the NVA Military Region 5 prisoner-of-war camp. This camp was generally located well to the southeast of Kham Duc, although it moved a few times over the years, remaining in the vicinity of the then provincial borders of Quang Ngai–Quang Tin. As at 3 July 1996, DPMO reported that 'SP4 Julius Long was the only American from the Kham Duc–Ngok Tavak battles who ever entered the MR5 POW camp.' On the basis that some credibility and emphasis had been given to the Nung exchange story and Perry's capture, John White was asked in 2006 to elaborate on his 1995 remarks. He added:

> I would not have said definitively that Perry was captured rather than say that I had heard that a couple of Nungs who had been severely wounded at Ngok Tavak were reportedly released some time later in the area of Dak To (I think) and they purportedly said that they were captured along with the other wounded and Tom Perry. I do not know if this story is true, as I never heard it backed up and I do not know why the NVA would have freed them. I did not give great credence to this story about Nungs being released but it does not mean that Perry was not captured.[8]

The second film that caused further agitation was *Kham Duc Victory*, from the Vietnamese Film Archives. There was great interest in a scene that allegedly showed Westerners/Caucasians, one of whom was identified as Specialist Fourth Class Julius Long, even though Long had said that he did not see any other American prisoners until he arrived at the Military Region 5 POW camp. The fact that several of the images could not be clearly identified raised the possibility that more prisoners from Kham Duc–Ngok Tavak might have been taken to the POW camp. In reply, DPMO said that discrepancies were noted in the film; for example, it had been spliced with what seemed to be scenes from other battles. What may have created some excitement among veterans was the DPMO statement that 'we have neither been able to associate these two images with particular individuals missing or presumed killed from Ngok Tavak or Kham Duc battles nor have we been able to rule out those lost in these battles'. Nevertheless, all of the Vietnamese witnesses who had been interviewed by JTF-FA said that there was only one American taken prisoner from the Ngok Tavak–Kham Duc battlefield to a prison camp. In addition, everyone agreed, including members of Team Bravo, the Vietnamese officers Du and Mai, and other NVA officers who had been interviewed by JTF-FA, that US aircraft bombed the Ngok Tavak camp and destroyed the bodies. The 1995 Team Bravo came away from that visit with a feeling of honesty, cooperation and friendship between them and the Vietnamese, and they had no reason to doubt the stories they had been told. What may have stirred in Tim Brown's mind was the thought that if the bodies had not been moved, maybe, just maybe, that meant some of the remains may still be on the hill, even though everyone agreed that the bombing had damaged everything and the ravages of time would have also assisted in the destruction of any human evidence. There must have been some hope.

Thomas Perry's case had created strong disagreements within and between organisations, to the point where, in 1996, DPMO was willing to nominate him as a 'Priority Discrepancy case'—General Vessey's initiative. DPMO wrote: 'The nomination would be based on three separate pieces of evidence, which, as already described are problematic. However, once we have coordinated our views with Joint Task Force analysts, the priority nomination will be made, and you will be notified.'[9]

'Americans like conspiracies,' said John McCain, who was shot down in October 1967 and incarcerated in the infamous 'Hanoi Hilton'. McCain's father was a four-star admiral and when the Vietnamese found out, he was called the 'crown prince', further evidence of their use of prisoners for propaganda advantage. As a US senator, McCain criticised the government for their accounting of prisoners of war. 'The war was over and everybody wanted to forget about it, including the Pentagon,' he said.[10] McCain's circumstances as a prisoner of war are also a very good guide to the value Thomas Hepburn Perry would have had as a means of helping the North's efforts to disturb the American people.

Nevertheless, no pieces of evidence have been produced that would support a definitive assessment that Perry was captured; everything was unsubstantiated speculation. Not one of the allied team that escaped from the hill in May 1968 saw what happened to Perry when he disappeared. They just knew he was not in the group. Jack Matheney and John White—the two who had discussed that he was missing—*thought* that Perry was back at the Ngok Tavak position.

Others have assumed—without verification, or proof—that Perry went back in the direction of the hill and was captured. This assumption is considered to be deficient. Investigations and studies of interviews and documents conducted and written over the years did not find anything that mentioned a prisoner being taken from Ngok Tavak. The VVA and Joint Field Activity personnel rated the Vietnamese witnesses as being reliable. On 18 June 2002, a joint American/Vietnamese team got information from a witness who said during the May 1968 battle that he had killed an American who 'was approximately 1.8 metres tall with blonde curly hair'. The location of the alleged killing was on the northwestern slopes of Ngok Tavak and away from the direction in which the escaping Allied force had gone. Although Perry is not mentioned by name, the information insinuated that it was the Special Forces medic, even though Perry did not have blonde curly hair. A JPAC report dated 30 March 2005 said, 'SFC Thomas Perry, was last seen alive tending to wounded; however, he is now assumed to have been killed in action at a location away from the fortified base.'[11] At the time Perry disappeared, the enemy was not following up the retreating allied force, but the NVA kept firing upon the hill area, especially with their mortars, as the 11th Company after action report noted: 'The enemy continued mortaring the FOB for approximately 90 minutes after it was abandoned.' Friendly attack air also covered the movement of the American force off the hill, and at that stage they would have been given a 'free fire' zone approval—everything on the hill was enemy. The danger for Thomas Perry was not capture, but death.

No speculative conclusion will appease everybody, as the continued argument over Perry's fate demonstrates. But it is more likely than not that Tom Perry was killed at Little Ngok Tavak hill either by enemy fire or attack air, and his remains destroyed by tactical air strikes, including napalm, which burnt some bodies beyond recognition. Mr Doan Ngoc Phuong, who had been a medic with the 40th Battalion in 1968 said in 1998, 'He went forward to recover friendly [NVA] wounded, he recalled seeing many bodies lying outside the fort, mostly Vietnamese . . . he saw bodies inside . . . some of which were badly burnt'.[12] B-52 sorties also struck the area early on 11 May 1968. It is thus likely that Thomas Perry's remains were lost under circumstances that would preclude them from being identified.

Politics not all on Capitol Hill

In 1996, while the search-and-excavate debate swirled through DPMO, JTF-FA and the VVA teams, George Duggins, vice-president of the VVA, had been requested to comment on, or to find, the Team Bravo report from February 1995. He had been appointed to President Clinton's delegation to Southeast Asia and his response was delayed until he had returned from Vietnam, Laos and Cambodia. He replied, 'I have no knowledge of a 117-page report from Team Bravo.' This incensed Dan Carr, who faxed off a strongly worded comment: 'Attached find copies of the cover sheets and introduction taken from this report. I would suggest that these be given to vice-president Duggins to encourage him to look a little harder.' In the space of one year it appeared as if the efforts of Team Bravo and their lessons learned had disappeared. Tim Brown then set up a meeting with DPMO in late April 1996, following which he was to be available to brief the VVA National Board meeting. To get back to the basics, Brown would set up video equipment, and have available full documentation that would provide compelling information regarding every one of the 32 cases from the Ngok Tavak–Kham Duc battles. Dan Carr was also concerned. He had travelled with the 1994 group that had opened the trail to Ngok Tavak and he was not about to let their efforts be wasted. Carr was worried that the Veterans' Initiative was losing its energy. He wrote:

My primary concerns within VVA regard the overall management (or lack thereof) of the Veterans Initiative and the obligation to include members of committees and the membership within this endeavour, as we are the ones who are ultimately supporting this program. We cannot become a microcosm of the bureaucratic government agencies that we have dealt with in regards to this issue. We owe our members, our missing brothers, the families, and our citizenry much more than that. Perhaps next week, VVA will come to that conclusion.[13]

Some of the communication now became more terse and angry. A few of the veterans felt that they were being ignored, misled, or worse when it came to getting more information on what the agencies knew and were willing to share with them. Team Bravo had travelled the trail, and they were not going to let any bureaucracy, be it government or otherwise, block the bridges. The main players now were Tim Brown, Don Waak and Dan Carr. Tim Brown expressed his frustration about the Kham Duc–Ngok Tavak project in a memorandum to the VVA POW–MIA Committee and Jim Brazee, the national president, on 21 May 1996. Brown listed his main concerns and requested a review of the course of the VVA actions. Although he now focused on Americans who might have been captured alive at Kham Duc, he had couched his letter around the fate of the 32 Americans killed/bodies not recovered, captured, or who are otherwise missing in action from the 10–12 May 1968 Kham Duc–Ngok Tavak battles. Dan Carr had also strongly censured John Horne, the Director of External Affairs at DPMO, about 'stonewalling' and 'non-responsiveness'. He also claimed that the previous 'DPMO reports on Ngok Tavak are fabricated', and he said, 'On Tuesday, 28 May [1996], I will begin to find other more responsive parties to assist us in encouraging your office to do the right thing.'[14] Unfortunately, the charges of fabrication and misleading conduct were not a one-way street. Concealing the detail to achieve an object is an age-old tactic and in this battle it was considered to be a necessary stratagem to win support for those who still lay at Ngok Tavak. It was difficult; every side believed that their claim was commendable and for the better, while the plans of others were plots wrapped in conspiracies. In some cases, interpersonal relations deteriorated to a spiteful level where some messages were delivered with the subtlety of a sledgehammer blow to the head. What went on behind the scenes in personal meetings cannot be determined here; however, the written words, as strange as it may seem, now started to show some agreement on the importance of the Kham Duc region. There was some dissension on priorities and the holding of the 'old line' on what happened at Ngok Tavak, but things were moving in the direction that some members of the VVA wanted, which was full accounting for the 32 lost in the May 1968 battles. Nevertheless, any further action at Ngok Tavak must have been doubtful following the 1995 trip, which proved to some veterans that it was probably a case of killed by hostile action/'bodies not recoverable'. If, however, an opportunity were presented for a forensic excavation of the hill, it would be grabbed with both hands and Team Bravo could rest with a clear conscience that they had been faithful to their brothers.

12 NGOK TAVAK PERCHANCE

Major Ken Royalty's team, Ngok Tavak, 1998

From 1996 through to early 1998 was a hiatus in the Ngok Tavak project. The JTF-FA and Vietnam veterans trips in 1993, 1994 and 1995 had fixed the battle site on the JTF task sheets. Nevertheless, a pragmatic doubt about the recovery of the bodies overrode the heart, and Ngok Tavak was placed in the nothing-more-can-be-done category. By 1997, the history of Ngok Tavak had faded as staff rotated through military assignments, as well as the bureaucracy; there were also many other sites that required attention. As fate would have it, an investigation into a helicopter incident that was possibly connected with Lieutenant Fleming's death led investigators back to the Kham Duc area. The initial discussions about this occurrence took place in a hotel in Hoi An on 24 May 1997. After that meeting the investigation moved to Phuoc My village, which was located just to the north of the Ngok Tavak airstrip, from where locals took a Joint Force team to a suspected crash site. The official report on that visit submitted by the Commander, JTF-FA, highlighted the following points:

> On 26 May 1997, a joint US/SRV team investigated a . . . crash site at grid coordinate . . . YC 96450 01015 . . . however no unaccounted for individuals are associated with this crash site. The unaccounted for individual in the case 1168 incident [Lieutenant Fleming] died in a fall from a rescue helicopter . . . Other items recovered possibly correlate to case 1167 [the bodies of those left behind on the hill in 1968].[1]

The grid coordinates mentioned above are the recorded global positioning system references to the 'old' Ngok Tavak LZ. Something didn't click in the investigative process until the team got to the location and walked over the hill into the old fort. That walk rekindled a flame to reinvestigate. Major Kenneth Royalty (today a lieutenant colonel) led the team. Ironically, one part of Colonel Royalty's current unit's motto-cum-warrior-ethos is, 'I will never leave a fallen comrade.' Royalty recalled what happened:

> I joined JTF-FA in the January of 1997. My team was the investigative team that actually located Ngok Tavak [rediscovered the site]. Our job was to find the site and then determine if it contained possible remains. Once I determined [if a] site was creditable, and remains were likely, I would recommend the site for recovery. What prompted us to reopen the investigation was my conversation with Mr [Tim] Brown, and my team sergeant's—Sergeant [Patrick A.] Franco—conversation with CPT White. The reason that I recommended the site for excavation was that the site looked remarkably undisturbed and in my conversation with the NVA soldiers that overran the site they told me that they left the American bodies where they died. They quickly scavenged what they could and hastily left the area fearing American air strikes.[2]

Contrarily, in this case, staff rotation and a lack of background experience worked in favour of the lobbyists who had for so long asked for an excavation. That desire still existed with several of the Team Bravo men, if for no other reason than to prove that everything that could be done had been done to account for the missing. The relics of the 1968 battle that remained on the hill energised the new team, and although they should have known of what had happened previously— especially the JTF-FA 1994 investigation—they didn't. This lack of historical experience turned out to be a good thing.

Richard 'Dickie' Hites, who was the J2-Casualty Resolution Specialist in Honolulu said, 'We went back through all of the files and examined a lot of material that we had on file.' The John White interview filmed by Harry Albert in 1995 was looked at again. The diagram of the position with the last known locations of the bodies—drawn by Dave Fuentes—

also reappeared. The information was well recorded; the site had been examined twice, and Dickie Hites had been on staff since 31 January 1994. One thing that JTF-FA had not done previously was to interview the Vietnamese officers General Phan Thanh Du and Major Mai, even though these officers had travelled to the battle site with the VVA members in 1995. Joint Field Activity teams reinvestigated the history of the battle through interviews and site inspections during April and June 1998. Ngok Tavak was checked for unexploded ammunition, again, on 29 June. More discussions took place with people who may have had some knowledge of what happened, either during the 1968 battle or afterwards, when the local militia cleared the battleground. No new information was uncovered and the Phuoc Son District People's Committee verified, in writing, that the 'residents of the above two villages [Phuoc Chanh and Phuoc Cong] do not know about any dead Americans during the war'. General Phan Thanh Du was interviewed again on 1 July 1998 during which he 'provided information consistent with information he provided . . . on 21 April 1998', except for one major difference. Du now is alleged to have speculated, 'that the US servicemen killed at Ngok Tavak are still there, and a joint team should excavate the entire upper operating base area'. While his latest supposition tied in with all of the anecdotal evidence that no one had known of any American bodies being buried or moved, the previous consensus of opinion had it that any remains would be unrecoverable.

The joint investigation element went back to Ngok Tavak and conducted a site survey on 9 July 1998 during which they found 'jungle boot pieces, cloth wrapped in a poncho and wet weather gear'. There were numerous pieces of weapons, helmets, ponchos and body armour scattered around the old battle site. Possible human remains were also found and sent off for further examination. Most of this search was done in the areas drawn by Dave Fuentes on a 1994 sketch of the hill on the 1968 after action report diagram. Paul Swenarski's identification discs were found among other items of material evidence that were photographed and left in place for the time being. Swenarski survived the battle. Of interest, some 105 mm artillery projectiles were also found, which would suggest that not all of the shells were fired prior to the guns' destruction in 1968. The projectiles were probably flung from the ammunition pit when it caught fire and exploded during the battle.

There were also quantities of 60 mm, 81 mm and 4.2-inch mortar bombs. Further analysis of what was first thought to be bone proved that it was not; nevertheless, the team recommended that the site be excavated.

A groundswell of opinion had now swung in favour of a full excavation. The feeling was positive that the team would find the remains of the Americans left behind in 1968. The investigators had matched the consistency of the detail provided by the American and Australian survivors of the battle with the information that the Vietnamese witnesses had given them and concluded that 'the probability of recovering remains at this site is high'. The possibility that thirteen bodies—including Thomas Perry's—may be contained within a well-defined space, which measured 50 by 70 metres, also supported a case for digging. Now that the site had been cleared of 'large amounts of ordnance', there was a concern that 'remains traders' would scavenge the area, which added to the new feeling of priority for Ngok Tavak. It was estimated that it would take somewhere between 100 and 120 days to excavate the hill. The magnitude of the effort that was about to be undertaken was huge.

The 52nd Joint Field Activity unit went to Ngok Tavak on 23 August 1998. Mr Richard Wills and Captain Steven R. Bunch led the American team. The team sergeant was Sergeant First Class Dwayne Bell. Mr Pham Van Ruyen headed the Vietnamese government contingent. This team cleared the northwest side of the 'lower and inner compounds', the area between the inner fort wall and the outer perimeter. They also established a soil screening area between the fort and the old LZ in an area known not to contain mines. The group found much of the obvious battle debris that had been seen previously, but they concentrated their efforts on those parts of the fort that were the last known positions of the missing Americans. Wet weather created soil screening difficulties and the examination was suspended on 19 September 1998. Nevertheless, the 52nd JFA did find possible human skeletal and dental remains, as well as numerous personal effects, issued equipment, weaponry and ammunition. The JPAC report on this field activity and those that were to follow emphasised that other diagnostic evidence, such as recovered footwear and personal equipment, was associated with the recovered remains.[3] And there were numerous pieces of personal belongings recovered, including some 'British Commonwealth (Australian?) coins'.

In mid-1999, a 24-person team made up the 55th JFA, which was headed by Mr Bradley Sturm, the team anthropologist and joint team leader with Major Matthew Fuhrer and Major Steven Bunch. On an earlier mission near the Laos border in 1997, Matthew Fuhrer explained how the leadership arrangement worked. Inside the grid, the anthropologist was king. He decided where and how deep to dig. He was also the person who may have to testify in court years down the road if someone contested the US military's efforts. Their Vietnamese counterpart was Mr Pham Cong Khoi. The 55th team also found possible human remains that were located near the last known positions of the bodies left on the hill in 1968. Numerous personal items were also recovered, some that probably puzzled the team and some that should have raised a smile as the team carried out the painstaking and tedious work. Film fragments from Bob Adams's 8 mm camera were uncovered—unfortunately, not viewable—as were two cufflinks from the Royal Military College, Duntroon, Australia. They were John White's. What purpose hair curlers were put to is anyone's guess, but four were found. Among the Vietnamese items were an NVA sergeant's epaulette rank bars and a shoulder patch for the 'second infantry division, (ARVN)'. If only that patch could talk. The 55th team remained on location from 6 May to 15 June 1998.

Brad Sturm and Matthew Fuhrer returned with the third and final JFA, which was identified as 56, and its task kept the team in the Ngok Tavak area from 13 July through to 27 August 1999. The site was now showing signs of deterioration caused by erosion, rodent and insect activity, as well as damage caused by plant root growth and ammunition explosions. An unexploded ordnance disposal pit had been established just to the south of the inner compound and by the end of the JFA it contained a good collection of unstable and dangerous pieces of munitions. There was also evidence of probable recent looting activity. Although the human remains that were found were generally concentrated within the communication trenches and bunkers, they were not in the locations noted on Dave Fuentes's sketch map. They were found, however, in depressions near the last known locations, which suggested that someone might have made an attempt to cover the bodies in 1968, or later. It was suggested that the Local Force unit that had been responsible for the battle site clearance might have made an attempt to bury, or protect the bodies. The people who lived in this area had also expressed their misgivings about the spirits that may haunt them if they collected items from the battlefield and it was suggested that they might have made the effort to cover the dead. However, the witness statements taken over the years did not support either of those possibilities. The team continued to find a lot of personal and military equipment scattered throughout the site, which made the search more difficult as there was a correlation between personal equipment and some remains, but it was not constant across the old fort. A final search was also conducted for Thomas Perry in the last known location as reported by Captain White, which was in the vicinity of the 'eastern area of the lower compound trenches'. John White's comments about Perry's disappearance contradicted the information that he had passed to the American military staff in Hanoi in 1995. What happened to Perry was not known. As discussed in previous pages, and in the many reports and papers written about his disappearance, no one saw Perry after the escaping group left the Ngok Tavak hill. Witness statements from interviews conducted with Vietnamese and Americans over the years did not discover any other reported evidence that Perry was captured, or taken and killed elsewhere, or that he returned to the hill and was in the eastern area of the compound. Nevertheless, the recovery team 'completely excavated' the eastern area of the lower compound, but nothing was found. Subsequent to this, in March 2005, a JPAC report on Case 1167 (Ngok Tavak) included this statement on Perry. 'The details of SFC Perry's demise are not known with certainty'; however, a credible report 'strongly indicates that his [Perry's] death occurred at a place outside, and some distance from, the outpost perimeter'. This information came via a memorandum from Mr Paul Mather to JPAC in August 2003. Other than a statement obtained in 2002 from a Vietnamese soldier who said he had killed an American in the vicinity of Ngok Tavak in May 1968, no other reference to this 'credible information' was found. 'On 27 August 1999, at the conclusion of the 56th JFA, the anthropologist/recovery leader, determined that the REFNO 1167 site has been excavated to the fullest practicable extent', and he closed the recovery operation down.

Although the field activities had accomplished a great deal, under very difficult conditions, there was still much to be done in the identification process. The soil around Ngok Tavak was tested as relatively non-acidic, but the preservation of remains varied from poor to good, which would have an effect on the more detailed laboratory process that had to follow. The recovered human remains were received at the Central Identification Laboratory in Hawaii on 8 September 1999. This laboratory undertook a series of detailed studies to identify the remains. Samples were submitted to the Armed Forces DNA Identification Laboratory, which reported that mitochondrial DNA (mtDNA) was obtained from seven of the fourteen samples. Some items were too small to be tested, others did not yield any useable data, while other results showed 'markers commonly associated with Asians'. One of the primary next of kin to one of the Marines had also passed away, which meant a relative had to be found who could provide DNA that would allow a full analysis to be completed. Forensic dental and anthropologic reports were completed in March 2004. In March 2005, Dr Thomas Holland, the scientific director of JPAC CIL, received consultancy advice from three external forensic experts who had been requested to review the case file. Their concurrences and recommendations were:

> Based upon mtDNA results, and dental and anthropological evidence, as well as circumstantial evidence, Cpl Gerald Eugene King, LCpl Joseph Francis Cook, LCpl Raymond Thomas Heyne, LCpl Donald Wayne Mitchell and LCpl Thomas William Fritsch are identified.

The circumstantial evidence and laboratory results established that the rest of the remains were not individually identifiable based on the 'limitations of current scientific techniques'. These samples, designated Group Remains, involved: Sergeant Glenn E. Miller, Lance Corporal James R. Sargent, Private First Class Thomas J. Blackman, Private First Class Paul S. Czerwonka, Private First Class Barry L. Hempel, Private First Class Robert C. Lopez and Private First Class William D. McGonigle. Dr Hugh Berryman also noted the circumstantial evidence that influenced his decision on why he did not include Lieutenant H. 'Bud' Fleming and Specialist Fourth Class Thomas Perry among the human skeletal remains.

> A thirteenth US serviceman [Perry] who was initially on site is now assumed to have been Killed In Action at some distance from the fortified base. A fourteenth US serviceman [Fleming] is known to

have died while being extracted from the battle zone and his remains are not thought to be among those at the fortified base.

Dr Lowell J. Levine, a doctor of dental science from Albany, New York, commended JPAC, 'on the enormity of the effort in the recovery and identifications that were accomplished in these cases'. That dental and skeletal remains were recovered from a dangerous jungle hilltop in quantities that were measured in centimetres and some in millimetres was a truly remarkable effort. It was a crusade that grew from the agony suffered by the families of the lost and the friends who made it home but didn't forget. Along the way there was disbelief, anger and suspicion. This was mixed with belief, political skill, compassion, friendship and plain old hard work, all of which turned an impossible task into a commendable achievement, which was commemorated on 7 October 2005 at Arlington National Cemetery.

13 THE FINAL JOURNEY

October wept

Arlington National Cemetery was cloaked in cloud on 7 October 2005, and the clouds wept as a hearse rolled slowly westward down Bradley Drive alongside Section 60 to a point immediately adjacent to MacArthur Drive. Rain and grey—a colour of mourning—seemed to be appropriate but perhaps a ray of sunshine should also have appeared because in the darkness of hurt there was some happiness. The men had come home. All funerals test our emotions, but somehow military funerals add an extra layer of feeling that mixes pride with love and remembrance, and gives strength to those who are left to grow old. A resplendent bearer party with a strong hold upon a coffin and a steady step comforts those who mourn. When a volley of three shots is fired—which can cause a jolt to those who do not expect a noise of war on such a day—it is a final salute; no matter what custom one believed it came from. At Arlington it is a signal that the dead have been cared for. The presentation of a folded flag of the United States of America to a family or friend is one of the most solemn moments of an American military funeral service. On 7 October 2005, twelve flags were handed over, eleven by Marines and one by a soldier. Each flag was perfectly shaped from thirteen folds, with the stars uppermost and in the shape of a 'cocked hat', which is thought to be a reminder of the soldiers who served under General George Washington, as well as the sailors and Marines who served under Captain John Paul Jones. On this day, the folded flags signified the end of the journey; the warriors had travelled a long road from the Ngok Tavak battlefield to peace.

'Taps'

Day is done
Gone the sun
From the lakes
From the hills
From the sky
All is well
Safely rest
God is nigh.

*—Union Army Brigadier
General Daniel Butterfield, 1862*

Although the Arlington National Cemetery headstone for the Ngok Tavak group at site 60-8234 displays twelve names, five identified remains were interred elsewhere. Raymond Heyne is immediately alongside the group in site 8233. The other Marines are: Corporal Gerald E. King, of Knoxville, Tennessee, and Lance Corporals Joseph F. Cook, of Foxboro, Massachusetts, Donald W. Mitchell, of Princeton, Kentucky, and Thomas W. Fritsch, of Cromwell, Connecticut.

There was also a good news postscript to the story about the two Australians who were left behind near Bien Hoa in 1965. The remains of Lance Corporal Richard Parker and Private Peter Gillson were recovered and returned to Australia in 2007.

HEROISM AND LEADERSHIP CITATIONS

United States Marine Corps

Meritorious Unit Commendation with 'V'

The preamble reads: 'Detachment X-Ray, Battery D, 2nd Battalion, 13th Marines, was awarded a Meritorious Unit Commendation with the letter 'V' authorised, for valour. The detachment was cited for extraordinary heroism in action against enemy Viet Cong and North Vietnamese forces during the defence of Ngok Tavak on 10 May 1968.'

The Navy Cross

Conklin, Richard F. The citation reads: 'For extraordinary heroism while serving as a field Artillery Batteryman with Battery D, Second Battalion, Thirteenth Marines, First Marine division (Reinforced), in connection with operations against the enemy in the Republic of Vietnam. On 10 May 1968, Corporal Conklin was a member of a detachment of two howitzers at the United States Army Special Forces camp at Ngok Tavak in Quang Tin Province. In the early morning hours, the camp was attacked by a reinforced North Vietnamese Army battalion which penetrated the camp's defensive wire in two places, and, utilizing grenades, mortars, B-40 rockets, and automatic weapons, attempted to overrun the hill-top position. Realizing the seriousness of the situation, Corporal Conklin manned a .30-caliber machine gun and delivered a heavy volume of accurate fire against the enemy reaching the crest of the hill. Sustaining heavy casualties from the machine-gun fire, the enemy concentrated its automatic weapons fire on his position and attacked it with grenades. Although seriously wounded by grenade fragments, Corporal Conklin resolutely remained at his position and continued to deliver effective fire on the assaulting North Vietnamese. Observing numerous grenades land in his position, he quickly retrieved them and threw them back at the enemy. Wounded a second time by grenade fragments, he temporarily lapsed into unconsciousness and slumped over the weapon, severely burning himself on the hot barrel. Regaining consciousness, he continued to deliver fire for another fifteen minutes until he collapsed from his multiple wounds. When he was subsequently evacuated, three unexploded grenades were found in his emplacement. By his exemplary courage, unfaltering determination, and steadfast devotion to duty at great personal risk, Corporal Conklin was instrumental in repulsing the enemy assault and upheld the highest traditions of the Marine Corps and the United States Naval Service.'

Schunck, Henry M. The citation reads: 'For extraordinary heroism while serving as a field Artillery Batteryman with Battery D, Second Battalion, Thirteenth Marines, First Marine division (Reinforced), in connection with operations against the enemy in the Republic of Vietnam. On 10 May 1968, Corporal Schunck was a member of a detachment of two howitzers at the United States Army Special Forces camp at Ngok Tavak in Quang Tin Province. In the early morning hours, the camp was attacked by a reinforced North Vietnamese Army battalion, which attempted to overrun the hill top position. Corporal Schunck unhesitatingly left his covered post adjacent to the command bunker and moved under intense fire to the 4.2-inch mortar emplacement in the center of the compound. Although wounded in the leg by grenade fragments en route, he resolutely continued to the mortar position and attempted to deliver mortar fire single-handedly. Suddenly, he was attacked by a North Vietnamese soldier armed with a flamethrower. Reacting instantly, Corporal Schunck mortally wounded the enemy with accurate rifle fire and then left the mortar emplacement to assist a comrade who had been wounded while attempting to reach the mortar. After moving the casualty to a covered position, he shifted to the 81 mm mortar, and with the aid of a companion, directed a heavy volume of fire against the attackers, inflicting several casualties as they launched a concentrated attack on his position. Although wounded a second time by grenade fragments, he selflessly disregarded his painful injuries in order to continue bringing effective fire to bear against the hostile force until his supply of ammunition was expended. Leaving the emplacement, he moved along his unit's defenses, distributing ammunition and moving casualties to the Fire Direction Center bunker for treatment. Throughout the remainder of the engagement, until the enemy had been repulsed, he continued to move along the defensive lines, encouraging and directing his companions. Then, weakened from his wounds and near exhaustion, he accepted evacuation. By his uncommon courage, unfaltering determination, and selfless devotion to duty at great personal risk, Corporal Schunck upheld the highest traditions of the Marine Corps and the United States Naval Service.'

Australian Army

Distinguished Conduct Medal

Cameron, Donald G. The citation reads: 'Warrant Officer Cameron served with The Royal Australian Regiment in Korea where he was awarded the Military Medal for bravery, and in Malaysia. He served in South Vietnam with the Australian Army Training Team from October 1965 for one year and rejoined the Team in February 1968 as a Platoon Commander with No 11 Mobile Strike force Company of the 5th Special Forces Group. On 10 May 1968, 11 Company was occupying an outpost at Ngok Tavak in Quang Tin Province near the Laotian border. A North Vietnamese Battalion attacked and partially over-ran the outpost, isolating the command post from Warrant Officer Cameron and the surviving defenders. At dawn, Warrant Officer Cameron organised and led a counter-attack, which broke through to the beleaguered command post and which eventually cleared the enemy from within the perimeter. Under constant fire, he calmly moved around the post reorganising the defences, controlling the clearing of pockets of resistance and encouraging and helping the Vietnamese soldiers. His outstanding leadership and exemplary conduct under fire contributed greatly to the success of the defence. On other occasions during his two years of service in South Vietnam Warrant Officer Cameron's professional ability, his bravery and his qualities of leadership have been of a high order and have brought great credit to him and the Australian Army.'

Military Medal

Lucas, Franklin J. The citation reads: 'Warrant Officer Lucas enlisted in the Australian Army in 1949 and has served in Korea with The Royal Australian Regiment and in South Vietnam with the Australian Army Training Team. He rejoined the Team in February 1968 and was posted as a Platoon Commander with No 11 Mobile Strike Force Company of the 5th Special Forces Group. On 10 May 1968, 11 Company was occupying an outpost at Ngok Tavak in Quang Tin Province near the Laotian border. A North Vietnamese Battalion attacked and partially over-ran the outpost and surrounded the command post. Warrant Officer Lucas disregarding the intense enemy fire, moved around his platoon position, encouraging and reassuring his troops. At dawn, the defenders counter-attacked and Warrant Officer Lucas personally killed three enemy soldiers in a machine gun position. He turned the captured weapon on the withdrawing enemy, killing several more before leading a small party along the trench line to clear the last of the enemy from the bunkers. Throughout the battle Warrant Officer Lucas displayed conspicuous gallantry and his aggressive leadership contributed greatly to the successful outcome of the battle. In his two years of operational service in South Vietnam, he has consistently shown himself to be a brave and inspiring leader and his professional ability has been of a high order.'

Mention-in-Despatches

White, John E. John White was mentioned in despatches. However, Lieutenant Colonel Ray Burnard, Commanding Officer, the Australian Army Training Team Vietnam, expressed disappointment with the decision not to give John White a Military Cross. He believed his actions were worthy of such an award. In his summary of Captain White's action, Colonel Burnard wrote: 'Captain White's conduct and bravery throughout the battle were an inspiration to all. The heavy casualties inflicted upon the enemy and the safe and orderly withdrawal of the survivors was due, very largely, to Captain White's professional skill, his calmness under fire and his outstanding leadership.'

GLOSSARY

AATTV Australian Army Training Team Vietnam

adjutant a staff officer on a headquarters, assistant to the CO

AK-47 Kalashnikov 7.62 mm Assault Rifle—fired a short round not exchangeable with NATO 7.62 mm

alert (Australia) stand to, to be prepared for an enemy action with load-carrying equipment on, in fighting positions and crew-served weapons manned

AO Area of operations, see TAOR

Arlington Arlington National Cemetery, Virginia

ARVN Army of the Republic of Viet Nam—the South Vietnamese regular army

A-team Special Forces detachment of twelve men commanded by a captain, usually designated as 'A-' followed by a set of numbers, e.g. A-105

AWM Australian War Memorial

B-52 US strategic eight-engine jet bomber

battery an artillery unit generally of six guns and 120–150 personnel

berm an earthen wall

BNR body not recovered

C-130 medium range four-engine tactical transport aircraft

cannon-cocker slang for artilleryman, also 9-mile sniper

Caribou C-7 short range, twin-engine, tactical transport aircraft

Charles also Charlie, Viet Cong

CH-46 Sea Knight helicopter flown by the USMC, often confused with CH-47 Chinook

CIA Central Intelligence Agency

CIDG Civilian Irregular Defense Group

CINCPAC Commander In Chief Pacific-US, a four-star appointment

Claymore an anti-personnel mine

CO Commanding Officer, usually a lieutenant colonel in rank

COMUSMACV Commander United States Military Assistance Command Vietnam, a four-star general

C-ration individual combat ration consisting of canned foods, a beverage mix, chewing gum and cigarettes

C-team Special Forces command and control detachment commanded by a lieutenant colonel—Company C in I Corps was a C-team

CTZ Corps Tactical Zone—the zones in South Vietnam were numbered I through to IV from the DMZ to the Mekong Delta

DASC Direct Air Support Center, command and control centre responsible for the direction of air operations

DCM Distinguished Conduct Medal, an Australian gallantry award second only to the Victoria Cross

DIA US Defense Intelligence Agency, established in 1961—manages defence intelligence matters

division a large military unit made of brigades, or regiments. In Vietnam, US divisions were 20–30,000 strong. 2nd NVA was less than 10,000

DK 75 see 75 mm RR

DMZ Demilitarised Zone—a 10-kilometre buffer zone around the 17th parallel in Vietnam

DPMO US Defense POW/Missing Personnel Office

Dustoff helicopter casualty evacuation

559th NVA logistics group named for the date of its formation in May 1959

50 cal heavy machine gun of point 50 calibre, or 12.7 mm

FAC forward air controller—mostly airborne in a light aircraft who could communicate with attack aircraft and ground troops; directed close air support

Firecracker an artillery shell that contained small bomblets that were ejected over a target area

Fleschette also known as Beehive, an artillery round that contained finned, small darts, something like a large shotgun shell

FMPac Fleet Marine Force Pacific, commanded by a lieutenant general

FOB forward operating base—a forward area that is used to support tactical operations

free fire zone an area clear of civilians into which weapons could be fired without further clearance on the understanding that all movement was considered to be hostile

grunt slang for infantryman

gunship a helicopter mounted with rockets and machine guns

Hanoi Jane a derogatory label applied to Jane Fonda due to her visit to North Vietnam during the war

HC smoke   hexachloroethane mixed with other substances in a shell to produce smoke when exposed to the air

HMM   Helicopter Marine Medium

howitzer   an artillery piece capable of firing at high angle; 105 mm is a calibre

HQ   headquarters

HQAFV   Headquarters Australian Force Vietnam, Saigon

Huey   Iroquois helicopter

I Corps   'Eye' Corps—a geographic region that contained the five provinces south from the DMZ: Quang Tri, Thua Thien, Quang Nam, Quang Tin and Quang Ngai

Imperial awards   British honours and awards that applied prior to 1975 in Australia; see VC, MC, DCM, MM, MID

JFA   Joint Field Activity

JPAC   Joint POW/MIA Accounting Command created through the merger of US Army Central Identification Laboratory and JTF-FA

JTF-FA   Joint Task Force-Full Accounting

KIA   killed in action

LAW   lightweight anti-armour weapon, 66 mm calibre rocket packed in a shoulder-fired container

LLDB   Luc Luong Dac Biet—South Vietnamese (ARVN) Special Forces

Local Force   VC guerrillas from the local hamlets and villages, sometimes indistinguishable from VC regional force; operated at platoon and company level within their home area, also known as militia

LZ   Landing Zone—in this book a designated helicopter landing area

M-16   standard issues American service rifle of 5.56 mm calibre capable of single shot or automatic fire and fed by a 20-round magazine

M-60   a belt-fed general-purpose machine gun that fired NATO 7.62 mm rounds

MACV   Military Assistance Command, Vietnam, commanded by a four-star general

III MAF   III Marine Amphibious Force—senior American HQ in I Corps, commanded by a lieutenant general

Main Force   VC regular units—well trained and usually operated at battalion level, not restricted to a local region. NVA units were also referred to as Main Force

map   military maps are divided into squares by grid lines, which are read across then up, or down to provide a reference to a location

map distance   map distances must be adjusted for gradient and changes of course to obtain true distance across the ground

Marines   as in 13th Marines, indicates a Marine regimental-sized unit

MC   Military Cross—an Australian gallantry award, the US Silver Star equivalent

MGF   Mobile Guerrilla Force—specially formed units of the Mike Force that were established to operate independently for extended periods

MIA   missing in action

MID   Mentioned In Despatches was an Australian award for gallantry or commendable conduct. Australian gallantry awards in order of precedence were: VC, MC, DCM, MM, MID

Mike Force   Special Forces multi-purpose reactionary-reconnaissance units which were also used in conventional combat operations

militia   see Local Force

minefield   mines generally placed in the ground to a pattern—difficult to lay, record, maintain and protect

MM   Military Medal was an Australian gallantry award, the US Bronze Star (V) equivalent

Mobile Strike Force   see Mike Force

Montagnards   Hill tribes people, also known as 'Yards', recruited into the CIDG

mortar   muzzle-loaded indirect fire weapon that fires bombs (shells) over short ranges in a high ballistic arc

MR5   a North Vietnamese political and military region that commanded a large area of the northern part of South Vietnam; considered to be an army corps equivalent

MSF   Mobile Strike Force; see Mike Force

Navy Cross   the second highest medal that is awarded by the US Department of the Navy for valour

NLF   National Front for the Liberation of South Vietnam, commonly called the Viet Cong

noticas   notification of casualty

Nungs   Chinese mercenaries resident in Vietnam, allegedly descended from the Chinese warrior class

NVA   North Vietnamese Army; also known as PAVN

NVA ranks   see p. 228, Chapter 10, note 3

OC   officer commanding—usually a sub-unit commander and major in rank (Aust.) or captain (US) or lieutenant (ARVN)

PAVN   People's Army of Vietnam—the military arm of North Vietnam; also known as NVA

PFC   Private First Class, US Forces—senior private

PLAF   People's Liberation Army Forces; see VC

province   a geographically defined political region

PSP   pierced steel planking that was interconnected to form a solid mat—generally used to surface a tactical airstrip, but also used as reinforcement on bunkers etc.

PX   Post Exchange—a duty-free store and commissary for soldiers

rank stars   particular to the US: one star brigadier, two stars major general, three stars lieutenant general, four stars general, five stars general of the army

RAR   Royal Australian Regiment, infantry

recon   reconnaissance—to obtain information about the activities and resources of an enemy either through visual observation, or other detection methods, e.g. air photographs and side-looking airborne radar

REFNO   reference number

RPG   rocket-propelled grenade fired from the shoulder

RVN   Republic of (South) Viet Nam

75 mm RR   recoilless rifle of 75 mm calibre—direct fire no recoil as blast exhausts to the rear of the weapon; Vietnamese DK 75

S   staff identification letter at battalion level, see below. At divisional level the letter is changed to G and in a joint command it is changed to J

S1   unit Personnel Officer (US)

S2   unit Intelligence Officer (US)

S3   unit Operations Officer (US)

S4   unit Logistics Officer (US)

SF   Special Forces (also USSF)

SFC   Sergeant First Class (US)

SFG   Special Forces Group

Silver Star   US third-highest award for valour

SOG   Studies and Observation Group—a deliberately designed misnomer for a secretive cross-border operations group

SOP   standard operating procedure—a standard set of procedures to perform a given task

'Spooky'   C-47 a [DC-3] fixed-wing close air-support gunship also known as Puff the Magic Dragon

2IC   Second-in-command

30-cal   a point 30 calibre machine gun that fired a .30-06 calibre round, replaced by the M-60. Some .30 calibre were re-chambered to accept NATO 7.62 mm

TAOR   Tactical Area of Responsibility, an assigned area of operations

Tet   Chinese New Year

tube   an artillery piece (also mortar tube)

units   military units run in size upwards from squad, platoon, company, battalion, regiment, division, corps

USMC   The United States Marine Corps—the forces from the Department of the US Navy that were initially formed to serve as landing forces with the fleet

VC   Victoria Cross—highest British Imperial Award for valour; Medal of Honor equivalent

VC   Viet Cong—from Viet Nam Cong San. The term Viet Cong, (for Vietnamese communists) was invented by the US Information Service in the late 1950s to rename the Viet Minh, a term it thought was too close to nationalism

Viet Minh   a contraction of Viet Nam Doc Lap Dong Minh Hoi (League for the Independence of Viet Nam). The term was applied to the Vietnamese resistance fighters of the First Indochina (French) War

VT fuse   variable time, or proximity fuse

VVA   Vietnam Veterans of America—founded in 1978 and dedicated to Vietnam-era veterans and their families

WIA   wounded in action

WO2   Warrant Officer Class Two—a rank below WO1, usually a company sergeant major in the Australian Army

XO   Executive Officer, the second-in-command of a military unit

NOTES

Prologue

1 The Rand Corporation, *A Translation from the French Lessons in Indochina, Volume 2*, Santa Monica, CA, 1967, p. 94.

Part 1   The Warriors

Chapter 1: Pathways to a battle

1 Douglas Pike, *People's Army of Vietnam*, Presidio Press, Novata, CA, 1986, pp. 88–9.
2 Harry Albert, video: A filmed record of Team Bravo's Mission to Vietnam, 1995. Ba Gia was a major battle in 1965 that decimated the 51st ARVN Regiment by the 1st VC Regiment, which was given the name as a battle honour.
3 Senior General Chu Huy Man, *Time of Upheaval*, People's Army Publishing House, Hanoi, 2004, p. 479.
4 MACV Command History 1964–1973, Military History Branch, Joint Staff Headquarters MACV, and III Marine Amphibious Force PERINTREP No 18-68, 5 May 1968.
5 Man, *Time of Upheaval*, pp. 477–8.
6 George L. MacGarrigle, The 2d North Vietnamese Division, unpublished, no date. Jack Shulimson et al., *U.S. Marines in Vietnam, The Defining Year 1968*, Headquarters, U.S. Marine Corps, Washington, D.C., 1997, Chapter 6. Also, see James F. Humphries, *Through The Valley, Vietnam, 1967–1968*, Lynne Rienner Publishers, Newton, MA, 1999, p. 156.
7 Shulimson et al., *The Defining Year 1968*, Chapter 8, p. 161.
8 Major General Spurgeon Neel, *Vietnam Studies, Medical Support of the U.S. Army in Vietnam 1965–1970*, Department of the Army, Washington D.C., 1991, Chapter III.

9 This information is gleaned from a variety of sources, such as: Marc Leepson with Helen Hannaford, *Dictionary of the Vietnam War*, Macmillan General Reference, New York, 1999; MACV Command History 1964–1973; Department of History, Ohio State University, <http://ehistory.osu.edu> Vietnam War; United States Marine Corps Command Chronologies.

10 Commanding General, Fleet Marine Force Pacific, Pacific Operations, General Officers Symposium Book, 1967, pp. 10–11.

11 Command Chronology, III Marine Amphibious Force, February 1968.

12 Man, *Time of Upheaval,* p. 477.

13 Operations of U.S. Marine Forces, April 1968, Fleet Marine Force, Pacific.

14 Herbert Y. Schandler, *The Unmaking of a President, Lyndon Johnson and Vietnam*, Princeton University Press, Princeton, NJ, 1977, pp. 92–3, 95.

15 Shulimson et al., *The Defining Year,* pp. 572–3.

16 William Loman correspondence dated 11 June 2006.

17 Conrad Kinsey correspondence dated 13 June 2006.

18 Bob Adams correspondence dated 13 June 2006.

19 Tim Brown correspondence dated 22 June 2006.

20 Colonel Francis J. Kelly, *Vietnam Studies, U.S. Army Special Forces 1961–1971*, Department of Army, Washington, D.C., 1989, Part 1, Chapter III, p. 46.

21 Peter Ray correspondence dated 1 May 2006.

22 Malcolm McCallum correspondence dated 13 May 2006.

23 Ted Gittinger interview with Jonathan F. Ladd, 24 July 1984, transcript Lyndon Baines Johnson Library, p. 69.

24 John Prados and Ray W. Stubbe, *Valley of Decision,* A Marc Jaffe Book, Boston, MA, 1991, p. 333.

25 Jack Shulimson, a personal opinion, correspondence dated 12 June 2006.

26 Command Chronology, 1st Marine Division, May 1967, Operational Documents—Relief/Reinforcement of CIDG Camps—CG III MAF 061504Z May 67.

27 Command Chronology, 1st Marine Division, October 1967.

28 Tropical Warfare Advisers' Course 11/67—course reports.

29 John White correspondence dated 15 March 2006.

30 Humphries, *Through The Valley,* p. 33.

31 Command Chronology, 1st Marine Division, 1 March to 31 March 1968.

32 5th Special Forces Group (Airborne), Operational Report for Period Ending 30 April 1968.

33 OPLAN 1-68 Golden Valley (Relief/Reinforcement of CIDG Camps)—change to—04 May 1968.

34 ibid.

35 Detachment B, 1st Military Intelligence Battalion, Special Study Kham Duc, 14 March and 7 April 1968.

36 HQ 5th SFGA, 1st SF, Nha Trang, RVN, Intelligence Estimate Update, 28 April 68.
37 Lieutenant General Nguyen Huy Chuong, Editorial Direction, *Second Division, Volume 1,* Da Nang Publishing House, 1989.
38 Man, *Time of Upheaval,* pp. 475, 477.
39 Chuong, *Second Division,* pp. 102–3.

Chapter 2: Into the cauldron

1 Department of the Army, Company C, 5th Special Forces Group (Airborne), After Action Report Battle of Kham Duc, 31 May 1968.
2 Wayne Long and Jim McLeroy correspondence dated 24 May 2006 and 21 May 2006 respectively.
3 Kenneth Benway correspondence dated 5 July 2006.
4 Detachment B, 1st Military Intelligence Battalion, Special Study.
5 John White correspondence dated 15 March 2006.
6 Kudelk, cartoon *The Australian,* date unknown.
7 White correspondence.
8 ibid.
9 Kenneth Benway correspondence dated 4 July 2006 and 5 July 2006.
10 ibid.
11 ibid.
12 Australian War Memorial 293, R723/10/4, Mobile Strike Force Danang Report, April 1968.
13 John White interview, Canberra 10 and 11 May 2006.
14 John White correspondence 15 March 2006 and interview, Canberra 10 and 11 May 2006.
15 Kenneth Benway correspondence dated 4–5 July.
16 ibid.
17 Australian War Memorial 95, 1-2-52, AATTV Monthly Report, April 1968.
18 Don Cameron tape recording April 2006.
19 Company C After Action Report, Battle of Kham Duc.
20 White interview.
21 5th Special Forces Group (Airborne), Intelligence Estimate Update.
22 Jack Shulimson et al., *U.S. Marines in Vietnam, The Defining Year 1968,* Headquarters, U.S. Marine Corps, Washington, D.C., 1997, p. 251.
23 Shelby L. Stanton, *Green Berets at War: U.S. Special Forces in Southeast Asia 1956–1975,* Presidio Press, Novata, CA, 1985—see Mobile Guerrilla Forces. Also, *Vietnam Studies, U.S. Army Special Forces 1961–1971,* Department of the Army, Washington, D.C., 1989, Chapter VI.
24 Major J.E.D. White, 'Venison and Valour', *Australian Infantry,* Jan–Feb 1972, p. 11.

Chapter 3: Battle plans

1 Author's interpretation of events that may have occurred based upon information in the documents listed throughout the endnotes and his imagination.

2 5th Special Forces Group, Memorandum, undated, with Lieutenant Colonel Schungel signature block among papers from US Center of Military History in date sequence, May 1968. Also included in a signal from Colonel Ladd, CO 5th Special Forces Group, to Major General L.C. Shea, Director I & CA, ODCSOPS, 22 May 1968. Declassified DAAG–AMR–D–#14 Date 2/27/85.

3 Major General David Ewing Ott, *Field Artillery, 1954–1973*, Department of the Army, Washington, D.C., 1975.

4 Headquarters 5th Special Forces Group (Airborne), 1st Special Forces, Lang Vei–Kham Duc Comparative Study (U), 20 July 1968.

5 Conrad Kinsey correspondence dated 14 April 2006.

6 Ott, *Field Artillery, 1954–1973*, p. 169.

7 5th Special Forces Group (Airborne), Lang Vei–Kham Duc Comparative Study, PW [prisoner of war] 60th Battalion, 1st VC regiment, statement.

8 Bob Adams correspondence dated 18 September 2006.

9 2nd Battalion, 13th Marines, Command Chronology 1–30 April 1968, dated 1 May 1968.

10 Tim Brown tape recording September 2006.

11 Bob Adams correspondence dated 20 May 2006.

12 Greg Rose correspondence dated 2 May 2006.

13 Brown tape recording.

14 William Loman correspondence dated 7 June 2006.

15 Adams correspondence dated 20 May 2006.

16 Adams correspondence dated 18 September 2006.

17 Captain Daniel Waldo, Jr., et al., End-of-Tour Interview, 18 June 1968.

18 John White correspondence dated 15 March 2006.

19 Rose correspondence.

20 Henry Schunck and Tim Brown tape recording 27 September 2006.

21 Brown tape recording.

22 John White correspondence dated 15 March 2006 and interview 2006.

23 'The Fall of Ngok Tavak', *The Advisor*, December 2006, published by the Queensland Branch of the AATTV Association. John White provided additional notes and corrections to Hardy Bogue's draft.

24 Brown tape recording.

25 Adams correspondence dated 20 May 2006.

26 Dean Parrett correspondence dated 2 May 2006.

27 Unsigned After Action Report, Ngok Tavak FOB 16 May 1968, attributed to Captain John White.

28 Adams correspondence dated 20 May 2006.

29 Henry Schunck and Tim Brown tape recording 27 September 2006.

30 John White in Harry Albert video, A filmed interview with John White, 1995.
31 Major J.E.D. White, 'Venison and Valour', *Australian Infantry*, Jan–Feb 1972, pp. 10–15.
32 William Loman correspondence dated 7 June 2006 and 23 October 2006.
33 Rose correspondence.

Chapter 4: The warriors clash

1 Information gleaned from Harry Albert video, A filmed record of Team Bravo's Mission to Vietnam, 1995; Unsigned After Action Report, 16 May 1968; and After Action Report, Battle of Kham Duc, 31 May 1968 signed by Lieutenant Colonel Schungel.
2 Greg Rose correspondence dated 2 May 2006.
3 Henry Schunck and Tim Brown tape recording 27 September 2006.
4 Bob Adams correspondence dated 20 May 2006.
5 Raymond Scuglik correspondence undated 2006.
6 Paul Swenarski correspondence dated 30 May 2006.
7 Adams correspondence.
8 Scott Thomas correspondence dated 3 May 2006.
9 Henry Schunck tape recording 26 October 2006.
10 Bruce Davies–David Fuentes telephone conversation on 8 November 2006.
11 Jim Garlitz tape recording 25 April 2006.
12 Lieutenant General Nguyen Huy Chuong, Editorial Direction, *Second Division, Volume 1,* Da Nang Publishing House, 1989, p. 104.
13 Dean Parrett correspondence dated 2 May 2006.
14 Charles Reeder correspondence dated 9 April 2006.
15 Unsigned After Action Report, 16 May 1968.
16 Project CHECO, Kham Duc, 8 July 1968. HQ PACAF, Directorate, Tactical Evaluation, p. 4.
17 CDR JTF-FA Honolulu, Administrative message, 5 October 1999.
18 Jack S. Ballard, *Development and Deployment of Fixed-Wing Gunships 1962–1972,* Office of Air Force History, Washington, D.C., 1982, p. 9.
19 Major Hardy Bogue wrote in 1968 that the inner fort was 33 by 50 yards. The joint POW/MIA Accounting Command report CIL 1999-060, TAPC-PED-H (628-2) 15 December 1999, recorded the area as approximately 24 by 45 metres.
20 14th Air Commando Wing History: 1 April–30 June 1968, Appendix to Volume II.
21 ibid., p. 58.
22 Reeder correspondence.
23 Davies–Fuentes telephone conversations on 8 and 10 November 2006.
24 Chuong, *Second Division,* p. 105.
25 Garlitz tape recording.

26 Captain Eugene Edward Makowski after action statement, two pages, undated, in documents from US Center for Military History.

27 Major General Patrick Brady, Medal of Honor, correspondence dated 9 May 2006.

28 Harry Albert video, A filmed record of Team Bravo's Mission to Vietnam, 1995.

29 Robert Mascharka correspondence dated 30 October 2006 and 20 January 2007.

30 Makowski, after action statement.

31 John White correspondence dated 15 March 2006 and 28 May 2007.

32 5th Special Forces Group, After Action Report–Battle of Kham Duc, p. 3.

33 Bobby Thompson correspondence dated 26 and 27 January 2007.

34 White interview Canberra, 10 May 2006.

35 Eugene Makowski correspondence dated 27 April 2006.

36 Jack Matheney correspondence dated 17 April 2006.

37 Bob Mascharka correspondence dated 20 October 2006.

38 Brady correspondence.

39 Bruce Davies–Jon Davis telephone conversation on 25 January 2007.

40 Harry Albert video, A filmed record of Team Bravo's Mission to Vietnam, 1995, a new translation by Khiet Nguyen, ex-ARVN Ranger, 2007.

41 Makowski correspondence.

42 William Loman correspondence dated 23 October 2006.

43 Rose correspondence.

44 Scuglik correspondence.

45 Albert video.

46 Matheney correspondence.

47 Major J.E.D. White, 'Venison and Valour', *Australian Infantry*, Jan–Feb 1972, pp. 10–15 and Albert video.

48 Matheney correspondence.

49 Makowski correspondence.

50 Davies–Fuentes conversations.

51 Rhett Flater, correspondence dated 30 September 2006 and Kham Duc Group Newsletter, November 2004.

52 Eugene Makowski correspondence dated 5 August 2006.

53 5th Special Forces Group, After Action Report–Battle of Kham Duc, p. 4.

54 5th Special Forces Group, Lang Vei–Kham Duc Comparative Study, 20 July 1968.

Chapter 5: Aftermath

1 *Kham Duc Victory*, a North Vietnamese film, undated, provided by Leslie Hines, Americal Division Association Historian (Vietnam).

2 Man, *Time of Upheaval*, pp. 466–7.

3 Senior General Chu Huy Man, *Time of Upheaval*, People's Army Publishing House, Hanoi, 2004, pp. 466–7.

4 Ray Burnard correspondence dated 1 November 2006 and Bruce Davies and Gary McKay, *The Men who Persevered*, Allen & Unwin, Sydney, Australia, 2005. p. 126.

5 Ted Gittinger with Jonathan F. Ladd, 24 July 1984, transcript Lyndon Baines Johnson Library, p. 72.

6 Geoff Skardon correspondence dated 14 April 2007.

7 Captain Nguyen Ky letter to Major Chi Huy Truong dated 22 February 1968.

8 Ray Burnard correspondence dated 24 April 2007.

9 Davies and McKay, *The Men who Persevered*, p. 123.

10 J.E. Glick, Brigadier-General, paraphrased press interview undated, contained within US Army Center of Military History papers.

11 Unsigned after action report, May 1968.

12 Leonard B. Scott, *The Battle for Hill 875, Dakto, Vietnam 1967*, U.S. Army War College, Pennsylvannia, 1988, p. 4.

13 Eugene Makowski correspondence dated 18 February 2007.

14 John White correspondence dated 20 February 2007.

15 William Loman correspondence dated 7 June 2006.

16 Greg Rose correspondence dated 2 May 2006.

17 Scott Thomas correspondence dated 3 May 2006.

18 Headquarters 11th Marines, Command Chronology, 1–31 May 1968, S-1 Report.

19 Truong Nhu Tang, *A Viet Cong Memoir*, Vintage Books, New York, 1986, p. 168.

20 Department of the Navy, Headquarters United States Marine Corps 3040, MHP-10, 25 May 1993. Joint Task Force-Full Accounting, Camp H. M. Smith, Hawaii, case 1167-0-01 through 13, narrative attached to document, 25 April 1994.

21 General Abrams to Lieutenant General Cushman, message 6 June 1968, Abrams Papers, Back Channel Files. Brigadier-General John Chaisson to Mrs Chaisson, 14 May 1968, Chaisson Papers.

22 Headquarters Military Assistance Command Vietnam, Monthly Summary, May 1968, p. 2.

Part 2   When the Captains and the Kings Depart

Chapter 7: Agony

1 *Saving Private Ryan*, Dreamworks Pictures and Paramount Pictures, an Amblin Entertainment Production, 1998.

2 Dennis King correspondence dated 21 February 2007.

3 ibid.

4 ibid.
5 ibid.
6 Ms Patricia Fritsch Zajack correspondence dated 10 March 2007.
7 Mrs Janice Kostello correspondence dated March–April 2007.
8 Jack Matheney correspondence dated 15 April 2007.
9 Ms Sherry Perry correspondence dated 23 March and 11 April 2007.
10 Southeast Asia Division, Defense POW/MIA Office, communication to VVA dated 3 July 1996.
11 Sherry Perry correspondence dated 18 April and 5 May 2007.
12 ibid.
13 ibid.
14 Kostello correspondence.

Chapter 8: Full accounting

1 *The Bright Light,* Joint Task Force-Full Accounting publication, 26 August 1998.
2 ibid. A synopsis of *Operation Homecoming.*
3 Americans Missing in Indochina: An Assessment of Vietnamese Accountability, prepared by Defense Intelligence Agency Special Office for Prisoner of War and Missing in Action, November 1992.
4 ibid., p. 7.
5 *Full Metal Jacket,* Warner Brothers, 1987. Gunnery Sergeant Hartman, USMC, was portrayed by Gunnery Sergeant R. Lee Ermey, a Marine Corps drill instructor, who used his own choice of words.
6 VVA Document, To the Members of The Vietnam Veterans of America, February 1995.
7 Tom Berger, Tim Brown's Vow, <www.articlebankonline.com/Article/Tim-Brown's-Vow/11139> [13 November 2007].
8 William Duker correspondence dated 19 June 2007.
9 ibid.
10 Tim Brown and Bruce Davies communicated frequently on this subject, by telephone, email and postal mail.
11 Duker correspondence.
12 The Veterans' Initiative Fact Sheet, undated, circa 1994.
13 Joint POW/MIA Accounting Command, Central Identification Laboratory, CIL 1999-060, Appendix A, signals May 1993.
14 Patricia Fritsch Zajack to USMC Casualty Officer, HQ USMC, 14 October 1993.
15 ibid.
16 US Government Archives, Vietnam War, Casualty List, and discussion with Ms Sherry Perry.
17 *USA Today,* Tuesday, 14 September 1993.

18 ibid. Also, Vietnam Veterans of America Inc. press release dated 14 September 1993.
19 The Veterans' Initiative, VVA resolution PM-5-93, adopted 7 August 1993.
20 ibid.
21 Garnett 'Bill' Bell and George J. Veith, 'POWs and Politics: How Much Does Hanoi Really Know', a paper presented on 19 April 1996 at Texas Tech University.
22 ibid.
23 Garnett 'Bill' Bell correspondence dated 6 July 2007.
24 Bell correspondence dated 5 July 2007.
25 Bell and Veith, 'POWs and Politics'.
26 Bell and Veith, 'POWs and Politics'.

Chapter 9: On the ground again, 1994

1 Vernon Valenzuela tape recording dated 16 June 2007.
2 ibid.
3 Colonel William H. Frizell, PAO 5300 Ser: 225-94 dated 12 April 94.
4 Tim Brown correspondence dated 7 July 2007.
5 Don Waak, 'From the Heart', an article written circa 1995 for *The Vet Center Voice*, Washington, D.C.
6 Tim Brown correspondence dated 7 July 2007.
7 Don Waak 'From the Heart'.
8 Headquarters Joint Task Force-Full Accounting, fax message dated 1458 local, 7 February 1994, from Colonel Frizell to Tim Brown.
9 CDR JTF-FA, OP 030718Z Jun 94 PSN 774607P31.
10 ibid.
11 ibid.
12 ibid.

Chapter 10: To Hanoi and beyond, 1995

1 Harry Albert, video, A filmed record of Team Bravo's Mission to Vietnam, 1995, pp. 212–36 passim. Subsequent quotes in the book are from this video.
2 Vietnam Veterans of America, Veterans' Initiative Task Force, Team Bravo After Mission Report on: Vietnam Trip February 5 thru February 18, 1995, p. 25.
3 NVA ranks differed from allied forces: one star indicated major general, two stars lieutenant general, three stars colonel general–senior lieutenant general, and four stars general–senior general.
4 Company C After Action Report, Battle of Kham Duc. Americal Division TOC log, May 1968. Also see, Lieutenant Metis report 196th Light Infantry Brigade undated.
5 Truong Nhu Tang, *A Viet Cong Memoir*, Vintage Books, New York, 1986, p. 168.

Chapter 11: Paperwork, analyses and politics

1 Vietnam Verterans of America, Veterans' Initiative Task Force, Team Bravo After Mission Report on: Vietnam Trip February 5 thru February 18, 1995, p. 5.
2 ibid., p. 9.
3 ibid., p. 16.
4 ibid., pp. 26–7, 29–30.
5 Project CHECO, Kham Duc, 8 July 1968, p. 63.
6 William Duker correspondence, dated 19 June 2007.
7 VVA-Memorandum via Fax to Julie Precious from VVA National Board of Directors, 11 April 1996, Questions, p. 4.
8 John White correspondence dated 19 July 2007.
9 DPMO letter to VVA dated 3 July 1996, p. 7.
10 Quoted in Christian G. Appy, *Vietnam: The Definitive Oral History Told From all Sides,* Ebury Press, Sydney, 2007, p. 483.
11 Joint POW/MIA Accounting Command, Memorandum CILOI 1771 30 March 2005, p. 6.
12 JTF-FA Detailed Report of Investigation of Case 1167, 29 June 1998.
13 Dan Carr facsimile to unknown recipients dated 18 April 1996.
14 Dan Carr facsimile to John Horne dated 28 May 1996.

Chapter 12: Ngok Tavak perchance

1 CDR JTF-FA, Honolulu, HI//J3// dated 5 August 1999. PSN 482972H32.
2 Ken Royalty correspondence dated 19 August 2007.
3 JPAC Central Identification Laboratory CIL 1999-060 dated 30 March 2005. Unless otherwise annotated, all of the detail about the recovery operations in 1998 and 1999 come from this document.

BIBLIOGRAPHY

Unpublished government records

Australian War Memorial

AWM 95, 1-2-52, AATTV Monthly Report, April 1968
AWM 293, R723/10/4, Mobile Strike Force Danang Report, April 1968

Private papers

Tim Brown collection
Janice Kostello collection
Sherry Perry letters
Patricia F. Zajack letters

Personal correspondence with the author

Letters and emails

Adams, Bob
Bell, Garnett 'Bill'
Benway, Kenneth
Brady, Patrick
Brown, Tim
Burnard, Ray
Cameron, Don
Carr, Dan
Duker, William
Garlitz, Jim

King, Dennis
Kinsey, Conrad
Kostello, Janice
Loman, William
Long, Wayne
McCallum, Malcolm
McLeroy, Jim
Makowski, Eugene
Mascharka, Robert
Matheney, Jack
Parrett, Dean
Perry, Sherry
Ray, Peter
Reeder, Charles
Rose, Greg
Royalty, Kenneth
Schunck, Henry
Scuglik, Raymond
Shulimson, Jack
Skardon, Geoff
Swenarski, Paul
Thomas, Scott
Thompson, Bobby
Valenzuela, Vernon
Waak, Don
Zajack, Patricia F.

Although not every piece of correspondence is included in this book, every letter and email helped to decipher a difficult pattern of events that was connected with the Ngok Tavak battle.

Unit histories

Davies, Bruce and McKay, Gary, *The Men who Persevered*, Allen & Unwin, Sydney, 2005
Chuong, Nguyen Huy, Lieutenant General, *Second Division, Volume 1,* Da Nang Publishing House, 1989
Military Assistance Command, Vietnam: Command Histories 1964–1973
Shulimson, Jack et al., *U.S. Marines in Vietnam, The Defining Year 1968,* Headquarters U.S. Marine Corps, Washington, D.C., 1997

Stanton, Shelby L., *Green Berets at War: U.S. Special Forces in Southeast Asia 1956-1975*, Presidio Press, Novata, CA, 1985

United States Marine Corps, Command Chronologies, 1967–1968

Official histories

Joint POW/MIA Accounting Command, Central Identification Laboratory, CIL 1999-060, 30 March 2005

Sams, Kenneth and Thompson, A.W., Major, *Kham Duc*, HQ PACAF, Directorate, Tactical Evaluation CHECO Division, 7th AF, 8 July 1968

Books and monographs

Appy, Christian, G., *Vietnam: The Definitive Oral History Told From all Sides*, Ebury Press, Sydney, 2007

Ballard, Jack, S., *Development and Deployment of Fixed-Wing Gunships 1962–1972*, Office of Air Force History, Washington, D.C., 1982

Chu Huy Man, Senior General, *Time of Upheaval*, People's Army Publishing House, Hanoi, 2004

Commanding General, Fleet Marine Force Pacific, Pacific Operations, General Officers Symposium Book, 1967

Humphries, James, F., *Through the Valley, Vietnam, 1967–1968*, Lynne Rienner Publishers, Inc., Boulder, CO, 1999

Kelly, Francis, J., Colonel, *Vietnam Studies, U.S. Army Special Forces 1961–1971*, Department of the Army, Washington, D.C., 1989

Maitland, Terrence, McInerney, Peter, et al., *A Contagion of War*, Boston Publishing Company, Newton, MA, 1983

Neel, Spurgeon, Major General, *Vietnam Studies, Medical Support of the U.S. Army in Vietnam 1965–1970*, Department of the Army, Washington, D.C., 1991

Ott, David E., Major General, *Field Artillery, 1954–1973*, Department of the Army, Washington, D.C., 1975

Pike, Douglas, *People's Army in Vietnam*, Presidio Press, CA, 1986

Prados, John, and Stubbe, Ray W., *Valley of Decision*, A Marc Jaffe Book, Boston, MA, 1991

The Rand Corporation, *A Translation from the French Lessons in Indochina, Volume 2*, Santa Monica, CA, 1967

Schandler, Herbert Y., *The Unmaking of a President, Lyndon Johnson and Vietnam*, Princeton University Press, Princeton, NJ, 1977

Truong Nhu Tang, *A Viet Cong Memoir*, Vintage Books, New York, 1986

Select list of journal articles, reports and filmed interviews

Albert, Harry, A filmed interview with John White, Danang, 1995

——A filmed record of Team Bravo's Mission to Vietnam, 1995

Brogue, Hardy Z., Major, 'The Fall of Ngok Tavak', *The Advisor*, AATV Association, Queensland Branch, December 2006

Department of the Army, Company C 5th Special Forces Group (Airborne), After Action Report Battle of Kham Duc, 31 May 1968

Joint Task Force-Full Accounting, Hawaii, *The Bright Light*, 26 August 1998

Vietnam Veterans of America, Veterans' Initiative Task Force Team Bravo After Mission Report on: Vietnam Trip February 5 thru February 18, 1995

Waak, Don, 'From the Heart', Veterans' Affairs Readjustment Counselling Service Newsletter, *The Vet Center Voice*, Washington D.C., 1995

White, J.E.D., Major, 'Venison and Valour', *Australian Infantry*, Jan–Feb 1972

INDEX